The American General Hospital

A Publication of the Francis Clark Wood Institute for the History of Medicine, The College of Physicians of Philadelphia

The American General Hospital

Communities and Social Contexts

DIANA ELIZABETH LONG
AND JANET GOLDEN, *Editors*

Cornell University Press

Ithaca and London

First published 1989 by Cornell University Press.

International Standard Book Number 0-8014-2349-X (cloth)
International Standard Book Number 0-8014-9604-7 (paper)
Library of Congress Catalog Card Number 89-7264

Printed in the United States of America

Librarians: Library of Congress cataloging information
appears on the last page of the book.

The paper in this book is acid-free and meets the guidelines for
permanence and durability of the Committee on Production
Guidelines for Book Longevity of the Council on Library Resources.

Contents

Illustrations and Tables

vii

CHARTS

TABLES

Preface

The American general hospital of the 1980s is a conspicuous institution, serving and symbolizing our biological and social needs. It is no wonder that our news media and social commentators are preoccupied with hospital politics, funding, and management. For reasons that run deep in our nation's history, the general hospital is as pervasive an American institution as it is a problematic one. Broadening our understanding of that history is the purpose of this book.

Numbering nearly 6,300 in 1986, general hospitals consume massive amounts of human and financial resources and dispense a variety of services, from performing surgical procedures to rearing abandoned AIDS babies. The federal government, through its Medicare, Medicaid, and other programs, subsidizes hospitals. Other federal funds pay for the training of physicians and nurses and support hospital-based medical research. State and local governments also underwrite hospital care. In 1986, insurance companies covered 181 million subscribers for hospital expenses, while another 15.5 million people made direct patient payments for hospital care. Whether hospitals are classified as public or private, they are supported by us all.

Hospitals concern us for personal reasons as well. Whether we admire the hospital as a social organization and workshop of skilled

professionals or fear its excessive costs, we all eventually expect to
spend time in its wards, clinics, medical offices, or emergency rooms.
It is hard to avoid the hospital, the birthplace of most Americans, the
site of most surgery and technologically intensive medical care, the
source of social services from nursing-home placements to counseling,
and the place of death for many Americans.

Yet the hospital has not always played so prominent a role in the
lives of Americans. The modern general hospital began to take shape
in the 1870s; over the decades it assumed new functions and responsibilities. The changing and expanding social and medical missions of
the general hospital are described in the ten essays in this book. The
historical evolution of the modern hospital helps us understand the
roots of many contemporary dilemmas, from the cost of care to the
ever more troublesome link between the hospital and the surrounding
community.

The essays explore the social world of the hospital, its place in the
surrounding environment as well as the layers of activity within it.
Together the contributors illuminate the conflicting intentions of hospital founders and workers as they struggled to create an institution
able to answer the medical and social needs of patients, practitioners,
employees, and administrators. These social actors wished to shape
and control the American hospital and, by implication, the society
around it, and they were not alone. Politicians, social reformers, and
others "outside" the hospital community had explicit moral and political agendas to which they saw this new American institution con-
forming. And of course members of the inner community of the hospital
were also part of the community outside the hospital walls; they brought
to their work the social and political values they used to negotiate
everyday life. To understand the development of the hospital is to
explore the increasing complexity of both its internal and its external
dynamics as well as the relationship between the two. As with the
study of all institutions, the conflicts and consensus between insiders
and outsiders deserve careful scrutiny.

The two parts of this book tell the story of the external and the
internal communities of the American general hospital. In Part I, we
focus on the period 1870 to 1920, when local hospitals first emerged
as community resources and then took shape as modern medical institutions. The articles in Part II explore how hospital workers trans-

formed the modern general hospital in the years from 1900 to 1970. Our study takes for granted the dominance in that institution after 1920 of scientifically trained physicians who effectively confronted infectious diseases with powerful technologies. We do not, however, accept the view that this technology was an independent variable or that physicians in that setting acted independently of their social world in the hospital community or in the world at large. As Gert Brieger pointed out at the 1984 conference "Hospitals and Communities," the hospital was important precisely because it was the meetingplace of these communities.

Charles Rosenberg, in the introductory essay, describes and evaluates the shifting balance between the hospital's moral and medical purposes. Surveying the general hospital in 1800, in 1920, and in the 1980s, he traces the social, technical, physical, and medical developments that have continually reshaped the image and the activity of the hospital. From an institution modeled on the family, responsible for the moral as well as the physical well-being of what were once called "inmates," the hospital has become a complex, bureaucratic medical facility based on an industrial-organizational model. Yet the moral dimensions remain. While there are no longer explicit attempts to influence the values of individual patients, the imperative to meet social needs through technical and medical measures means that the hospital must continue to weigh its obligations to social welfare against those to efficiency. Calling the modern general hospital both "rigid" and "indispensable," Rosenberg insists that we study its history in order to understand the origins of our present-day concerns.

Part I contains two case studies of local hospitals in transition, a photographic essay of life in these community hospitals, and an account of the attempt to move black hospitals into the mainstream. Joan Lynaugh describes the contrasting goals of hospitals in Kansas City in what she calls the "domestic" era of respectable care and the "medical" era of diagnostic and therapeutic efficiency. She recaptures a vital stage in the transition from the nineteenth-century to the twentieth-century institution. Following the rapid proliferation of hospitals linked to religious and ethnic communities and the related development of nurse training schools, hospital management came to be the shared responsibility of the hospital administrator, the superintendent of nurses, and the representatives of the medical staff. Within a few decades the balance shifted as pressures for standardization were felt. As medical staffs came to hold the power to direct patients to specific institutions, the doctors took control. Their ascendancy marked the beginning of the modern hospital, even as their continued dependence on nurses and administrators allowed the hospital to maintain its necessary complexity.

Edward Atwater makes a similar statement about the stages of development of the community hospital in upper New York State. Like Lynaugh, Atwater sees standards set by the American College of Surgeons for accreditation of hospitals as a crucial instrument in shifting power within these institutions to the scientifically trained doctors as hospitals set their management in order after 1920. Lynaugh and Atwater emphasize the special social and economic conditions that led local religious leaders on the one hand, and local matrons and businessmen on the other hand, to organize an institution that brought pride to the community. While Atwater's study of "this worthy enterprise" shows the central place of both women and the general surgeon as innovators in hospital history, his story contrasts the town and county hospitals with those in metropolitan areas in important ways. For economic reasons the rural hospitals encouraged all local physicians to care for their patients in the institution, thus generating revenue and creating a social environment adapted to local circumstances.

The growth in the number of hospitals between 1870 and 1930 and the movements to standardize their activities are evidence of a social transformation in both medical care and institutional services. Yet each individual institution was founded for a specific reason that cannot be seen simply by viewing national patterns. We must explore the patient records, the minutes of meetings, the account books, and the other documents that provide a window into the world of the hospital. Photographs also supply important information. In an illustrated essay Rima Apple gives us a visual tour of life in the general hospital and discusses what can be learned from studying photographs.

The twentieth-century movement toward the standardization and accreditation of hospitals swept away many small, inefficient institutions, often without regard for the particular needs of their patients and staffs. The movement as a whole, Vanessa Gamble argues, most profoundly threatened the black hospitals and the black physicians and nurses who worked in them. Responding to the threat of extinction, black medical and hospital leaders, activists within the National Medical Association and the National Hospital Association, initiated a standardization movement designed to save the healthiest of the black hospitals. Gamble concludes that while the activities of these leaders, "in concert with philanthropies and government agencies, produced some significant changes in the status of black hospitals by World War II," the successes were those of only a few institutions. In the wake of World War II, integrationist sentiment, decreasing numbers of black medical school graduates, and problems within the surviving black hospitals compelled many of them to close.

The second set of essays explores the shifting roles of physicians, nurses, administrators, and other workers in the late-nineteenth- and the twentieth-century American hospital. In the opening essay Joel Howell describes the adoption of the X-ray and electrocardiograph machines at the Pennsylvania Hospital in the early twentieth century. Howell concedes that this new technology became central to both medical diagnosis and the dominance of physicians. Yet he concludes that the use of machines depended as much on the organization of the hospital as on any medical or scientific imperative. Specifically, the creation of new types of patient records and charts allowed the information gathered from machines to become useful. By implication, these new records, which contained medical information rather than the traditional remarks about the social and moral condition of the patient, were a signal that medicine had superseded social welfare as the primary purpose for admission to the hospital ward.

The remaining essays examine the negotiation of relationships and power in the twentieth-century American hospital from the perspective of three communities: nurses, administrators, and workers. In essays described above, Lynaugh and Atwater cogently argue that trained nurses made the transition to the modern community hospital possible but were not able to establish autonomy from physicians after World War I. By focusing on the nursing agendas for science, Susan Reverby helps us to understand why nurses remained caught in the gender hierarchies that limited their authority. The professionalizing elite in nursing understood the leverage that science could give them. Nevertheless, it proved impossible to overcome the sentimental view of nursing as a womanly art or to challenge the economic value of an orderly hospital labor force provided by the traditional hospital nursing-school program. Reverby focuses on the "science-interested" curriculum of Isabel Stewart and the "science-oriented" curriculum of Virginia Henderson and explains why both efforts failed to gain professional autonomy for nurses.

Hospital administrators also redefined their roles and responsibilities in the interwar period. David Rosner contends that this group of professionals faced conflicting demands posed by the need for fiscally adept institutional management as well as a socially adequate response to the needs of hospital patients. Rosner describes the friction that arose as administrators tried to respond to both sets of responsibilities, tracing how they came to acquire formal, university-based training in business and management, even as they were expected to preserve their commitment to the welfare of their patients.

Brian Greenberg, looking at Local 1199, a union of hospital workers that came of age in the 1960s, introduces us to a third adaptation to the new world of scientific medicine and bureaucratic life. In attempting to meet their managerial responsibilities hospital administrators often found it necessary to hold down labor costs. But labor eventually organized and demanded better pay. The strategy of organizing that developed in the 1930s for other labor groups did not affect hospitals until after the Taft-Hartley Act of 1947, which specifically excluded them. In the late 1950s, however, hospitals, as the low-wage employer of last resort, began to yield to the organizing tactics developed by Elliott Godoff at Montefiore.

Union success brought new challenges and questions. One issue was whether all hospital employees should belong to a single union or whether a guild system was necessary for organizing white-collar workers. A second critical point concerned the link between demands made on behalf of a largely black hospital labor force and the ongoing civil rights struggle. Strikes, negotiations, and tactics developed in an era of massive public spending for health care would not be as effective in later years when government cuts, new management strategies by hospital negotiators, and internal struggles slowed 1199's momentum.

Greenberg illuminates the interaction of this sometimes successful effort in the 1960s with the search for a "peaceable kingdom" in the hospital.

The concluding essay turns our vision from a past period of revolutionary change in the American general hospital to the present. The 1970s seem to have signaled the coming of a new kind of hospital, one controlled more than ever by third-party payers, government-elected and appointed officials and, with an increase in the number of for-profit institutions, stockholders. On the one hand, Rosemary Stevens provides us with information about present shifts in funding, personnel, communities, roles, and service that suggest a possible end to the hospital as we know it. On the other hand, she documents the more conservative elements within the hospital. The dominance of the medical profession that began after World War I is perhaps little changed today, even as corporations move to take over large parts of hospital management. The diversity of hospitals since the "domestic era" arguably remains a continuing source of their strength and adaptability in the 1980s. Her conclusion is worth pondering for its policy implications as well as its historical insights. "American hospitals, collectively, are thriving institutions. Their ambiguity of function and of ideology; their responsiveness to a wide range of communities of interest, marked in particular by the flow of funding; their uses of prevailing ideology; and the enthusiasm of their adherents for the latest rhetoric characterize the hospitals of the 1980s just as much as they did in earlier decades."

Present concern with the American hospital has stimulated and responded to new scholarship in the field. One sign of this scholarly concern was the conference on which this book is based. The 1984 conference "Hospitals and Communities" at the College of Physicians of Philadelphia was the first on the history of the American general hospital and the first of the new Francis Clark Wood Institute of the College.

Participants at the conference provided insights and efforts that could not all be accommodated in one volume. We are grateful to Gert Brieger, Peter Buck, Sidney Lee, Barbara Melosh, and Barbara G. Rosenkrantz for their contributions to the conference and to Alan Astrow, Michael Frisch, A. McGehee Harvey, Andrew Pattulo, and Morris Vogel. Chairs of the sessions were Henry Nicholas, Albert W.

Snoke and—from the College of Physicians—Robert Austrian, Steven Peitzman, and Robert Pressman.

Research assistance was provided by Rosalind Valentin, Virginia Montijo, and Sarah Tracy. We gratefully acknowledge the conference grant from the Research Division of the National Endowment for the Humanities, which made the conference possible.

DIANA ELIZABETH LONG
JANET GOLDEN

Philadelphia

INTRODUCTION

Community and Communities: The Evolution of the American Hospital

CHARLES E. ROSENBERG

We have no comprehensive and analytical history of *the* hospital in America, though we have histories of individual hospitals in abundance.[1] To write of *the* hospital rather than *a* hospital is to imply a detached and critical point of view: most historians of American hospitals have hardly been that. But these chroniclers have not been alone in their uncritical stance. Until comparatively recent years the hospital has seemed a given to most Americans, a logical product of social need and technical necessity, free of the arbitrariness of history and the sordidness of interest. The hospital has been seen by the great majority of its historians, administrators, and clients as a necessary and thus proper institution.

In the last generation these attitudes have begun to change: criticism from every part of the political and intellectual spectrum has made the

1. The following pages are based largely on the author's *The Care of Strangers: The Rise of America's Hospital System* (New York: Basic Books, 1987), which covers the period between 1800 and 1920. *In Sickness and in Wealth: American Hospitals in the Twentieth Century* (New York: Basic Books, 1989) is a "companion" study by Rosemary Stevens emphasizing the period between 1910 and 1965. Two local studies of particular interest are Morris J. Vogel, *The Invention of the Modern Hospital: Boston 1870–1930* (Chicago and London: University of Chicago Press, 1980), and David Rosner, *A Once Charitable Enterprise: Hospitals and Health Care in Brooklyn and New York 1885–1915* (Cambridge: Cambridge University Press, 1982).

contemporary hospital a problematic and no longer an inevitable institution. Growth in medicine's technical capacity no longer seems
unambiguously laudable; ethicists, economists, and social activists
have all turned their critical attentions to contemporary health care.
One need not be a political extremist or quixotic Luddite to question
the particular form, the social role, and the presumed benefits of American hospitals in the 1980s.[2]

Many ordinary Americans have come to see it as a mixed blessing—
a technological and bureaucratic brontosaurus with an enormous ap-
petite, an inadequate heart, and a minute social brain. In any case, the
hospital has become too important a social and economic reality to
escape careful scrutiny, in part because of its substantive importance,
in part because it illuminates fundamental aspects of the society it
reflects and embodies. The history of the hospital illustrates precisely
the linked interactions of technology, bureaucracy, and science which
have so drastically altered the shape of American society during the
past century.

THE HOSPITAL IN 1800

When Thomas Jefferson was inaugurated as president there were
only two American hospitals—one in Philadelphia and the other in
New York. These novel institutions filled only a minor role in providing
medical care. The bulk of inpatient beds were provided in almshouse
wards, and even these were comparatively few in number. The great
majority of Americans still resided on farms and in rural villages.

Though marginal in this demographic sense the hospital was nevertheless a characteristic product of the society that nurtured it. The
hospital could not help but reproduce fundamental social relationships
and values in microcosm. Early America was a society in which relationships of class and status prescribed public demeanors and specified the particular responsibilities of individuals and the community;
it was a society in which bureaucracy and credentials meant little,
bearing and social origin much. Even in America's largest cities traditional views of Christian stewardship shaped assumptions of a proper

2. This critique of the twentieth-century acute-care general hospital is by no means
novel; it has built on an older tradition of criticism by advocates of social medicine and a
generation of sociologists who studied the hospital's internal life after World War II.

reciprocity between rich and poor. It was an urban world in which benevolence could still be imagined—if not always realized—in a context of face-to-face interaction between the giver and receiver of charity.

Allied with medicine's limited technical resources, it produced a medical system minimally dependent on institutional care, in which dependence and social status, not diagnosis, determined the makeup of institutional populations. Sickness in itself did not imply hospitalization—but only sickness or incapacity in those without a stable home or family members to provide care. Certification by a hospital contributor or board member was still a prerequisite to admission; without such personal knowledge and the stable place in society that this visibility implied, it was assumed that a prospective patient should occupy an almshouse pallet and not a private hospital bed.

Late-eighteenth- and early-nineteenth-century hospital advocates felt two kinds of motivation. One was the imperative of traditional Christian benevolence in urban communities already burdened with large numbers of "unsettled" individuals needing care. The other grew out of the clinical and educational needs of an elite in the medical profession; both lay and medical supporters of private hospitals contended that there could be no conflict between the hospital goals of laymen and physicians, for citizens of every rank would ultimately benefit from the clinical instruction that could be most effectively organized around the aggregated bodies of the poor.

Such optimistic words were not enough to banish conflict. From its earliest years the hospital was marked by a structured divergence of interests—between those of the pious laymen who bore the moral and legal responsibility for the institution and those of the medical men who practiced and taught within it. Drawn largely from the same social circles, attending physicians and lay authorities shared most values and assumptions, but in regard to professional matters, such as autopsies or admission policies, they could and did differ.[3] Where they did not, however, was in their assumption of stewardship and the mingled authority and responsibility that constituted it. Wealth and social position implied both the right and duty to direct the lives of dependent fellow citizens.

3. For a more detailed discussion see Charles E. Rosenberg, "Inward Vision and Outward Glance: The Shaping of the American Hospital, 1880–1914," *Bulletin of the History of Medicine* 53 (1979): 346–91.

The hospital was, insofar as its trustees and attending physicians could manage, a reflection of such relationships and responsibilities. Patients, nurses, attendants, and to an extent junior house pupils, were considered moral minors in need of direction and guidance. Trustees felt a personal responsibility for every aspect of the institution—and regularly inspected its wards and interviewed patients just as they personally oversaw admissions and settled accounts.

Day-to-day management was delegated to a lay superintendent who bore a paternal responsibility for the institution and its "inmates." In theory at least, the web of relationships within the hospital was always seen in terms of a family writ large. The superintendent was presumed to exert a paternal authority over all his "children." It is no accident that the hospital building was referred to as the "house," and its few paying patients as "boarders." It is no accident that the superintendent was expected to live in the hospital with his own family, and his wife was ordinarily expected to serve as matron, in charge of servants, food, and laundry—women's traditional area of responsibility. Apothecary and house staff ate at the superintendent's table, acting out the root-conception of the hospital as extended family.

The superintendent was not trained for his multi-faceted role in any specific way, but was expected to be a man of prudence and piety, ideally but not necessarily possessing appropriate business experience. Moral stature, not a specific credential, was the primary requirement for hospital administration.

Poverty and dependence were the operational prerequisites for hospital admission. (Regular exceptions were made only for the insane; in mental illness a different gradient determined the willingness of respectable Americans to hospitalize family members.) Sickness was a necessary but insufficient condition; aside from the occasional trauma victim even the laborer or artisan preferred to be cared for at home—if he had a home and family to provide that care. It was only to have been expected that men should have far outnumbered women among nineteenth-century hospital patients; urban America's abundant supply of single laboring men provided the bulk of hospital admissions.[4] If age and sex justified the father's authority in an ordinary home, so

4. Sex ratios were not so disproportionate in the growing number of community hospitals founded at the end of the century. The same is true of early specialty hospitals. Both social and technical factors made a hospital stay less stigmatizing in such institutions.

gender and class identity legitimated that authority in the hospital and implied the unquestioned deference that patients were expected to show toward the superintendent, attending physicians, and trustees.

The intimate scale of these early-nineteenth-century institutions provided a context in which these more general social realities could reproduce themselves. It was expected that the superintendent would see every patient every day, that he would know their names and be aware of their personal situations, just as he knew the cook, laundress, and coachman, who all resided in the hospital. Not surprisingly, many of these employees worked for long years at their jobs and were paid on a quarterly or semiannual basis. Like the patients they cared for, the hospital's workers bartered independence for security. This unyielding quid pro quo provided a measure of stability in a world that offered few such choices for the great majority of Americans who worked with their hands.

The hospital was part of an institutional world that minimized cash transactions and subsisted instead through a network of less tangible interactions. Physicians were paid in prestige and clinical access, trustees in deference and the opportunity for spiritual accomplishment; nurses and patients in creature comforts—food, heat, and a place to sleep. Patients offered deference and their bodies as teaching materials. Few dollars changed hands, but the system worked.

This was possible in part because the prebellum hospital was not burdened by a capital-intensive technology. There was little that could be done for a patient in the hospital that could not be provided at least as well in the home—and without the stigma of having received charity or the family having failed in its collective duty. Just as medical care was not segregated in the hands of a licensed and trained corps of practitioners, so the provision of acute care was not limited to a specific institutional setting. The boundaries of prebellum medicine were ill defined; domestic and irregular practice were a significant part of medical care, a vital reality even in families well able to employ trained physicians.

Boundaries between hospital and home were similarly indistinct, a consequence of limited technology as well as traditional social attitudes. In architecture as well as in terms of social organization, America's early hospitals differed little from a large home or welfare institution. As late as the Civil War much surgery was still done on the wards; laboratories, X-ray units, and sterile operating theaters were far in the future.[5] Many prebellum hospitals did not even have specific spaces adapted to the treatment of emergencies or the evaluation of patients for admission; a limited technology demanded little in the way of functionally differentiated space. Until the twentieth century hospital expense budgets were dominated by the cost of food, heat, light, and labor—costs little different from those of an orphanage, boarding school, or rich man's mansion.

Medical ideas and skills were widely disseminated in the community as well and not segregated in the profession, justifying in part the hospital's marginality and paralleling its lack of internal differentiation. Every educated gentleman was presumed to know something about medicine; every woman was something of a general practitioner. Medicine provided a striking example of a traditional society's general lack of specialized roles. In terms of authority, technology, administration, and even architecture, the hospital was very much a living sample of the community that produced it. The boundaries between community and hospital, and between medicine and its clients, remained indistinct in American cities until mid-century, and in rural areas until much later.

MEDICALIZING THE HOSPITAL AND
HOSPITALIZING MEDICINE

All this had changed drastically by 1920. The hospital was no longer exclusively a resort for the dependent; diagnosis as well as social location had begun to determine hospital admissions. Technology had provided new tools and, equally important, a new rationale for centering acute care in the hospital. Medical men and medical skills had come to play an increasingly prominent part in the institution, gradually supplanting older patterns of lay control. Bureaucracy had reshaped the institution's internal order: a trained and disciplined nursing corps,

5. The rationale for construction of early-nineteenth-century surgical amphitheaters was primarily pedagogic and, to a limited extent, aesthetic, removing the patient from the eyes and ears of ward mates. For an excellent introduction to the history of the hospital as physical entity see John D. Thompson and Grace Goldin, *The Hospital: A Social and Architectual History* (New Haven: Yale University Press, 1975).

a self-consciously professionalizing hospital administration, and an increasingly specialized profession had all played a role in transforming the nineteenth-century hospital.

Many social functions were moving from the home and neighborhood to institutional sites in late-nineteenth- and early-twentieth-century America, but none more categorically than medical care. And in no other case was the technological rationale more compelling. From a late-twentieth-century perspective, the resources of hospital medicine in the era of World War I may seem primitive, but they were impressive to contemporaries. Antiseptic surgery, the X ray, and clinical laboratories represented a newly scientific and efficacious medicine—a medicine necessarily based in the hospital. Few practitioners could duplicate these resources in their offices or make them available in the homes of even their wealthiest patients. Successful physicians had come to assume, and convince their patients to assume, that the hospital was the best place to undergo surgery and in fact to treat any acute ailment. Meanwhile, America's cities had grown, providing more patients without the means or often even the room to be cared for at home.

It was not only the urban hospital that had assumed a new prominence in medical care. By 1910 few enterprising towns of any size failed to boast a community hospital; it had become an accepted part of medical and especially surgical care for farmers and small-town Americans as well as for their urban contemporaries.

These changes in technology and patient population had consequences for every aspect of the hospital. An increasingly sophisticated technology—both medical and nonmedical—implied higher capital and operating costs and thus a ceaseless quest for reliable sources of income. For many nonprofit and every proprietary institution, rising costs meant a continued or growing dependence on income from the care of private patients.

Within the hospital, medical men and medical values became increasingly important in decision making. Though no abrupt or categorical shift, the general trend was clear enough; even where lay authorities still controlled public or private governing boards, they deferred to medical men in a way that would hardly have been approved by their self-confidently intrusive predecessors a century earlier. The growing complexity and presumed efficacy of medicine's tools seemed to make the centrality of physicians in hospital decision making both inevitable and appropriate.

But in most hospitals the power of attending staffs did not go uncontested. Like many other institutions in this period, the hospital was also becoming increasingly bureaucratic—governed by a new kind of chief executive officer with the aid of a middle management composed of a nursing superintendent, senior residents, and a comptroller. Management was negotiated as well as imposed.[6]

No single change transformed the hospital's day-to-day workings more than the acceptance of trained nurses and nurse training schools. A disciplined corps of would-be professionals entered wards previously dominated by the values and attitudes of a patient population different in class and often ethnicity from their social superiors who populated lay boards and attending staffs.[7] It was a nursing staff, moreover, whose social position reflected but could not rival the growing status of a male-dominated medical profession. Central to the professional self-consciousness of trained nursing was a relentless emphasis on discipline and efficiency—paralleling medicine's newly scientific self-image. This emphasis and the trained nurses who embodied and enforced it helped impose a new social order in hospital wards and rooms. Nursing added an additional layer to hospital management, which on balance enhanced rather than undermined the growing power of medicine in the hospital.

The increasing prominence of technology and the medical men who employed it expressed itself as well in a symmetrically preeminent role for acute care in the general hospital (and a reciprocal concentration of chronic cases in county, municipal, and, in the case of tuberculosis and mental illness, state hospitals).[8] More intrusive therapies, espe-

6. In smaller community hospitals a trained nurse often served as administrator and nursing superintendent. Attending staffs in such institutions could often exert an authority undiminished by the power of a male executive and well-established middle management.

7. Cf. Susan M. Reverby, *Ordered to Care: The Dilemma of American Nursing, 1850–1945* (Cambridge: Cambridge University Press, 1987), for a careful and comprehensive study of American nursing. See also Rosenberg, *Care of Strangers*, esp. 212–36, and Barbara Melosh, *"The Physician's Hand": Work, Culture and Conflict in American Nursing* (Philadelphia: Temple University Press, 1982).

8. This distinction was far older, but the rapidly increasing capacity for the delivery of acute care in the late nineteenth and early twentieth centuries only exacerbated the gap between municipal and private voluntary hospitals—with the responsibility for chronic and

cially surgery, helped to both shorten hospital stays and attract a new sort of hospital patient. Both therapeutic innovation and new admission patterns drastically altered the average patient's social and biological experience.

Diagnosis was also becoming self-consciously scientific, determined increasingly by medical men and medical categories. By World War I diagnosis had replaced dependency as the key to hospital admission. Socially-minded critics of the early-twentieth-century hospital were already contending that the patient was in danger of being reduced to his or her diagnosis—to a discrete biopathological phenomenon. The hospital and those who practiced in it were, they charged, losing sight of the patient as an individual with a family and an idiosyncratic social, psychological, and physiological identity. But although such critics never disappeared they were to exert comparatively little influence in the next half-century; the undeniable power and increasing efficacy of scientific medicine had an extraordinary appeal for physicians and their patients alike. The hospital had become the embodiment of—and in a measure the justification for—powerful new hopes and expectations.

The hospital had been transformed not only socially and technically, but physically as well. New medical tools coupled with a new industrial and building technology made the early-twentieth-century hospital a physical artifact very different from its forerunners a century earlier. The needs of radiology and clinical pathology, of hydrotherapy and electrotherapy, and, most importantly, of antiseptic surgery demanded reorganization of the hospital's interior. In an effort to increase what they termed efficiency, architects and administrators arranged the hospital's interior so as to minimize steps for its medical and nursing staff. The growth of fee-for-service practice in the hospital required examining and consulting rooms more private than facilities previously available in ward and outpatient departments. The presumed needs and desires of valued private patients led to the creation of more private and semiprivate accommodations. And like every other large institu-

---

geriatric care resting disproportionately on public institutions. For an introduction to the history of America's municipal hospitals see Harry F. Dowling, *City Hospitals: The Undercare of the Underprivileged* (Cambridge: Harvard University Press, 1982). On the special case of mental illness and state policy see Gerald N. Grob's indispensable studies: *Mental Institutions in America: Social Policy to 1875* (New York: Free Press, 1973) and *Mental Illness and American Society, 1875–1940* (Princeton: Princeton University Press, 1983).

tional structure at the time, hospitals were built with electric lights, dynamos, elevators, and partially mechanized laundries and kitchens. In addition to the cumulative impact of a mid-century reform movement that had underlined the need for improved modes of heating and ventilation, these new technological realities were turning the American general hospital into a capital-intensive and internally differentiated physical entity—mirroring in a different sphere the changes in professional organization and the distribution of knowledge that were reshaping medical care more generally.

Medical knowledge, like medical practice, was gradually but inexorably becoming segregated in professionally accredited hands. No longer was it assumed that an educated man would understand something of medicine, or that midwives would provide the bulk of care during childbirth and early infancy. Drugs were purchased, not gathered, and even in rural areas Americans turned to physicians sooner than they would have several generations earlier. Within the medical profession, too, knowledge was gradually segregating itself, so that average practitioners were no longer presumed to be omnicompetent (even if they might have to ignore such limitations in rural areas or choose to ignore them in cities). The specialist had become a significant part of medical care.[9] Practitioners as well as educated laymen assumed that the hospital was and must be the site of medicine's most advanced, efficacious, and specialized care.

If the hospital had been medicalized, the medical profession had been hospitalized in the years between 1800 and 1920. This intra-professional process has attracted far less attention from contemporary historians than the hospital's social evolution, but it is no less significant. These two spheres of change are in fact inseparable—for the hospitalization of medical men and medical ideas was a key element in the institution's social transformation. Late-nineteenth- and early-twentieth-century reforms in medical education meant that an ever larger proportion of American physicians was being socialized and educated in hospital wards and rooms.[10] This had been a gradual but

    9. See Rosemary Stevens, *American Medicine and the Public Interest* (New Haven: Yale University Press, 1971), for the most detailed survey of the development of medical specialties in the United States.

    10. The hospitals, with their growing scale and need for in-house medical care, exerted their own role, pulling more and more physicians into their wards. The push of individual

steady process, well advanced by the 1910 publication of the Flexner Report, which called for increased clinical experience at the under-graduate and graduate levels.

Hospital service had always been central to the ambitions and careers of America's medical elite; by World War I it had become central to the education and practice of a much larger proportion of the profession, which was itself becoming more tightly organized, uniformly trained, and systematically licensed. Since the eighteenth century hospitals had played a key role in disseminating as well as accumulating medical knowledge, serving as a mechanism to communicate ideas and techniques from a metropolitan elite to a new generation of practitioners. With an ever larger proportion of physicians serving as interns and residents, the twentieth-century hospital became an increasingly effective tool for the diffusion of ideas and skills. But it was more than that. With its ability to provide an intense shared experience, the hospital provided a context that helped create a social and emotional community among physicians—a community bound together and legitimated by shared knowledge as well as shared experience. Sociologists have in the past quarter-century studied the texture of hospital training in detail as they sought to illuminate the social character of medicine; historians of medicine need to concern themselves with the same questions in the past. Not only shared social functions, but specific shared experiences, ideas, and skills created and recreated the subcommunity we call the medical profession.

More generally, the twentieth-century hospital has moved into a marketplace of discrete and impersonal cash transactions—to a style of benevolence that would have seemed inappropriate to the sort of men who managed hospitals in the first third of the nineteenth century. Efficiency, not stewardship, threatened to dominate the early-twentieth-century hospital. Some administrators boasted, in fact, of applying personnel and management skills learned in factories and the military to hospital organization, thus providing ultimately more benevolent, because more rational and cost-effective, care.

---

ambition and educational reform was consistent with these needs. Cf. Kenneth M. Ludmerer, *Learning to Heal: The Development of American Medical Education* (New York: Basic Books, 1985); William G. Rothstein, *American Medical Schools and the Practice of Medicine: A History* (New York: Oxford University Press, 1987); and Rosenberg, *Care of Strangers*, 190–211.

But the hospital never entirely assumed this particular guise in the first three-quarters of the twentieth century. It was never managed as a factory or department store. The hospital continued in the twentieth century, as it had begun in the eighteenth, to be clothed with the public interest in a way that mocked categorical distinctions between public and private. Private hospitals had always been assumed to function for the community at large—treating the needy and dependent, training a new generation of medical practitioners, and attracting a varied and eclectic assortment of subventions from city, county, and state authorities. The late eighteenth and early nineteenth century had in any case never understood absolute distinctions between the public and private spheres; the idea of commonwealth subsumed something of the commonhealth—and thus collective responsibility for that health. It was natural for most hospital authorities to assume that they should continue to receive public funds, just as they assumed they should be free of local taxes and the constraints of tort law.

The hospital's transactions involved pain, sickness, and death as well as the public good. An insulating sacredness surrounded the activities of the twentieth-century hospital; its "products" were, in a literal sense, beyond material accounting. The newly intensified expectations of scientific medicine were both material and transcendant; Americans hoped and expected that this new institution would provide a refuge from the sickness and premature death that had always seemed immanent in man's corporeal body. It is not surprising that the private hospital's operations (except for a minority of clearly proprietary institutions) have never been entirely disciplined by the impersonal logic of profit maximization or easily bent to communally determined demands for planning and cost control.

Nor is it surprising that transactions within the hospital continued until World War II to be structured around the exchange of labor and status. The hospital was in, but not of, the marketplace. Nurses and house staff still exchanged their labor for credentials; attending physicians bartered their ward services for prestige and admission privileges in private services. Nonprofessional workers traded a measure of autonomy and the higher wages they might have received on the commercial labor market for the security and paternalism that presumably characterized the hospital. Thus, even as it was being transformed into an increasingly technical and seemingly indispensable institution, the hospital remained clothed with a special and sacred quality that removed it from both normal social scrutiny and the market's discipline.

ROOTS OF CONTEMPORARY PROBLEMS

If the hospital in Thomas Jefferson's or Andrew Jackson's America had been a microcosm of the community that nurtured it, so is the hospital of the 1980s. Although we live in a very different sort of community, the hospital remains both product and prisoner of its own history and of the more general trends that have characterized our society. Our mingled concern with health and high technology have in fact created expectations and material interests that have made the hospital a substantive if not irritatingly visible element in the nation's economy. Its origins are hardly recognizable in its quaint forerunners.

The hospital is a necessary community institution strangely insulated from community. It is instead a symbiotically allied group of subcommunities bound together by social location and the logic of history. This insulated character is typical of a good number of social institutions, such as schools, the federal civil service, and large corporations. But there are some special aspects of the hospital that have exaggerated its ability to look inward, to pursue its own vision of social good. This institutional solipsism has taken place in ironic if not logical conjunction with the hospital's function of dealing with the most intimate and fundamental of everyday human realities.

To most contemporary Americans rising costs have been the key element in transforming the hospital from personal solution to social problem. But spiraling costs are no more than a consequence of the hospital's particular history as it evolved within America's more general social and economic structures.

Like the Defense Department, the hospital system has grown in response to perceived transcendant need, in comparison with which normal budgetary constraints and compromises have come to seem niggling and inappropriate. Security, as any absolute and immeasurable good, makes enormous demands on our resources. Both health and defense, moreover, have become captives of high technology and worst-case justifications. In both instances, the gradient of technical feasibility becomes a moral imperative.[11] That which might be done, should be done. Absolute ends do not lend themselves to compromise; and the bottom line is that there has been no bottom line.

This analogy can, of course, be carried too far. The hospital has a special history incorporating and reflecting the evolution both of the medical profession and our social welfare system. The relationship between nursing and medicine, the development of health insurance and third-party payment, and the gradual involvement of the federal government have all helped create the hospital's special character. The high status of medicine has been built into the hospital—not only in the form of an undifferentiated social authority but in the shape of particular historically determined intellectual and career choices. An increasingly proliferative specialism and an emphasis on laboratory research and acute care, for example, have played an important role in the profession, and thus in the hospital. So complex and interwined are these interrelationships that changes in any one sphere inevitably affect other areas. Some aspects of modern medicine seemed at first to promise little eventual economic impact. One, for example, was the increasing ability of physicians to disentangle specific disease entities. Yet we have seen a complex and inexorably bureaucratic reimbursement system grow up around these diagnostic entities; sickness does not exist if it cannot be coded. The current controversy surrounding Diagnosis Related Groups (DRGs) can be seen in part as a natural outcome of the intellectual and institutional history of the medical profession. The ideas that rule the worldview of medicine and its system of education and research have very practical connections with the pragmatic world of medical care and medical costs.

The development of third-party payment and the subsequent intrusion of the federal government have only intensified these patterns. They have provided funds on the provider's terms without fundamentally changing the provider's orientation. And these terms have, until recent years, assumed an identity of interest among the medical profession, the hospitals, their employees, and their patients. Only in the past decade has it become clear to the public how profoundly these interests can differ.

---

11. And the carrying out of that imperative has, of course, created economic and institutional interests committed to it—and thus another source of rigidity in the system.

Within the last generation the hospital has been forced to leave the world of paternalism and traditional values. Unions, a more assertive nursing profession, ever-increasing capital costs, a growing dependence on federal support, and even the need to pay house staff have moved hospitals into a position increasingly analagous to that of other social institutions, and exposed them to the prospect of increasing external control. Clothed with a public interest and promising transcendant social goods, the hospital remains a rigid and intractable, yet indispensable, institution. It will not go away. As students of its peculiar history, our task is to try to understand it and to communicate that understanding but perhaps not to forgive all.

Part I

THE AMERICAN HOSPITAL
IN TRANSITION

I

From Respectable Domesticity to Medical Efficiency: The Changing Kansas City Hospital, 1875–1920

JOAN E. LYNAUGH

As the members of the board of directors at St. Luke's Hospital in Kansas City pushed back their chairs to end yet another stormy meeting, A. E. Stowell assured his colleagues that the decisions just taken would "develop this institution to a high plane of efficiency; taking it away from the invalid home idea; also from the [image of a] high class boarding house for chronic cases."[1] For, after three years of argument, the board in 1917 finally decided to change policies at St. Luke's and limit admissions to paying patients sent by members of a self-selected medical staff; furthermore, the only free-care patients admitted would be those approved by a management committee. Stowell and the board were changing the hospital's original emphasis on benevolent, custodial care of the deserving sick to a more self-sufficient, therapy-oriented focus on care of acutely ill patients. Their decision also reordered the internal direction of the hospital. Lou Eleanor Keely, the superintendent of nurses, now had to share power with a management committee made up of a board member, a new hospital manager, and a medical-staff appointee. She promptly resigned.[2]

1. Minutes, March 16, 1917, Archives, St. Luke's Hospital, Kansas City, Mo.
2. Miss Keeley, who had managed the hospital since its founding in 1902, left Kansas

21

St. Luke's story illustrates the steady reorientation of the turn-of-the-century hospital to an exclusive focus on care of the acutely ill and surgical patients. This description of hospitals in postbellum Kansas City, Missouri, reveals how these community hospitals began and how they changed in less than two generations. Much of hospital history to date tends to telescope the story of the changing American hospital so that it seems as if hospitals were transformed directly from shelters for the chronically ill and homeless poor into highly technologic, medically dominated curative institutions.[3] On closer examination, a critical intermediate stage in this transition appears that I have chosen to call the "domestic" era of hospital development. This period spanned the decades from 1875, when hospitals began to be acceptable as substitutes for care at home, to 1920 when the technologic era of surgical treatment and medical diagnostic services began to dominate hospital affairs. The domestic era was characterized by an emphasis on building safe, accessible institutions and providing reliable, respectable caretakers. The case of Kansas City's hospitals and nurses helps us understand why hospitals proliferated, why nurses played a critical role in this transitional period, and how the nineteenth-century hospital was reinvented in the first decades of the twentieth century.[4]

HOSPITAL GROWTH IN KANSAS CITY

As the dust settled after the political division and violence of the Civil War, signs of rejuvenation began to appear in Kansas City. The 1870 population had soared from an immediate postwar low of three

City to direct a contingent of nurses in France during World War I. Later she served as superintendent of three rural hospitals in Missouri.

3. A renewed interest in the history of hospitals has been led by Charles Rosenberg, Morris Vogel, Rosemary Stevens, and David Rosner, among others. See, for instance, Charles Rosenberg, *The Care of Strangers: The Rise of America's Hospital System* (New York: Basic Books, 1988); Morris Vogel, *The Invention of the Modern Hospital, Boston 1870–1930* (Chicago: The University of Chicago Press, 1980); Rosemary Stevens, "'A Poor Sort of Memory': Voluntary Hospitals and Government Before the Depression," *Millbank Memorial Fund Quarterly* 60 (Fall 1982): 551–84; and David Rosner, *A Once Charitable Enterprise: Hospitals and Health Care in Brooklyn and New York, 1885–1915* (Cambridge: Cambridge University Press, 1982).

4. This essay is drawn from data collected for my dissertation, *The Community Hospitals of Kansas City, Missouri, 1870–1915* (Ann Arbor, Mich.: University Microfilms International, 1982). A facsimile version is forthcoming from Garland Press.

thousand inhabitants to twenty-five thousand people. Completion of the Hannibal Bridge (1869), which carried the all-important railroad over the Missouri River at Kansas City, made it certain that the town was to be the hub of commerce and transportation for westward development.[5] As people crowded into the alternately dusty or muddy town it became an instant city with all the problems of urban growth already seen in older, eastern cities.

The city built its first hospital in 1870 to cope with destitute sick persons. There were fifteen beds in a single room divided by a curtain to screen women patients from men. After a fire destroyed this rudimentary facility in 1875, a larger, brick hospital of twenty-eight beds was built. An 1880 city ordinance required the municipal hospital to admit only destitute city residents; wage earners or travelers had to look elsewhere for care when they fell sick or were injured.[6]

Kansas City's citizens multiplied rapidly; they were widely diverse in origin, religion, and race. In 1880 the population doubled that of 1870, reaching 55,785. The people came from rural Missouri, the Middle Atlantic states, the border states of Kentucky and Tennessee, and the Southeast as well as from Ireland, Germany, and Great Britain. Numerous voluntary associations sprang up among this burgeoning and heterogeneous population. Historian A. Theodore Brown estimates that there may have been as many as 482 associations in Kansas City by 1880.[7] Some groups intended to improve and expand commercial enterprises; others concentrated on the social welfare of segments of the city's population.

5. Details of late-nineteenth-century Kansas City abound in two works published by local historians during the years encompassed in this study. Theodore S. Case's *History of Kansas City, Missouri* (Syracuse, N.Y.: D. Mason, 1888) and Carrie Westlake Whitney's *Kansas City, Missouri: Its History and People* (Chicago, 1908) indicate public and private priorities related to social problems and offer much descriptive information about the environment and its population. A. Theodore Brown and Lyle Dorset survey the history of the city in their *K.C.: A History of Kansas City, Missouri* (Boulder, Colo.: Pruitt, 1978).

6. Kansas Citians who were in a position to decide chose to limit governmental responsibilities to the sick and infirm. The obligation to be self-supporting and the preference for voluntary association to achieve collective goals is exemplified by the remarks of Theodore Case, first president of the Provident Association, a charity organization founded in 1880 to assist Kansas City's needy. He stated the mission of the association as "not only to alleviate suffering and distress, but to ferret out and expose a class of beggars who constantly impose upon the confidence and liberality of the people." Case, *History of Kansas City*, 169.

7. Brown and Dorset, *K.C.*, 74.

This pattern of private, voluntary association also characterized community response to the sickness care needs of the city during the last quarter of the century and beyond. Between 1874, when a Catholic order of nuns opened a hospital on the bluffs overlooking the junction of the Kansas and Missouri rivers, and 1915, when hospital development finally slowed down, twenty-two hospitals opened their doors. This census of hospitals excludes the various rest homes, refuges for alcoholics and drug addicts, temporary railroad hospitals, and pesthouses in the city during the period.[8] Eleven of the hospitals were founded by religious and ethnic groups as voluntary and charitable organizations. By 1915, three of these had failed. One, St. Luke's Hospital, was reorganized and reopened. Eight other hospitals were founded by physician entrepreneurs. These tended to be ephemeral; none lasted more than ten years. Three city hospitals, Kansas City General, Kansas City General, No. 2 (the black public hospital), and a tuberculosis hospital represented the only tax-supported public initiatives in institutional care of the sick.

The hospital boom in Kansas City mirrored the national pattern of hospital development. From less than two hundred hospitals in the 1870s, the number of institutions nationwide rose to more than five thousand by 1915. Most of this growth was due to private sector initiatives by individuals or groups who relied on income from patients, charitable donations, and voluntary labor.

Why this rather sudden American enthusiasm for hospitals? The Kansas City experience substantiates the argument that a substitute for home care during illness was needed because the necessary elements of care—space, equipment, and caretakers—were missing at home.[9] Rapid population growth created housing shortages, men following jobs found themselves without family support, and their serious illnesses could not be managed in ordinary public accommodations.

The roster of patients admitted to St. Joseph's Hospital, the first voluntary hospital in Kansas City, reveals that in 1874–75 the large majority (80 percent) were men under the age of fifty. These were

8. This number (19 private, 3 public) is derived from a survey of hospital records, newspapers, city directories, various local histories, medical journals, nursing histories, and memorabilia.

9. Morris Vogel makes this point particularly well in his *Invention of the Modern Hospital*, 97–119.

working men, including not only the railroad conductors and section hands so important to Kansas City at the time, but also farmers, clerks, police, and laborers. Home care, usually requiring a female relative or servant as care giver, was often not available to these men. Many of St. Joseph's patients listed as their home address that of their employer or foreman. The few women who appear on the hospital registers listed themselves as domestics or shopkeepers. These employed women might well have also found themselves in a solitary social situation that forced them to seek hospital care when ill.

The patients admitted to St. Joseph's and to the German Hospital (opened in 1887) were seriously ill, judging by hospital records. Consumption (tuberculosis), malaria and unspecified fevers, typhoid, and orthopedic problems, especially fractures, led the list of reasons for admission.

Most likely, people in Kansas City, as elsewhere in the United States, would have preferred to be cared for in their own homes when ill or injured. Failing that, they chose care in hospitals related to their ethnic and religious affiliation. At Roman Catholic and Irish-dominated St. Joseph's, where each patient's nationality was recorded, Irish-Americans were admitted most frequently, followed by foreign-born Irish, and then persons of German descent. Similarly, the house committee of the German Hospital reported that more than half of the 246 patients admitted in 1890 were German.[10]

Ethnic and religious groups spent scarce resources to found and maintain their own hospitals. There were three Roman Catholic hospitals; St. Joseph's was dominated by Irish Catholics, St. Mary's was run by an order of nuns of German origin, while St. Vincent's, founded in 1909 to care for women, claimed no specific ethnic orientation. The German Hospital, labeling itself a nonsectarian institution, opened in 1887. The Methodist Episcopal Church South sponsored an early hospital and was imitated by other Methodists in 1904. The Episcopal Hospital, St. Luke's, originally opened as All Saints Hospital in 1885, but failed financially in the depression of 1889. Swedish Lutherans organized their hospital after the turn of the century. Thus the voluntary hospitals reflected the varied religious, ethnic, and, to a lesser extent,

10. Patient Registers, 1874–94, and 1895–1900, Archives, Sisters of St. Joseph of Carondelet, Provincialate, St. Louis, and "Report of House Committee, German Hospital Association, 1890" in Missouri Valley Room, Kansas City Public Library, Vertical File.

racial mix of the city. More significantly, religious and ethnic groups invested in hospitals to an extent that seems surprisingly large, given their numbers.

The foreign-born population of early Kansas City was mostly Irish, German, and English. These immigrants joined a wave of native Americans migrating from the Middle Atlantic states and the upper South as well as rural Missouri. Germans constituted about 4 percent of the 1880 population; by 1900 they surpassed the Irish to become the largest single foreign-born group. "Colored" people made up about 15 percent of the 1880 population and about 10 percent of the 1910 census. The misleading drop in percentage of blacks reported in the 1910 census is due to removal of American Indians and Hispanics from the "colored" category, where they were located in the 1880 census. The 1890 census counted 11,900 Roman Catholics, 4,490 Baptists, 3,195 Methodist Episcopalians, slightly over 1,000 Presbyterians, a like number of Protestant Episcopalians, about 800 Lutherans, and 895 Jews.[11] This roster of communicants represents close to one-fourth of the total population (132,716), but it should be noted that they were divided among dozens of religious organizations. There were 101 church buildings in Kansas City in 1890. A picture emerges of numerous, rather small clusters of people bound together by religion or ethnic origin.

These groups justified their commitment to hospitals in both moral and practical terms. The sisters of St. Joseph relied on the rule of their order, dating from 1693: "They shall embrace the services of hospitals, the direction of orphan homes, the visiting of the sick poor."[12] The Church Charity Association, the Episcopal group that opened All Saints Hospital, declared itself ready to "associate for benevolent and purely charitable purposes" and "provide the benefits of the hospital to all without regard to sect, religion, country or sex. . . . The work is to be essentially charitable, for while pay patients are to be received, all sums obtained from them are required to be expended with the institution, and will go to aid in the support of the free wards."[13] The

11. Lawrence H. Larsen, *The Urban West at the End of the Frontier* (Lawrence, Kans.: The Regent Press of Kansas, 1978), 22–31 passim.

12. Sister Dolorita M. Dougherty, C.S.J. et al., *Sisters of St. Joseph of Carondelet* (St. Louis: B. Herder Book Co., 1966), 28.

13. "Amendments to the Articles of Agreement for Formation and Incorporation of the Church Charity Association of Kansas City," Archives, Medical Library, St. Luke's Hospital, Kansas City, Mo., and *Kansas City Sunday Times*, September 17, 1882.

Kansas Conference of the Lutheran Church put it a different way. Due to "the many excellent doctors who are residing in Kansas City and the many of our countrymen, who from different localities visit them and have to stay for a shorter or longer time and the non-existence of a good Swedish boarding house, there is a deeply felt need of getting a good Swedish hospital as soon as possible."[14] The founder of the Sisters of St. Mary, Mother Mary Odilia, conducted a five-year program of sick care in the homes of the poor. By 1877, however, she diverted her group toward hospital work, believing that institutional care of the sick would be less expensive than giving care at home, would provide a safe refuge for their patients, and would be less exhausting and more efficient for the nun nurses.[15]

Proliferation of these ethnically and religiously sponsored hospitals can be partially explained as an extension of tradition, especially for Roman Catholics and Lutherans, whose European hospital experience was translated to the new country. It can also be seen as a competitive response since the popularity of hospitals both as benevolent works and for personal use continued to grow. American Protestant denominations, such as the Episcopalians and the Methodists, saw hospital work as a powerful justification for their continuation in a period of increasing secularization and as a recruiting attraction for new members interested in charitable works. Competition among hospital developers is clear in the publicity for All Saints Hospital when the Episcopal *Church News* of May 1883 reminded its readers that the only other private hospital in Kansas City was the Roman Catholic St. Joseph's. The Catholic hospital administration "was not deemed as satisfactory," and Episcopalians were encouraged to contribute to All Saints as a way of rectifying the situation.[16]

Small, sectarian, and ethnic hospitals put much emphasis on security and respectability. They primarily offered nursing care, shelter, and food rather than complex medical services. Their organizational plans were simple, the numbers of personnel were small, and hospital work

14. E. H. Hashinger, "Trinity Lutheran Hospital," *Jackson County Medical Journal* 6 (December 3, 1932): 6–10.

15. Sister Mary Gabriel and Jane Berdes, *But What Is Greatness?* (Milwaukee: Marquette University Press, 1959), 68–103.

16. *The Church News*, May 1883, Archives, Medical Library, St. Luke's Hospital, Kansas City, Mo.

was undifferentiated. Nuns and nurses cared for patients, did laundry, cleaned, prepared food and medicines, and assisted at surgery. They also admitted and discharged the patients, raised funds, and managed the institutions. Domestic era hospitals for paying patients developed in the private sector as a way of creating an accessible, safe place in which to be sick. They responded to pressing community needs for personal services that families could not provide. Beyond the very existence of these new institutions the most innovative and interesting aspect of their development was the nurse training school idea. Finding an economically feasible way to provide direct personal care acceptable to the middle-class citizens of Kansas City preoccupied hospital leaders during the domestic era.

NUNS AND NURSES AS CARETAKERS

Hospital founders used a variety of strategies to solve the caretaker problem. For nearly twenty years, private voluntary hospitals relied exclusively on nuns and their assistants to nurse the sick. This strategy seems not at all unusual in the case of the Roman Catholic hospital but it is somewhat surprising to find the German Hospital Club hiring Roman Catholic Franciscan nuns from Illinois to give care in their avowedly nonsectarian hospital. The German Hospital specifically forbade unrequested visits from clergymen in its bylaws. In negotiating with the nuns who gave care, however, hospital founders contented themselves with stipulating that "the Sisters shall not make any religious propaganda toward non-Catholic patients."[17] As part of the development of All Saints Hospital in 1885, an attempt was made to establish an order of religious women to run the hospital and nurse the sick. The Order of the Holy Cross consisted of only two dedicated members of the Episcopal parish responsible for All Saints, and one of them, Sister Isabel Fitzgerald, ran the hospital during its brief existence. Both the hospital and the sisterhood failed after only four years.

Scant details survive about any individual nursing sister of the period

17. Sister Mary Gabriel Henninger, S.S.M., *Sisters of St. Mary*, (St. Louis: Sisters of St. Mary, 1979), 113. The contract between the sisters and the board of directors of the Hospital Club was translated by Otto Steinwauchs in 1976 and is reprinted in full in Sister Henninger's account of the order's activities.

before 1900. Most of the sisters of St. Joseph working in Kansas City were Irish-Americans, supplemented by a few recruits from Ireland. Everything these nineteenth-century nuns did, whether private or public, came under the authority of the sister superior of the hospital. The Provincial Superior General of the sisters of St. Joseph, who presided from St. Louis, directed a national network of hospitals, orphanages, and old-age homes that were run by the order. When she sent nuns to open the first private hospital in Kansas City in 1874 it became the western outpost of a chain of forty-seven institutions.[18]

The sisters of St. Mary, who succeeded the Franciscans at the German Hospital in 1895 and then opened their own St. Mary's Hospital in 1909, were almost all of German descent or nativity. Their order, with a tradition of smallpox and cholera nursing in France and Germany, found its niche among the German immigrant population of the midwest. German language, diet, and custom survived within the order well into the twentieth century. One of the obvious attractions of the sisters of St. Mary to the German Hospital Club was their affinity with German life, especially their ability to speak the language.

The nuns' lives were inseparable from their hospitals. Apparently, they worked a seven-day week, lived in the hospital, and attended the chapel within its walls. Training was on-the-job and ongoing. The nuns at St. Joseph's took classes from physicians, assisted at operations, and gave anesthesia. Several nuns trained as pharmacists.

In the Roman Catholic hospitals the management of hospital affairs was entirely in the hands of the sister superiors. Their autonomy stands in sharp contrast to the control exercised by hospital trustees over lay women hospital superintendents. The nuns' ownership of their hospitals and their retention of control over internal management, including patient admissions and medical staff membership, restrained efforts on the part of physicians and others to divert them from their goals. As we shall see, however, they were not immune to external pressures to change.

Secular nursing in the form of nurses' training schools became the dominant strategy for patient care beginning in the 1890s. The key to nursing school development was recruitment of a trained nurse to head the school, find and teach students, and quite often to supervise the

18. Dougherty, *Sisters of St. Joseph*, 427–28.

entire hospital. Emma Cushman pioneered the training school movement in Kansas City when she opened the Scarritt Hospital Training School (Methodist Episcopal Church South) in 1892. St. Joseph's, St. Luke's (successor to All Saints), Kansas City General (the city hospital), the German Hospital, and the Swedish Hospital all started training schools between 1901 and 1906.

Insofar as it was regimented and thoroughly authoritarian, life in the training schools emulated that in the religious orders. Superintendents of training schools assumed parental authority over pupil nurses. Hours of sleep, meals, recreation, days off, as well as classes and patient care duties, were laid out in detail. Lou Eleanor Keely, superintendent of the Hospital and Training School at St. Luke's, proclaimed her authority unequivocally. "The Superintendent . . . has entire control over everything pertaining to the discipline and duties of nurses, including their instruction and conduct at all times. . . . The work of nursing demands intelligence, good temper, an orderly habit of mind, thorough trustworthiness, and a willing spirit. No one should enter upon this work except with a strong sense of duty and a readiness to conform to the necessarily strict rules of discipline."[19] Young women entered the training schools, completed their apprenticeships of two years (later three years), and then usually sought employment as private duty nurses in patients' homes or in the hospitals. A few became visiting nurses in private social agencies or superintendents in hospitals. Hospital jobs were not available.

Student nurses provided the day-to-day care in hospitals, while learning a skill that would make them self-supporting. Most were farm girls. Rosters of students from several hospitals reveal that a significant proportion of the students migrated to Kansas City from small towns in Kansas and Missouri as well as Wyoming, Colorado, Oklahoma, and New Mexico. Hospitals recruited students with apparent ease. Perhaps it seemed better than farm work, or the city was alluring. This rural to urban migration of young women is exemplified by the decision to delay the opening of St. Mary's Training School from September to October because the "girls' work on the farm prevented them from coming until some of the crops were in."[20]

19. *Annual Report, St. Luke's Hospital and Training School* (Kansas City, Mo.: St. Luke's Hospital, 1915), 28–30.
20. Grade Book "x," 1905–39, Medical Library, St. Joseph's Hospital, Kansas City,

The curriculum included lectures supplemented by heavy doses of apprenticelike training at the bedside. Students were admitted to each school in numbers sufficient to care for that hospital's patients. Most Kansas City training schools required one or more years of high school for admission. Typical physician lectures dealt with anatomy, physiology, pharmacology, first aid, specialty areas such as gynecology, obstetrics, eye, ear, nose, and throat diseases, and pathology. Nurses taught dietetics, nursing ethics, bacteriology, and hygiene. In actuality, though, students thought most of their learning came from older students or physicians on the hospital wards. After all, student time and energy was primarily spent in active ward work. Student grades on general hospital work went into a permanent record kept by the superintendent or sister in charge of the school.

Women entering the training schools sometimes failed to complete the rigorous program. Fatigue, homesickness, and a dislike of the work or the environment took a toll. At St. Joseph's, for instance, the grade books reveal a high attrition rate from 1906 to 1916; as many as fifty percent of the students dropped out in some years. Some simply left; others were dismissed. Occasionally a reason for departure was recorded such as "married," "smoking," or "inefficiency." Part of the attrition was due to the hazards of the work. Two pupil nurses and two young nuns died at St. Joseph's during the ten-year period.[21]

The training school met the hospitals' voracious appetites for caretakers and the students' need for entry into a respectable, remunerative occupation. Twenty-five years after Emma Cushman pioneered the concept in Kansas City there were fifteen different training schools preparing nurses. This paralleled the national trend as the training school idea swept the United States. By 1909, there were 1,129 schools of nursing; virtually all of them were based in hospitals.

Thus the domestic era of hospital development in Kansas City created a series of clean and safe health-care institutions, many of which were organized under religious and/or ethnic auspices. The era also saw the

Mo.; *The Scalpel*, 1908 and 1909, University Medical College, Medical Library, University of Missouri at Kansas City, Mo.; and Sister Mary Gabriel Henninger, "St. Mary's Hospital and Its Schools of Nursing" (typescript, 1977), 35, Medical Library, St. Mary's Hospital, Kansas City, Mo.

21. Grade Book "x" and Diary of Sister Irmina Dougherty (1904), Medical Library, St. Joseph's Hospital, Kansas City, Mo. Sister Dougherty founded the training school at St. Joseph's in 1901.

development of the training school idea. Headed by a woman vested
with authority over patient care and the lives of the student workers
in the hospitals, the training school solved the crucial labor problems
of the domestic era hospital. Furthermore, the training school was a
good fit with the occupational and social mobility aspirations of young,
rural women in Kansas and Missouri who had no chance for employment in their own small towns.

FROM DOMESTICITY TO EFFICIENCY

But around 1910 or so the language of annual reports extolling the
virtues of the hospitals began to change. Words like "modern" and
"sanitary" replaced "homelike" and "restful." The first generation
of hospital founders deliberately stressed a "hospital as home" metaphor. Their successors were more likely to represent their institutions
as sanitary temples of scientific cure. It was more than a symbolic
gesture or advertising ploy. The focus had shifted slowly from personal
care, domestic services, and shelter to medical diagnosis and treatment,
and more specifically, to surgical intervention. Hospital leaders built
new buildings; the Germans, the Swedes, the Catholics, and the Episcopalians all moved or built anew between 1905 and 1917. More
important, the buildings filled up with operating rooms, X-ray facilities, and laboratories, as well as beds. Other changes, such as the
introduction of marble and tile surfaces for easy cleaning, promoted
antisepsis and aseptic surgical conditions. Obstetric wards opened as
women began to turn to obstetricians for care during childbirth. The
renovated house of the nineteenth century was abandoned in favor of
imposing, sometimes massive structures. New construction often
meant a change of neighborhood as hospitals moved with their constituencies away from downtown Kansas City toward the southern
suburbs.[22]

Demographic changes in Kansas City began to affect the various
hospitals' constituencies. This is especially evident in the older hospitals that originally served the Irish or German segments of Kansas

22. David Ward, among others, demonstrates the steady drift of turn-of-the-century
city residents away from the city center and along mass transportation routes. In Kansas
City this movement was south and east, and the hospitals followed. David Ward, *Cities
and Immigrants* (New York: Oxford University Press, 1971), esp. 105–17 and 126–39.

City. Late in the 1890s and increasingly after the turn of the century, the ethnic and to some extent the religious match of hospital founders and patients faded. By 1895 only 15 percent of St. Joseph's patients were listed as Irish. At the German Hospital in 1912, 75 percent of the patients were listed as American. St. Mary's, the newer Roman Catholic hospital, recorded only 25 percent of its patients in 1914 as Catholic.[23] The apparent decline in ethnic and religious distinctions among the hospitals corresponds with falling numbers of foreign-born persons in the local population. Perhaps religious and ethnic insularity became less important as the use of hospitals gained in social acceptability. Perhaps Americanization of second- and third-generation Kansas Citians reduced the need for ethnically and religiously safe havens. There was one important exception to this apparent assimilation. Older Kansas City hospitals began to serve somewhat more of a cross section of the population, but black Kansas Citians still found a need for a hospital of their own. They opened Wheatley-Provident Hospital in 1913.

As a result of the hospitals' growing size, increasingly complex services, and training schools, new managerial structures were required. Indeed, if the period from 1875 to 1900 can be called the domestic era, the period from 1900 to 1920 and beyond might well be called the managerial era of hospital development.

The internal organization of the early hospital was relatively simple, involving an active board of directors and a nurse superintendent; in the case of the Catholic hospitals a sister superior oversaw the entire operation. After the turn of the century the hospitals grew much more complex. The training schools contributed to this complexity, of course, because school management required superintendents, assistants, schedules, nurses' homes, and special budgets. A more critical stimulus was the growth of the institution. St. Joseph's new hospital, for example, had 250 beds where it once had 12. German Hospital doubled its original 100 beds, and even St. Mary's, one of Kansas City's newest hospitals, boasted 50 beds. A rapid escalation in the proportion of patients admitted for surgery similarly contributed to the internal complexity. Surgical patients required more operating room

23. Henninger, *The Sisters of St. Mary*, 15; 25th Annual Report, German Hospital, Kansas City, Mo. (Kansas City, Mo.: The Bishop Press, 1912); and "Report, St. Joseph's Hospital, 1895–96," Archives, Sisters of St. Joseph of Carondelet, St. Louis.

space and equipment, and more intensive nursing for short periods of time.

Management evolved into a triumvirate made up of a hospital administrator, the superintendent of nurses, and representatives of the medical staff. This later addition acknowledged the increasing power and role of medicine within the hospital. By the beginning of World War I all but the Catholic hospitals had switched from a system where female superintendents wielded most of the internal authority to a system where the hospital administrator and the medical chief directed the hospital and the medical care leaving the nurse superintendent with authority only over the nurses and nursing care.

In nineteenth-century Kansas City hospitals physicians held hospital staff membership, advised board members and superintendents, visited charity patients, occasionally ran clinics, and often did surgery, but rarely did they dominate decision making inside the hospitals. Patients used the hospitals primarily for nursing care, observation, food service, and shelter rather than for medical diagnosis and treatment.

The physician's new power can be attributed to two things—the advent of the surgical patient who was directed to a specific hospital by his physician, and twentieth-century pressures for standardizing medical and diagnostic services. Physicians forced hospital boards to consider a new type of social cost accounting. They agitated for closed medical staffs in an effort to persuade the hospital boards to limit hospital admissions to patients of specific physicians selected and policed by the physicians themselves. In return for this privilege the physicians' implicit promise was that they would keep the hospital full and would, moreover, admit patients who could pay for care. Access to hospital beds was increasingly necessary to successful medical practice. Hospitals had the laboratories, the X-ray machines, the surgical suites, and the nurses that the physician of 1910 had to have in order to compete effectively. Limiting the size of the medical staff and establishing rules for access to beds meant that a physician with a hospital staff appointment could get a bed for his patient when he needed it.

In the minutes of board of directors' meetings from the German Hospital and from St. Luke's Hospital the argument over hospital admissions is raised again and again. Board members' need to generate sufficient income to maintain their institutions eventually caused them to limit charity services and accede to more physician control over the use of hospital beds.[24]

The German Hospital was the first community hospital to make the transition to physician control of medical staff membership. In 1900 the medical staff insisted that the board of directors exclude the patients of a physician of whom the rest of the medical staff disapproved. German Hospital's board members refused, saying that they should retain the authority to decide which physicians would visit patients in their hospital. In 1901 the entire medical staff resigned over the issue, forcing the board to hire a physician to care for the hospital's charity patients. A compromise between the board and the physicians was not reached until 1903 when a new medical staff was appointed. This new staff gained the right to recommend candidates for the medical staff to the board of directors.[25] Similar conflicts persisted at St. Luke's Hospital from 1906 to 1917. At first, the board of directors through its president, Bishop Edward Atwill, named the medical visiting staff. In 1915 a proposal to establish a closed medical staff was made; it was not adopted until 1917 when Director Stowell finally convinced his fellow board members that institutional survival warranted a reduction of their powers.

The impact of a closed medical staff on the powers of the board and the superintendent at St. Luke's was considerable, since the new policy limited patient admissions to those sent by medical staff members and to charity patients approved by a hospital committee. Formerly, any physician could send patients to St. Luke's and actual decisions regarding admission were left to the superintendent of the hospital.[26] Argument over admission of charity patients, patients with chronic illnesses, and the powers of the superintendent, which had

24. Minutes of the German Hospital Society, *Grapevine*, September 1969, Missouri Valley Room, Kansas City Public Library; Minutes, December 10, 1907, Sidney C. Partridge to Jay M. Lee (1914); and Minutes, March 16, 1917, Archives, Medical Library, St. Luke's Hospital, Kansas City, Mo. For further discussion of hospitals' fiscal problems see Rosner, *A Once Charitable Enterprise*, 36–61.

25. Franklin Wakefield, "Research Hospital Medical Staff," *Jackson County Medical Society Bulletin* 50 (June 30, 1956): 1553–55; Richard Helman, [untitled article], *Grapevine*, September 1969, Missouri Valley Room, Kansas City Public Library; and typescript staff list, Medical Library, Research Hospital, Kansas City, Mo.

26. The "terms upon which any chamber or bed in said Hospital shall be occupied . . . shall be vested in the superintendent." Bylaws, 1902, Archives, Medical Library, St. Luke's Hospital, Kansas City, Mo.

persisted for ten years, resulted in board consensus favoring a more businesslike and affluent institution, even though it meant that control over admissions by the board of directors and superintendent was relinquished to the medical staff.

Kansas City surgeons saw the hospital as the ideal place to perform surgery. Eventually, as we have seen, the hospitals responded to the surgeons' needs for beds and equipment and, in some instances, to their demands for more authority. A review of the numbers of surgical procedures compared to total admissions helps explain why. In 1899 468 operations were performed among 693 patients admitted to German Hospital. In Scarritt Hospital 158 out of 205 patients had operations. Even the founders of St. Luke's, with their limited facilities in 1902, saw 75 surgical procedures performed, although their patient census that year was only 118. St. Joseph's Hospital found it necessary to enlarge and refurbish its operating room and to install new incandescent lamps there as early as 1896. Sixty appendicitis operations performed at St. Joseph's that year showed that surgeons were becoming more aggressive; treatment steadily became less "watchful waiting" and more interventionist, at least for some illnesses.[27]

Scientific and technologic changes obviously facilitated changes in treatment. Development of successful and reasonably safe methods of anesthesia enabled surgeons to convince patients of the desirability of surgical treatment, while pain control allowed them to take more time and do more complex procedures. Equally important, a clean hospital atmosphere for surgical procedures reduced morbidity and mortality from wound infections. The prospect of a relatively painless treatment without the unpleasant and dangerous aftermath of infection must have appealed to sufferers from hernias, tumors, gallstones, various gynecological problems, and dozens of other physical misfortunes that became amenable to turn-of-the-century surgical treatment.

As Kansas City physicians sought to control medical staff membership in hospitals and thereby access to hospital beds for their own patients, they were indirectly aided by the newly formed American

27. Report, St. Joseph's Hospital, Kansas City, Mo., November 1, 1894, to November 1, 1896, Archives, Sisters of St. Joseph of Carondelet, St. Louis, and "Report of the Various Hospitals of Kansas City for the Year of 1899," *Kansas City Medical Index-Lancet* 21 (February 1900): 64–66.

College of Surgeons and its hospital classification scheme.[28] Record keeping, laboratory verification of diagnosis, and control over medical staff constituted the central core of hospital standardization. Although it was not until 1920 that teams of surveyors from the American College of Surgeons actually visited Kansas City hospitals, the preceding years reveal something of a scramble to meet anticipated standardization requirements.

St. Luke's, for instance, circulated a letter to physicians in 1914 that described the technologic and nursing capabilities of the hospital and concluded, "The hospital will aim, as nearly as possible, to comply with the requirements of the Clinical Congress of Surgeons of America."[29] Most Kansas City hospitals anticipated the College's visits by drawing up staff organization plans and adjusting their record-keeping systems. All but one switched to a closed staff. This arrangement meant that only doctors who belonged to the staff organization could admit patients; moreover, a patient who preferred a certain hospital had to seek out a physician on that hospital's staff.

Only St. Joseph's Hospital held out. The superior of the sisters of St. Joseph retained the right to appoint the medical staff, administer the clinical work of the hospital, and give final approval of all recommendations from medical staff committees. St. Joseph's did conform to the standardizers' record-keeping and laboratory recommendations. Decisions on staff membership, however, remained in the hands of the nuns. A new building, a strong local reputation, and centralized power in an "all Sister" board of directors probably enhanced St. Joseph's autonomy in relation to the medical community.[30]

The language of standardization and modernization recurs often in the publications of the hospitals and in the local medical literature after

---

28. Rosemary Stevens, *American Medicine and the Public Interest* (New Haven: Yale University Press, 1971), 85–87. Franklin Martin, M.D., founded the American College of Surgeons (first called the Clinical Congress of Surgeons) in 1910. In 1912, Martin and his colleagues adopted a plan to standardize surgical practice, select surgeons for certification, and establish standards for hospitals.

29. Reverend Sidney Partridge to [local physicians], May 12, 1914, Archives, Medical Library, St. Luke's Hospital, Kansas City, Mo.

30. "Constitution, St. Joseph Hospital, Adopted at the Meeting of the Medical Staff, January 8, 1917" in *Minute Book-Governing Board*, Medical Library, St. Joseph's Hospital, Kansas City, Mo.

1910. Hospitals that were slow to conform were derided as "boarding homes"; the "grade A" hospital was extolled. Phrases such as "case records complete in every detail" and "fully standardized" applied to the good hospital.[31] A new aura of permanence and confidence based on medical standards, modern buildings, and efficiency rather than homelike security and charitable service came to surround Kansas City's voluntary hospitals. The modern hospital was now the home of scientific medical care built on a foundation of skilled nursing.

The domestic era of community hospital development was finished in Kansas City by the end of the second decade of the twentieth century. The old homelike hospital gave way to the new "temple of science." In the process some fundamental changes can be identified. Volunteers, especially hospital board members, were replaced by professionals— nurses, managers, accountants, and technicians. The patient population changed from chronically ill, dependent, and long-term patients to acutely ill, surgical, obstetrical, and short-term patients. The ethnic and religious identification of the hospitals was tempered by profes- sionalization and somewhat subsumed in a changing community en- vironment. The leadership role of women was diluted by the rising influence of physicians and the introduction of professional managers, but the place of the nurses training school as a solution to the hospital labor problem became firmly established. There was widespread ac- ceptance of the idea of institutionalization in times of serious illness. And finally, the hospitals had achieved a level of community recog- nition that enabled them to occupy a semipublic role as essential com- munity institutions.

The confidence and optimism felt by hospital leaders of that second generation can be found in the pages of their new journal *Modern Hospital*, established in 1913. Henry Hurd, of Johns Hopkins Uni- versity Hospital, himself the personification of the managerial era, proclaimed "the day of the home care of the sick can never return. Social conditions forbid that hospital care will become superfluous."[32]

---

31. "St. Joseph's Hospital," *Jackson County Medical Journal* 26 (April 23, 1932): 8– 13; Minutes, Church Charity Association, March 16, 1917, Archives, Medical Library, St. Luke's Hospital, Kansas City, Mo.; and Editorial, *Jackson County Medical Society Bulletin* 9 (March 29, 1915).

32. Henry Hurd, "The Hospital as a Factor in Modern Society," *Modern Hospital* 1 (September, 1913): 33.

Domestic era hospitals successfully substituted for home and family in the care of the sick; they also helped create a new occupation for women. Vehicles for ethnic and religious pride, they became as vital to their communities as Henry Hurd claimed. But the responsiveness of domestic era hospitals to their various constituencies faltered in the face of fiscal exigency. As Charles Rosenberg cogently observed, they turned "inward," leaving care of the chronically ill, the poor, and the aged to others.[33] Hospitals today have, of course, not become superfluous, but their limitations as socially responsive institutions force contemporary society to turn to home care of the sick, nursing homes, and other strategies to assist its dependent members whom the modern hospital has excluded.

33. Rosenberg, "Inward Vision and Outward Glance: The Shaping of the American Hospital, 1830–1914," *Bulletin of the History of Medicine* 53 (Fall 1979): 346–91.

2

Women, Surgeons, and a Worthy Enterprise: The General Hospital Comes to Upper New York State

EDWARD C. ATWATER

A new kind of hospital came to small American towns in the years between 1880 and 1930, one that was used by all citizens, not just the poor, and by all doctors, not just the chosen. It was quite different from its metropolitan counterpart that provided free care for the sick poor. The coming and the presence of the small-town hospital provides a chapter in American social and professional history, as well as in medical care. The story has several distinctive aspects: the essential role of women, as sponsors, as managers, and as nurses, the rise of the general surgeon as a dominant figure in the hospital hierarchy and among his professional peers, a dramatic increase in the number of "private" patients who paid both the hospital and the doctor who attended them, the opening of hospital staffs to all qualified physicians, and the recognition of the hospital as a central social institution, the primary focus of community good work.

The need for hospitals in small towns had long been recognized by both lay and medical leaders; the problem was how to pay for them. The crucial difference between the classical metropolitan hospital and the small-town institution was how the latter solved this problem. Though hospitals in larger communities accepted, indeed encouraged, payment by patients for room and board, their clientele in most cases

This study of regional hospital history has been supported in part by grant no. 5-ROI-LM 04455-03 from the National Institutes of Health.

was poor. Such hospitals were supported by public appropriations and by private philanthropy of a scope not possible in small towns. Since physicians were not allowed to charge professional fees for in-hospital care and since most physicians were not even on the hospital's staff, patients who could afford to pay when sick were usually cared for at home. The community hospital, on the other hand, welcomed all qualified physicians and allowed them to charge any of their patients occupying private (and more expensive) rooms for their services.[1] Most patients paid something, at least, for room and board. The hospital remained a charitable or eleemosynary institution, however, because it still depended on alms or subsidies from its sponsors.

In many towns, the establishment of a hospital was made possible through the cooperative effort of socially diverse groups who worked together for the first time. This effort was forerunner to the "community chest" concept that evolved at the end of World War I. Before the coming of the hospital, charitable activity in small towns had been parish-oriented; only on a community-wide basis was it on a scale sufficient to fund something as costly as a hospital. The many roles of women, initially crucial, diminished as the hospital evolved from a domestic establishment to a technical one increasingly dependent on physicians. In the beginning it was common for physicians, in ad-

---

1. Allowing patients to pay the doctor was a subject on which many held passionate views and a matter that is central to the role of the hospital in society. The classical view of the hospital as a charitable trust for the poor was well presented by Henry Jacob Bigelow (*Boston Medical and Surgical Journal* 120 [1889]: 377–78). If doctors charge for services, why not nurses and residents? Since the question of a hospital appointment for every qualified physician was then unthinkable, allowing those who held such appointments to collect professional fees for their services was considered unfair competition; professional prestige was sufficient reward. In communities where there were no medical schools or professors and fewer sources of philanthropy, the situation was different. Most smaller community hospitals organized after 1880 allowed physicians to charge professional fees to private patients from the first. "Gratuitous services will be given only to charity patients" (1st Annual Report, Vassar Brothers Hospital, Poughkeepsie, 1887–88). "The fees for medical or surgical care in private rooms shall be arranged by the attending physician and patients" (Bylaws, Samaritan Hospital, Troy, 1899). "Ward patients, or those paying less than five dollars per week are not allowed to fee or select a physician in the hospital" (House Rules, St. Luke's Home and Hospital, Utica, 1888). "It shall be the privilege of any recognized graduate in medicine to send and treat his patients in the private rooms of this hospital" (Report of the Trustees of St. Peter's Hospital, Albany, 1880). See also Medical Staff Bylaws, Buffalo General Hospital, 1889. For a detailed discussion of this problem as the larger city hospitals later faced it, see Morris J. Vogel, *The Invention of the Modern Hospital: Boston 1870–1930* (Chicago: University of Chicago Press, 1980), 103–4; 108–11.

dressing the lady managers, to speak of "your hospital"; soon it became "our hospital." Though women's role as managers declined, they continued to provide the central service of the hospital as nurses.

Three factors contributed to the growing control of hospitals by physicians: (1) the importance of the private patient who paid for hospital services but whose admission to the hospital depended on his physician's advice; (2) the coming of abdominal surgery and the rise of the general surgeon to a position of dominance among his professional peers, of prominence in the community, and of economic importance to the hospital; and (3) the growth of laboratory medicine, a diagnostic and therapeutic technology that the hospital provided, but which required a physician to interpret. The physician soon saw the advantages of associating with a hospital. An increasing number of special services were provided at no cost, such as trained nurses, an operating room, postoperative nursing care, X-ray and clinical laboratory facilities, and the convenience of a central location for the sickest patients.

The hospital remained a unifying social and charitable activity as long as there was only one such institution in town. When a second hospital was established in a small community, the effect was quite the opposite. The hospital became, instead of a cooperative venture, a symbol, even a weapon, in factional disputes both within the medical profession and in the community at large. Physicians probably did not consciously manipulate community feelings for their own professional ends. It is clear, however, that the ascendency of the general surgeon in the small-town hospital in the early twentieth century and growing social tensions in small industrial communities coincided in a way that made second hospitals seem necessary. With two hospitals there were the benefits of competition, but also community polarization and divisiveness.

Today second hospitals are disappearing from small towns as a result of economic and technical forces. The single dominant surgeon is gone, dispatched by specialization. The hospital is no longer an eleemosynary institution dependent on the efforts of a voluntary board and the contributions of local citizens; it is run on business principles, funded by third parties, regulated by civil authorities, and managed by professional administrators. The one constant has been the role of woman as nurse. From a poor but respectable domestic, to a surrogate mother with some schooling, to a technically sophisticated professional person, the nurse has remained the enduring person in the hospital hierarchy.

THE NEED FOR COMMUNITY HOSPITALS

In 1880 hospitals were found almost exclusively in cities with over 30,000 inhabitants. They were little different from what they had been for centuries. There the sick poor were given more adequate food, shelter, and warmth than was possible in their homes and were provided with such medical attention as was available, at no cost to their families and at greater convenience to the physicians who attended them. In return, patients were used for teaching clinical medicine to younger physicians. It was a sign of limited means to be admitted to such an institution, and more prosperous citizens, almost anyone with at least a clerical job and a family, would have been cared for at home, by kin or servants.

Small towns had little need of such places. There were no anonymous poor; everyone knew someone who would help in time of trouble. There were no people with special training as nurses; people nursed their own. Surgery was done in the patient's home. What led small towns to perceive the need for a hospital? At first they sought to provide a place for injured workers, accident victims, and transients who fell ill at the local hotel—a category that grew as the commerce and industry of small towns increased. The popular concept of health and cleanliness was also changing, and the importance of having a clean place in which to care for the sick grew in the public mind. By the early twentieth century, with the coming of aseptic surgery and safe abdominal surgery, the hospital was used by all people who needed an operation or trained nursing care. It could be run at small cost, and the people needed to manage and staff it were available.

The railroad brought industry to town and together these brought injuries and transients. Though the occasional catastrophe—a train wreck, factory explosion, or epidemic—made the need of a hospital vivid, it was the daily problems of individual industrial and railroad injuries, of alcoholism, and of contagious disease that were most vexing. The number of injuries to railway workers in the United States increased annually from 20,000 in 1888 to 70,000 in 1910.[2] In some villages, such as Hornellsville, N.Y., where the main repair shops of the Erie Railroad were located, the hospital was established primarily to care for injured workers.[3] Railroads and mills became good supporters of local hospitals, contributing to capital drives and often annually donating a "railroad" or "mill" bed to which sick or injured employees might be admitted without personal cost. Some early small-town hospitals were even called "emergency" hospitals and often consisted of little more than a room or two, perhaps staffed only in time of need.

By the turn of the century, a broader need was beginning to be apparent—for a central place, always staffed, available, and clean, in which to perform increasing numbers of aseptic surgical procedures. The appendectomy was the exemplary operation. Hitherto, most surgery involved the female genitourinary organs, the musculoskeletal system, or the integument. The appendectomy, virtually unknown in 1890, became almost epidemic by 1910, a fact that is strikingly apparent if one examines, even at random, the annual reports of small community hospitals. By 1910, it was the most common major surgical procedure in most hospitals, matched in frequency only sometimes by gynecological operations and later by tonsillectomies, though the latter were considered minor.[4] The operating room became the focal place of the institution and, in most hospitals, surgical patients predominated. Centralized surgery and fees charged by physicians for attending their hospital patients were responsible for the inexorable shift in emphasis from home and doctor's office to hospital. Even by the standards of

2. Annual Reports, U.S. Interstate Commerce Commission, 1888 and 1910 (Washington, D.C.: Government Printing Office, 1889 and 1911).

3. Archives, St. James Mercy Hospital, Hornell, N.Y. [Undated newspaper clipping.]

4. At the Arnot Ogden Hospital in Elmira no case of appendicitis was diagnosed in 1893 or 1894, 1 patient died from it in 1895 and 1 in 1896; in 1897 there were no cases. In 1899 there were 8 appendectomies, 22 in 1905, 33 in 1906, 39 in 1907, 43 in 1908, 49 in 1909, and 48 in 1910. In this last year there were 235 operations, major and minor, including X-ray examinations. Hence, 20 percent of all these procedures were appendectomies. By 1913 the number had more than doubled, to 102. At Troy's Samaritan Hospital 9 (3 percent) of 316 major and minor operations in 1899–1900 were appendectomies. By 1906–7 the number had risen to 77 (10 percent) of 766. In 1908 at Newburgh Hospital there were 10 salpingo-oophorectomies, 13 hysterectomies, 21 herniotomies, 24 amputations (including breast), and 103 laparotomies, of which 44 were appendectomies. At Saratoga Hospital 25 (17 percent) of 148 operations in 1909 were for appendicitis. (See annual reports of the respective hospitals for the years specified.)

the day the cost of an operation was relatively small—salaries were modest, most student nurses were unpaid, and little equipment was needed. In 1915, for example, the per diem ranged from $.90 to $1.70 in most upstate hospitals staffed by sisters, and $1.50 to $2.70 for most others.[5]

At the turn of the century, small towns encompassed a broader spectrum of society than they do now, and included among their inhabitants owners of local industries, businesses, and banks. This ownership class provided a group of unusually able young matrons who could organize, support, and manage the hospital. They may have perceived their own lack of fulfillment in the male-dominated society and found some purpose to their lives by running the hospital. These matron-managers were used to directing their own domestic establishments with servants, however few in number, and traditionally cared for the sick. Managing the hospital was a natural extension of the activities to which they were already accustomed.

To set in motion and sustain a hospital, women were needed not only as leaders and administrators but also as providers of direct nursing care to patients. Florence Nightingale brought social acceptability and English discipline to nursing, a profession that had hitherto been work for domestics in time of peace and prostitutes in time of war. For the first time there was escape from farm or factory for those young women who were unequipped or disinclined to teach school but who wanted or needed employment or, perhaps, hoped to look further afield for a husband. Most hospitals established a nurse training school and used their student nurses to staff the facility. Without this large and willing group of people to do the daily work of the hospital, for which there was little reward but a modicum of training and the satisfaction of service, the institution could hardly have succeeded.

In addition to the need for trained nurses, able managers, and an aseptic operating room, there was the idea of the hospital as a clean place. This association of health and cleanliness, the hygiene or sanitary movement, evolved over several decades in the later nineteenth cen-

5. The per diem cost per patient for 101 upper New York State hospitals in 1915 ranged from $.90 to $4.00, with all but 7 less than $2.80, and three-quarters less than $2.30 (derived from Report of New York State Board of Charities for the year ending September 30, 1915 [pp. 768–802] by dividing total current annual expenses by total patient treatment days.)

tury. It certainly did not characterize the older large metropolitan hospitals. Its roots and its evolution may be traced to the health reform movements of the midcentury. Examples of these might include Water-Cure establishments (health resorts at which patrons combined exercise, good diet, and the internal and external application of local spring water in quest of better health) and the vegetarian principles made popular by Sylvester Graham; the physical education and physiology courses introduced into the collegiate curriculum; and the series of antebellum national sanitary conventions that gave impetus to a public health movement quite apart from late discoveries of asepsis and bacteria. Publicly sponsored central municipal water supplies, piped into the house, available at the twist of a valve, relatively safe to drink, and sufficient for frequent bathing, a water closet, and a sewer all promoted cleanliness. Furthermore, an interest developed in providing better ventilation. The work of such men as Louis Pasteur and Joseph Lister and the subsequent discovery of bacteria and their role in producing disease, affirmed what the sanitarians had been preaching and provided the theoretical explanation for what Lister had recognized. The association of filth and bacteria with disease, and of cleanliness with health, made identification of the hospital as "the clean place" logical.

GROWTH OF COMMUNITY HOSPITALS

In 1870 only the seven largest cities, excluding New York City and Long Island, had hospitals. These cities—Buffalo, Rochester, Syracuse, Utica, Troy, Albany, and Yonkers—were stretched out across state on the east-west axis of the Erie Canal and Mohawk River, with Yonkers adjacent to New York City. Yonkers, with a population of 19,000 was the smallest of them. There were eleven hospitals in these cities: seven were church-sponsored (six Roman Catholic and one Episcopal), one was city-sponsored (Utica), and only three were private voluntary institutions (Buffalo, Albany, and Rochester) (table 2.1). The oldest, Sisters of Charity Hospital in Buffalo, had been open a mere twenty-two years (figure 2.1). They all accepted paying patients and some allowed private patients to have physicians of their choice, but none permitted physicians to charge for that care and, as a result, they had few private patients, serving primarily the indigent population.

Table 2.1.
Sponsorship of community hospitals in upper New York State, 1870 and 1930

Year	Total	Voluntary association	Roman Catholic	City or county	Proprietary	Industrial	Fraternal
1870	11	4*	6	1	0	0	0
1930	169	98+	27	21	21	1	1

* Includes one hospital sponsored by the Protestant Episcopal church.
+ Includes three hospitals sponsored by the Protestant Episcopal church.

By 1930, 107 communities had 169 hospitals. Only three of fifty-five upstate counties (Hamilton, Lewis, and Schoharie) were without at least one general hospital. The large majority were now sponsored by voluntary associations, ninety-eight in all, including seven homeopathic hospitals. Twenty-seven were run by Roman Catholic orders, twenty-one were municipal or county-operated, twenty-one were proprietary, and two were industrial or fraternal in ownership. Chart 2.1 plots the years in which general hospitals were opened in different towns.[6]

In the decade of the 1880s, towns with 10,000 inhabitants were opening hospitals and, in the lower Hudson Valley, especially Westchester County, villages with as few as 3,000 or 4,000 had them. By 1920, there were few communities of 5,000 in New York State without a hospital. Each of the seven largest cities had one or more voluntary

6. This study excludes hospitals in the five boroughs of New York City and on Long Island. Chart 2.1 does not include hospitals for tuberculosis, nervous and mental diseases, contagious diseases, maternity cases, or other special types; general pediatric institutions are included. Thanksgiving Hospital, a fifteen-bed institution organized in 1868 in the village of Cooperstown, closed in 1875 and reopened in 1896. St. Luke's Hospital, in Utica, opened in 1869, but was primarily domiciliary until 1886. Clifton Springs opened in 1850 as a Water-Cure and was established as a conventional hospital in the 1890s.
The hospital roster and statistical data about hospitals were derived from several sources, including: *The Medical Register of New York, New Jersey, and Connecticut*, vol. 12 (New York, 1874–ƒ); *American Medical Directory*, vol. 1 (Chicago: American Medical Association, 1906–ƒ); American College of Surgeons, *Year Book* (Chicago: American College of Surgeons, 1920–ƒ); Hospital Service in the United States 1931, *Journal of the American Medical Association*, March 28, 1931; J. C. Fifield, ed., *American and Canadian Hospitals* (Minneapolis: Midwest Publishers, 1933); New York State Board of Charities, Annual Reports (Albany, 1873–1934) (called State Board of Social Welfare in later years); American Medical Association, *Hospital Service in the United States* (Chicago: American Medical Association, 1921–40); and various printed and manuscript materials related to individual hospitals.

Figure 2.1. Sisters of Charity Hospital, Buffalo, New York. The first general hospital in upper New York State. Opened in 1848, this building functioned as a hospital until 1876. Now remodeled into apartments. From an old drawing reproduced in *Buffalo Historical Society Publications* 16 (1912): 192.

Table 2.2.
Sponsorship of community hospitals in upper New York State multiple-institution communities, 1870–1930*

First Hospital	Subsequent Hospitals			
	Voluntary association	*Roman Catholic*	*City or county*	*Proprietary*
Voluntary association	15	0	8	2	5
Roman Catholic	2	1	0	0	1
City or county	2	1	2	0	1
Proprietary	2	0	1 +	0	3
		2	11	2	10

* Does not include the seven largest cities or Lackawanna.
+ Absorbed proprietary predecessor.

hospitals and a sisters' hospital; all but one had a homeopathic hospital, and all but three a city-sponsored hospital. Twenty-one smaller cities established twenty-five second or third hospitals. The most frequent sequences were for a sisters' hospital or a proprietary hospital to open in a town that already had a hospital sponsored by a voluntary association (table 2.2).

During the period between 1870 and 1895, church-sponsored hospitals were the most common. In the days before trained nurses and charity that crossed denominational boundaries, only the bishops of the Roman Catholic church and, to a lesser extent, those of the Episcopal church, had sufficient authority to establish and fund a hospital and had, in nuns, persons suitable to staff it. Church-sponsored and operated hospitals were usually established by an order of nuns at the request of the local bishop. The Roman Catholic Sisters of Charity, of Mercy, of St. Francis, and of St. Joseph, and the Canadian Grey Nuns of the Sacred Heart were the orders most active in New York. Though these institutions usually each had a governing board of some kind, the sister superior had virtually unchallenged authority. The hospitals were usually poorly funded, but they had, and often still have, an atmosphere of care and concern for patients that is sometimes less obvious in secular institutions.

Some towns received their hospital as a gift from prosperous citizens. The building itself might be the old family home of the donor, as in the case of Brooks Memorial Hospital in Dunkirk or Arnold Gregory

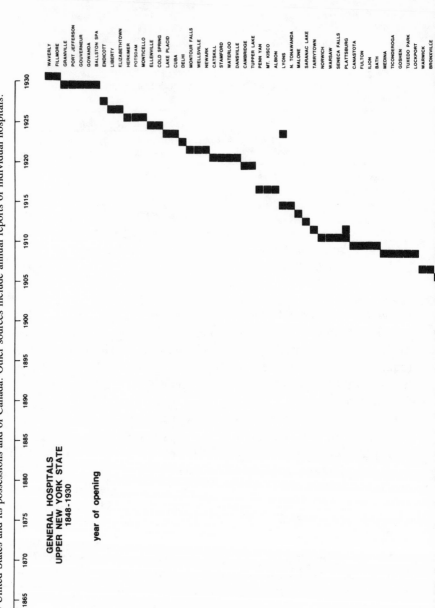

Chart 2.1. Location and year of opening of general hospitals in upper New York State, 1848–1930. From James Clark Fifield, ed., *American and Canadian Hospitals* (Minneapolis: Midwest Publishers, 1933). This reference book gives historical, statistical, and other information on the hospitals and allied institutions of the United States and its possessions and of Canada. Other sources include annual reports of individual hospitals.

GENERAL HOSPITALS
UPPER NEW YORK STATE
1848-1930

year of opening

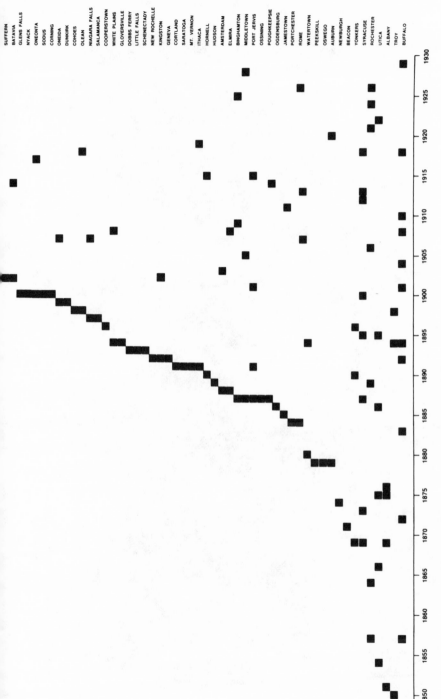

YEARS

Figure 2.2. Cambridge Hospital, Cambridge, New York. This hospital opened on January 5, 1919. These and subsequent pictorial images are from postal cards of the period.

Hospital in Albion. At the other extreme were hospitals such as Mary McClellan in Cambridge, Frederick Ferris Thompson in Canandaigua, and Arnot Ogden in Elmira, each of which had not only a modern brick structure but an endowment that sometimes generated as much as 20 or 25 percent of the annual budget.

The eastern New York State community of Cambridge had a population of about 1500 in 1915. A former hometown boy, Edwin McClellan, had prospered in the Buffalo-based but internationally known Foster-Milburn proprietary medicine company (makers of Burdock Blood Bitters and of a liniment called Dr. Thomas's Eclectric Oil), and decided to donate a hospital to the village in memory of his mother. The four-story, sixty-bed, fireproof building, designed by the donor's architect brother-in-law, had the latest in appointments, including an electric elevator, a 125,000-gallon water reservoir, facilities for handling three classes of contagious diseases, an up-to-date pathology laboratory, and an endowment of $229,100. Seven male citizens of Cambridge directed the well-funded operation. The chief of staff was a New York surgeon, friend and classmate of the donor, who performed all nonemergency major surgery once a week (figure 2.2).

Brooks Memorial Hospital in Dunkirk, on the other hand, was an antiquated if elegant old house, the downstairs of which was shared with the public library. It was bequeathed by its owner, a locomotive maker, with only a small endowment. An operating room was added to the back. Patients had to be carried up and down a narrow back stairway until a water-powered elevator was donated. After an endowment of $100,000 was given, the town relaxed its fundraising efforts and the hospital was perpetually underfunded and undermaintained, though it continued to serve the community.

It is difficult to enumerate the proprietary hospital census with precision. Often without peer recognition, such institutions were not always listed in published rosters. Since they received no public funds for indigent patients, they were not required to submit annual reports to the State Board of Charities, and in fact, most of them do not seem to have kept records. They also tended to be ephemeral—dependent on the health of the proprietor—and were victims of increasingly stringent state codes and the requirements of third-party payors. None remain today except those that became voluntary hospitals, notably the Myers Community Hospital in the village of Sodus.

The voluntary community-supported hospitals were the backbone of the system and were by far the most numerous, accounting for almost 60 percent of the total. Occasionally they were established by doctors or businessmen. Often, the matrons of a community recognized the need, persuaded their husbands to participate, raised the money, and ran the day-to-day affairs of the hospital once it opened. In 1900, the King's Daughters, a service organization of the local Baptist Church in the western New York village of Batavia, sent inquiries to similar groups belonging to other denominations asking if they were interested in trying to organize a hospital. They were, and what followed was the first instance of interdenominational cooperation in Batavia for a common cause, a fact as notable as the institution it produced.

Most of the voluntary nondenominational hospitals were governed by a board of directors that included men, although at least ten were run entirely by women. In the case of sisters' hospitals the board usually included the bishop, perhaps a local attorney, and the leading Roman Catholic physician of the community. But the sisters had unchallenged authority, and the board served as financial, legal, and political adviser. The day-to-day operations were overseen by a superintendent, a dietitian, a janitor, and a small staff of nurses who were replaced to the extent possible by student nurses enrolled in a training school. The superintendent, usually a nurse, was directly responsible to a board of "lady managers." Physicians had little to say about the operation at first. In smaller towns the staff was open; all qualified physicians, including homeopaths, were welcome and encouraged to admit patients.

The physical development of the community hospital was surprisingly uniform, the sequence depending mostly on when the hospital was started. The first concern was for patient beds. There was usually a women's ward, a men's ward, perhaps a maternity ward, a few private rooms, a kitchen, a matron's office, a waiting room, and an operating room. It is easy to see why a large house often served as the first hospital in a small community. A laundry came next, followed by a home for student nurses, a contagion cottage, and finally, by the 1890s or 1900s, a more sophisticated operating room and an ambulance. Except for cases of severe contagious disease or appendectomy, children were usually cared for at home. Later, X-ray facilities and clinical laboratories were added. The sequence, almost monotonous in its regularity, delineates the evolution of the hospital and of contemporary medical practice.

The advent and increasing popularity of the colored picture postal card after the 1890s coincided with the period in which community hospitals were being established. As civic enterprises of which each town was proud (the hospital was often its most impressive undertaking), it is not surprising that a substantial photographic record exits. It is sometimes possible to trace the external evolution of the hospital, the addition of operating rooms, new wings, and new buildings, as they appear in sequential pictures. The wide diversity of architectural imagination is also apparent (see figures 2.3 and 2.4).

INCREASING PHYSICIAN CONTROL

By the second decade of the twentieth century the pattern of hospital control was changing, and the physician was taking a more active role. At the same time, fundamental changes were occurring in the social structure of small industrial communities, changes that were to affect the image of the hospital and the professional ambitions of the surgeon. In Batavia, for example, confrontations, ruptures, and their ramifications went far beyond what seemed, at first glance, to be an internal hospital dispute. There were several unsuccessful attempts by physicians in 1914 and 1915 to participate more in the management of the hospital, which in their view was not keeping pace with the times. The senior surgeon, William D. Johnson, stated that sterile techniques in the operating room were chronically inadequate and resulted in a high postoperative infection rate. The County Medical Society, prodded by Dr. Johnson, prepared a list of complaints and called for the resignation of the superintendent and her assistant. The board appointed a committee of its own that meticulously investigated and categorically explained or refuted each allegation. When three senior society members, including Dr. Johnson, were received with reluctance by Alice G. Fisher, still board president after a dozen years, Mrs. Fisher is said to have raised her lorgnette and announced that the board saw no cause

Figure 2.3. Community hospitals using converted houses, from simple to elegant, ca. 1900–12. *Left to right*: City Hospital, Oneida; Emergency Hospital, Herkimer; Medina Hospital, Medina; Myers Hospital, Sodus; St. Mary's Hospital, Amsterdam; Brooks Memorial Hospital, Dunkirk.

Figure 2.4. Community hospitals occupying structures designed as hospitals, ca. 1900–12. *From top left*: Little Falls Hospital, Little Falls; Higgins Memorial Hospital, Olean; Nathan Littauer Hospital, Gloversville; Corning Hospital, Corning; Arnot Ogden Hospital, Elmira; Frederick Ferris Thompson Hospital, Canandaigua.

for dismissal of the superintendent. The matter seemed, for the moment, to be settled.[7]

Dr. Johnson withdrew from the staff and worked for a while at a small local private hospital he established. In the meantime, a former active board member of the Batavia Hospital, Rose Jerome, left her house to the Sisters of Mercy, who established St. Jerome's Hospital in it, with Dr. Johnson as chief of staff. The medical profession and the community took sides, thereafter often bitterly divided on what soon became largely partisan lines, polarized between Roman Catholics and Protestants. Batavia, then a town of 13,000, had (and still has) two hospitals.

The immovable object and the irresistible force had met. Community leaders—sometimes business, sometimes social, occasionally both—created the hospital, not doctors. The founders, however, failed to grasp the need for innovation as hospital activities became more sophisticated. It was difficult for them to accept that the hospital (as the Medical Society pointed out) was no longer their possession, but had become an essential community institution. The confrontational presentation of demands from the medical profession, which had hitherto been more than willing to let the women do the work and in fact even doubted that the hospital venture could succeed, had decisive consequences that reached far beyond the hospital and were to be felt for many decades. The doctor-hospital issue did not cause all the trouble, but its timely occurrence in a period of great social change helped to polarize other antagonistic forces.

Until the 1880s the population of Batavia was fairly homogeneous; the Protestant majority accepted and assimilated the Irish-born and German-born Roman Catholics. The influx of Italian and Polish immigrants at century's end, hired for semiskilled jobs in local farm-machinery factories, resulted in a population that was, by 1910, 50 percent foreign-born or first-generation American, predominantly non-English-speaking, and sufficient to warrant three new Roman Catholic parishes between 1904 and 1908, where there had been but one. For a village of about 10,000 such a rapid change was difficult to assimilate, not only for the Protestant majority but also for the English-speaking

7. *Batavia Times*, June 10, 1916; *Batavia Daily News*, July 12, 1916 (editorial). David B. Johnson, M.D. (son of W. D. Johnson, M.D.), personal interview, September 1984.

Roman Catholics. The cooperative spirit that had existed in 1900 all but disappeared, replaced by dissension and antagonism. A physician who returned from medical school to practice in Batavia in 1915 recalled it as a narrow, bigoted town. The 1920s even saw crosses burning on the lawns of Roman Catholic parishes, placed by local Ku Klux Klan members.[8]

Similar tensions could be found in Auburn, a large farm-machinery manufacturing town eighty miles to the east where a second hospital was opened, also by the Sisters of Mercy, in 1917. In Hornellsville, now Hornell, the population was predominantly of Italian and Irish birth or descent, and the first hospital to be established was sponsored by the Roman Catholic church. As far as one can tell from the record and from oral tradition, it was well run and quite adequate for its purpose. Nevertheless, in 1915 a determined, if prolonged and barely successful, effort was mounted to establish a nonsectarian (actually poly-Protestant) hospital. In the northeastern New York village of Plattsburgh a hospital was opened in 1910, only to be followed by a second one a year later. A majority of the members of the Medical Society, under the leadership of surgeon Cassius Silver, declined staff appointments at the first hospital ostensibly because its directors, consistent with the common practice of the time, were unwilling to accept physicians as members of the board. The following year Dr. Silver became chief of staff at the second hospital, where he remained for forty-four years. Here too, sectarian divisions played a role, not only between Roman Catholic and Protestant, but also between Catholics of French and of Irish descent.

HOSPITAL STANDARDIZATION

As hospital standards were established at state and national levels, the matter of hospital control ceased to be a local contest. From at least the mid-nineteenth century the State Board of Charities had authority to inspect and set minimum standards for any hospital receiving public funds. By 1915 this included about two-thirds of the private voluntary hospitals of the state, proprietary hospitals being the main

8. Taped interview with Dr. Edith Ryan, December 27, 1985; *Batavia Daily News*, December 26, 1923.

exception. After the organization of the American College of Surgeons (ACS) in 1913, surgeons were to take an increasingly active role in hospital standardization.

The College set out to examine all general hospitals in the United States, starting in 1915 with those having over one hundred beds, much as Nathan Colwell and, later, Abraham Flexner had done to medical schools a decade or more earlier. The first public report of the ACS committee was to be presented at the 1919 annual meeting, but the results were so appalling that the directors destroyed the report and merely announced that only 12.9 percent of the nation's 692 largest hospitals had been approved. The following year, the situation improved.

The requirements for approval hardly seem stringent: (1) Physicians working in the hospital must be licensed graduates of recognized schools, must be competent, of good character, ethical, and must not split fees; (2) there must be a staff organization that meets monthly, with regular periodic reviews and analyses of clinical experience involving both free and paying patients; (3) accurate, accessible, and complete written records must be kept for all patients and should include patient identification, complaints, personal and family history, history of present illness, physical examination, record of special examinations such as consultations, clinical laboratory and X-ray results, provisional or working diagnosis, proposed medical or surgical therapy, gross and microscopic pathology findings, progress notes, final diagnosis, condition on discharge, follow-up, and in case of death, autopsy findings; and (4) there must be diagnostic and therapeutic facilities under competent supervision, for performance of chemical, bacteriological, serological, pathological, X-ray, and fluoroscopic examinations. These requirements, of course, have long been accepted as standard practice; that they were uncommon in 1920 gives some idea of hospital conditions at the time.[9]

In 1920, only 3 of approximately 43 upstate New York 100-bed hospitals passed, with 11 more receiving conditional recognition. Gradually, smaller hospitals were included, and by 1930, 61 percent of upper New York State general hospitals were at least conditionally

9. American College of Surgeons, *Year Book* (Chicago: American College of Surgeons, 1919 and subsequent years).

Table 2.3.

Size and sponsorship of community hospitals in upper New York State accredited by the American College of Surgeons, 1930

	Total	Number fully approved	Number conditionally approved	% with some approval
Total	163	85	15	61
By size				
40 beds or more	118	85	15	85
39 beds or less	45	0	0	0
By sponsorship				
Church	28*	17	5	79
Independent association	96	57	9	69
City or county	23	10	1	48
Proprietary	12	0	0	0
Fraternal	2	1	0	—
Industrial	2	0	0	—

* 26 Roman Catholic; 2 Episcopal.

Sources: American Medical Association Census of Hospitals, 1930 (*Journal of the American Medical Association*, March 28, 1931), and ACS *Yearbook*, 1931.

Note: Includes all general hospitals except those in New York City and Long Island. Excludes all special hospitals, e.g., maternity, tuberculosis, nervous and mental disease, army, etc. Includes three pediatric hospitals (Albany, Syracuse, Buffalo), fraternal, and industrial hospitals.

approved. Size was an important factor: no hospital with fewer than 40 beds (there were 45 such institutions) received approval; 85 percent of 118 hospitals with 40 beds or more were approved. The percentage for church-sponsored and independent voluntary hospitals was higher than for those that were city- and county-operated. No proprietary hospital was approved, but all except 3 had fewer than 40 beds (table 2.3). Recognition was not pro forma and, once given, was often withdrawn. At least 30 institutions were on probation or disapproved after having had at least conditional acceptance. The standardization effort of the ACS clearly denoted the new power of physicians in hospitals.

EVOLUTION OF NURSE TRAINING SCHOOLS

While the ever-impoverished community hospital was becoming the focus of community charitable endeavor and was embroiled in disputes concerning control, it continued to function. This was due more than anything else to the work of its nursing staff, whose effort formed the essence of the place. During the period 1880–1930, nursing evolved from domestic service to professional status. Because it was apparent that the virtually free labor of student nurses would be economically essential, most larger hospitals started a nurse training school soon after opening their doors to patients. Between 1877 and 1925 at least seventy-five hospitals started nurse training schools, with the peak between 1887 and 1910.

The training school at the hospital in Little Falls was typical. It functioned from 1897 until the late 1920s, when, like many of its kind, it fell victim to increasingly costly state educational requirements. A young woman was expected to read, write, cipher, and complete a year of high school. After a two-month probationary performance that met with the superintendent's approval, a candidate might enroll for the two-year course, agreeing to live in the hospital, to obey all rules, and to perform any duty assigned her. Pay consisted of room, board, laundry, and six dollars a month, which was increased to eight dollars in the second year. The working day was from seven to seven, and when on night shift a student had to be in her room between 9 a.m. and 4 p.m. There was an occasional afternoon off and part of Sunday, which was to include church attendance except for sufficient reason. The hospital served in loco parentis. Essential qualities were "punctuality, personal neatness, general order, a gentle voice and manner, and a patient temper." In return for her services, a student nurse learned to do dressings, fomentations, poultices, cups and leeches; to administer enemas and to use the catheter; to manage appliances for uterine complaints; to apply friction to the body and limbs; and to manage helpless patients—making their beds, changing their clothes, giving baths in bed, preventing and dressing bedsores, and managing various positions. Learning to make bandaging, lining splints, nursing sick children, and preparing, cooking, and serving "delicacies for the sick," completed the course.[10] A graduate had a marketable skill by the time she was through, and many later went to work in private homes. Many hospitals rented students out for this purpose, and some institutions acquired significant income from this practice. Once a school was registered, as was the one in Little Falls in 1906, the

10. *Training School for Nurses of the Little Falls Hospital* (Little Falls, N.Y., 1897).

graduate could take state examinations and become a registered nurse, which conveyed even higher professional recognition.

The life of a nurse was a hard one, though more interesting than the drudgery of domestic service and easier than industrial working conditions. Both the number of training schools and the number of students more than quadrupled between 1900 and 1920, but the system gradually deteriorated as hospitals became increasingly dependent on this inexpensive source of labor.[11] The problem was that nurse training was an apprenticeship in which the patient's needs had to come before the student's learning if the hospital were to depend primarily on students. The 1928 Committee on Grading of Nursing Schools put it this way: "Hospitals run training schools for two reasons. The first reason is that it is cheaper to run a poor school than it is to employ graduate nurses. . . . It is an extraordinary thing, but it seems to be a fact, that hospitals regard the suggestion that they pay for their own nursing as unreasonable. They have been receiving free service from students for so many years that they regard it as an inalienable right. . . . The second reason . . . is that it is easier to handle the nursing service of a hospital with student nurses than with graduate nurses."[12] The annual demand for such students also resulted in an enormous overproduction of nurses.

CHANGING IMAGE OF THE HOSPITAL

As the years passed, the image of the hospital continued to change, from being merely a clean and comfortable place in which to be cared for to a place where beneficial intervention by physicians might occur. The hospital became less an alternative and more a necessity, a place to which all expected access. Yet, as can be seen in chart 2.2, the hospital became increasingly dependent on patients who could pay. When the Depression came, this vulnerability and the need for a sounder

11. *Nursing and Nursing Education in the United States*, Report of the Committee for the Study of Nursing Education, Josephine Goldmark, Secretary (New York: Macmillan, 1923).

12. Committee on the Grading of Nursing Schools, *Nurses, Patients, and Pocketbooks*. Report of a Study of the Economics of Nursing Conducted by the Committee on the Grading of Nursing Schools, May Ayres Burgess, Director (New York: [The Committee], 1928), 435–36.

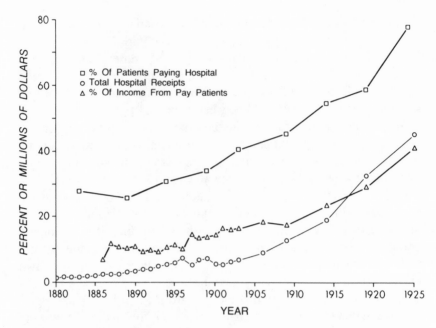

Chart 2.2. Increasing dependence of general hospitals on paying patients, New York State, 1880–1925. Data derived from hospital statistics in Annual Reports of the State Board of Charities, Albany, 1881–1926.

system of financing were all too apparent. Along with this temporary financial embarrassment came a change in social philosophy. The idea of insurance, whether for unemployment, retirement, or sickness, became fashionable. Earlier there had been cooperative hospital insurance ventures between certain work and fraternal groups, but Blue Cross, which began in the 1930s, was the first broadly conceived plan. Though only 8 1/2 percent of businesses had such insurance on the eve of World War II, this increased rapidly. By the 1950s most hospitals had a dependable source of income that became even broader with the coming of Medicare and Medicaid in 1965. These insurance plans radically changed the character of the hospital. The doctrine of *respondeat superior*, by which an organization is held responsible for the negligence of its employees, and from which American hospitals, as eleemosynary institutions, had long been exempted by the courts, began to be applied to them after a 1957 New York State Court of Appeals decision, a clear sign that the hospital was no longer privileged.[13] With reliable income, the image of the hospital as a charitable institution was soon replaced by that of the hospital as a business establishment.

New institutions fill new needs. Now there is the supermarket, providing one-stop food and household shopping as well as banking and pharmacy services. The fast-food emporium serves the members of a mobile family—grazers who seldom sit to eat. There are palatial nursing homes to look after grandma while the rest of the family works. Perhaps most impressive of all is the modern medical center, a supermarket of its own kind, now run on business principles and delivering a sophisticated product, perhaps even replacing the church as the place to which most resort for help in time of trouble—a far cry from what women built so many decades earlier.

The voluntary hospital that was established between the Civil War and World War II holds a distinctive place among social institutions. It established a clean haven of health for the community and a place to house the injured and very sick, but its success was only in part a medical phenomenon. The hospital filled the nonmedical needs of several groups in the community it served. Its functions were more diverse in small towns than were those of its metropolitan counterpart. In order for it to exist at all, it needed a broad base of support. A small town could not afford a philanthropically supported hospital that would serve only the poor. This problem was solved by allowing physicians to accept professional fees from those hospitalized patients who could afford to pay. As a result, all kinds of people came to the hospital. It was in the small town, not the city, that all citizens were introduced to hospital care and that hospitalization became socially acceptable. The consequent economic interest that small-town physicians developed in the hospital in the early twentieth century changed the role physicians played from passive to active, in fact dominant. Most community hospitals had open staffs from the beginning, which created a professional meeting ground where contacts were more fre-

13. Bing *v.* Thunig, 2 New York Reports, 2d Ser. (1957), 656–64.

quent than those provided by meetings of the Medical Society. It also led to earlier resolution of the dissension between regular physicians and homeopaths.

The hospital was the vehicle by which the medical profession was propelled to dominance in the world of health and under whose control it ultimately became a citadel, given, in the words of one historian, to "inward vision," becoming unresponsive to extramural social needs.[14] This turning inward was probably inevitable. In the case of larger institutions that came under the control of medical schools after the turn of the century, it resulted from the increasingly dominant interests of the educational-research bureaucracy; at smaller hospitals such turning inward reflected the growing control of the staff physicians, whose increasing influence challenged that of the volunteer boards of directors.

Women, not physicians, made the community hospital possible. The hospital, in turn, offered women a cause, some purpose beyond household and family. It provided the first common activity for the many elements of an increasingly diverse and denominationally fragmented society. Everybody worked together for the local hospital, although in several of the more industrialized towns, especially those with a large number of Roman Catholics, there came to be two hospitals that ultimately symbolized the polarity between newcomers and established residents. The hospital offered escape from farm or factory to young women who needed employment; it provided work, gave training and discipline, and broadened horizons. The success of the community general hospital resulted from what it offered the patient, the doctor, the nurse, the voluntary supporters, and the community as a whole.

14. Charles E. Rosenberg, "Inward Vision and Outward Glance: The Shaping of the American Hospital, 1880–1914, *Bulletin of the History of Medicine* 53 (1979): 346–91.

3

Picturing the Hospital:
Photographs in the History
of an Institution

RIMA D. APPLE

The value of photographs to historical study was recognized almost from the invention of photography. In the nineteenth and early twentieth centuries some historians and educators urged the preservation of the photographic record specifically for later historical investigation and promoted the development of research methodologies that acknowledged the significance of photographs as primary source documents.[1] Despite these recommendations, researchers and teachers still used photographs primarily for illustrative purposes.[2] Recently, though, increasing numbers of historians have begun to view the photographic record as research material, finding in photographic images new data and new historical questions.[3]

1. Alan Trachtenberg, "Introduction: Photographs as Symbolic History," in United States, National Archives and Records Service, *The American Image: Photographs from the National Archives, 1860–1960* (New York: Pantheon, 1979), esp. ix–xi; Marsha Peters and Bernard Mergen, " 'Doing the Rest': The Uses of Photographs in American Studies," *American Quarterly* 29, no. 3 (1977): 280–82.

2. See, for example, such illustrated textbooks as Philip A. Kalisch and Beatrice J. Kalisch, *The Advance of American Nursing* (Boston: Little, Brown, 1978); and Glenn Sonnedecker, *Kremers and Urdang's History of Pharmacy*, 4th ed., (Philadelphia: J. B. Lippincott, 1976). Also, articles in journals such as the *Wisconsin Magazine of History* and *Medical Heritage* frequently contain photographic illustrations.

3. See, for example, Madelyn Moeller, "Photography and History: Using Photographs

Photographic research is particularly appropriate and useful in studying and presenting the history of hospitals. Hospitals underwent significant structural, technological, and social change in the second half of the nineteenth century and the early years of the twentieth century. Proud administrators and amateur photographers excited over technical advances in photography celebrated and preserved in photographs many of the hospital's developments. In addition, historical photographic research contributes much to the study of people and relationships not discussed in more regularly researched materials such as monographs, serials, diaries, letters, and the like. Photographs enhance our understanding and knowledge of daily life for hospital patients and staff. They present details of the hospital environment not described in written and oral records, and express emotional elements of hospital affairs rarely disclosed in other types of sources. But, as with all historical documents, photographs must be analyzed cautiously.

We typically see the camera as neutral and objective, unlike other visual art forms, such as painting, which are "subjective." After all, it is said, the photograph appears to present an undistorted, realistic image, simply duplicating what the camera lens sees (unless the negative is retouched).[4] Nonetheless, the same conscious and unconscious biases that affect other sources also affect the production and preservation of photographs. Photographers position the camera and manipulate the scene in order to produce the desired image.[5] Even without this overt management of process, the mere presence of the camera may cause the subjects to modify their stance, expression, or action.

Furthermore, the photographic record is incomplete and scattered.

---

in Interpreting Our Cultural Past," *Journal of American Culture* 6 (1983): 3–17; Cathy Slusser, "Women of Tampa Bay: A Photo Essay," *Tampa Bay History* 5 (1984): 47–63; Walter Rundell, Jr., "Photographs as Historical Evidence: Early Texas Oil," *American Archivist* 41 (1978): 373–98; Rima D. Apple, "Pictorial Essay," in *Women and Health in America*, ed. Judith Walzer Leavitt (Madison: University of Wisconsin Press, 1984), 285–97.

4. For an analysis of this point in relation to the development of commercial photography, see David E. Nye, "Early American Commercial Photography: Origins, Techniques and Esthetics," *Journal of American Culture* 6 (1983): 2–12. For a humorous example of the application of modern technology to the photographic image, see Douglas Davis, "Seeing Isn't Believing," *Newsweek*, June 3, 1985, 68–70.

5. For interesting analyses of this phenomenon, see Donald E. English, *Political Uses of Photography in the Third French Republic, 1871–1914* (Ann Arbor, Mich.: UMI Research Press, 1984); and Peter Bacon Hales, *Silver Cities: The Photography of American Urbanization, 1839–1915* (Philadelphia: Temple University Press, 1984).

Owing to accident or plan, some photographs are treasured and carefully stored, while others disappear from sight. Few hospitals retained and maintained comprehensive iconographic collections. Historical images of one institution may be housed in an unrelated institution's archives, may be relatively inaccessible in some private collection, or unnoted in a family scrapbook. For reasons of privacy, sensibility, or lack of interest, many aspects of hospital life were infrequently, or never, photographed. Therefore we have very few early, unposed photographs of such common practices as emptying bedpans and preparing a patient for surgery. The fragmentary nature of the photographic record forces researchers to be extremely careful in judging the relative importance of each individual image.

Frequently the photograph is without further data—it is undated; the photographer is unidentified; and the reason for taking and preserving the photograph is unknown. Without such information our historical interpretation is uncertain and it is difficult to evaluate how "realistic" a reflection of hospital life we are examining. Consequently, photographs reproduced with accompanying text in annual reports or newspaper articles can sometimes be more useful to researchers than original prints or negatives without supporting documentation. For example, hospital annual reports were highly self-conscious publications intended to promote the institution and its work. The inclusion of specific images signified what contemporaries believed was important about their hospital. Analyses that juxtapose the photographs with their captions or with the text often disclose unstated assumptions. Recognizing the bias of the published record gives the historian another source for interpreting the views of the people involved in the development of the hospital. Similarly, the contents and arrangement of photographs in albums and scrapbooks give some indication of what collectors considered memorable.[6] The photographic record frequently acts as a catalyst for further inquiry, suggesting additional areas of investigation.[7] A photograph used to exemplify one point or generally accepted

6. On analyzing and interpreting photographic albums of an earlier era, see Alan Trachtenberg, "Albums of War: On Reading Civil War Photographs," *Representations* 9 (1985): 1–32.

7. In addition to sources cited in notes 1 and 3, see Jill Gates Smith, "Women in Health Care Delivery: The Histories of Women, Medicine and Photography," *Caduceus: A Museum Quarterly for the Health Sciences* 1, no. 4 (Winter 1985): 1–4; James S. Terry, "Dissecting Room Portraits: Decoding an Underground Genre," *History of Photography*

historical interpretation may inform us about other issues as well. But, as with analyses of other historical sources, photographic research is not an end in itself but rather an approach to historical study. Though historical photographs may be more difficult to locate than other sources, the search is well worth the effort, as the accompanying photographs indicate.

William Harvey King exemplifies the illustrative function of photographs, both for contemporaries and for historical study.[8] In figure 3.1 we see the hospital staff attending patients in the maternity ward of Flower Hospital, New York, in 1905. A carefully posed group portrait, this photograph suggests what King felt would be an impressive manner of presenting homeopathic medicine. From their relative positions we can sense the relationships, or at least the idealized relationships, among the staff and between the staff and the patients. The care of the infants is most interesting. In other hospitals at this time bassinets were hung on the ends of beds in maternity wards keeping newborns close to their mothers. At Flower, however, infants apparently were separated from their mothers, though looked after in the same maternity ward. (Hospitals did not generally care for infants in separate nurseries until later in the century.) Which form of care was common? Were newborns typically kept near their mothers in

---

7 (1983), 96–98; John D. Stoeckle and George Abbott White, "Plain Pictures of Plain Doctoring: An Overlooked Archive Comes to Light," *The Sciences*, May/June 1985, 24–33; Jon Wiener, "Paris Commune Photos at a New York Gallery: An Interview with Linda Nochlin," *Radical History Review* 32 (1985): 59–79; Hilary Russell, "Reflections of an Image Finder: Some Problems and Suggestions for Picture Researchers," *Material History Bulletin* 20 (1984): 79–83; Michael Thomason, "The Magic Image Revisited: The Photograph as a Historical Source," *The Alabama Review* 31 (1978): 83–91; James West Davidson and Mark Hamilton Lytle, "The Mirror with a Memory: Photographic Evidence and the Urban Scene," in *After the Fact: The Art of Historical Detection* (New York: Alfred A. Knopf, 1981); James S. Terry, Antol Herskovitz, and Daniel M. Fox, "Photographs Tell More Than Meets the Eye," *Journal of Biological Photography* 48 (1980): 111–15; Rima D. Apple, "Image or Reality? Photographs in the History of Nursing," in *Images of Nurses: Perspectives from History, Art, and Literature*, ed. Anne Hudson Jones (Philadelphia: University of Pennsylvania Press, 1988), 40–62; John D. Stoeckle and George Abbott White, *Plain Pictures of Plain Doctoring: Vernacular Expression in New Deal Medicine and Photography* (Cambridge: MIT Press, 1985). For some of the shortcomings of historical photographic analysis as published today, see Robert M. Levine, "Semiotics for the Historian: Photographs as Cultural Messengers," *Reviews in American History* 13 (1985): 380–85.

8. William Harvey King, *History of Homeopathy and Its Institutions in America*, 4 vols. (New York: Lewis Publishing Co., 1905).

Figure 3.1. Maternity ward, Flower Hospital, New York, 1905. Reprinted from William Harvey King, *History of Homeopathy and Its Institutions in America*, 4 vols. (New York: Lewis Publishing, 1905).

bassinets or separated from them, attended by nurses? This photograph suggests such questions about turn-of-the-century hospital maternity care.

Photographically illustrated annual reports are equally suggestive and useful. Probably administrators hoped that views of pleasant, "homelike" private rooms and of sleek, well-equipped operating rooms would attract patients to the hospital. In the early twentieth century, annual reports were filled with pictures of private rooms furnished with rugs, flowers, and other domestic touches. When a nurse was included in such a picture, she was often posed behind a patient or handing a meal to a patient, giving credence to the concept of nurse-as-servant, an image current in today's historiography, which emphasizes the domestic, housekeeping aspect of nursing at the turn of the century. Over the following decades the image of nurses slowly changed. By the 1930s hospitals increasingly stressed that their nurses were educated women, trained to care for patients. Figure 3.2 documents this shift from "domestic" to "professional." This photograph from the 1930 annual report of Montefiore Hospital shows a class of student nurses observing a clinical lecture by an intern, Dr. Furman. The text of the report proudly claims that such bedside clinics play an important role in the education of nurses at Montefiore.[9] The positioning of the students around one side of the bed and the angle at which the instructor is standing reveal the influence of the photographer on the image. But even such a carefully arranged scene suggests much about the relationships between physicians and nurses, and the interactions of staff and patients. And, although focused on the students and the instructor and depicting the idealized view of the educated nurse, the photograph also reveals something of the daily life of patients convalescing at Montefiore.

Photographs also capture images of uncommon occurences in the hospital. Figure 3.3 is a case in point. This image has been preserved in a scrapbook inscribed "To Kittie L. Pond, Compliments of J. L. Whitcomb, M.D., Bellevue Hospital [New York], Christmas 1890–1891." We know little more than that about the album or its photographs. Who took the pictures? Whitcomb, who interned at Bellevue

9. I wish to thank Dorothy Levenson, Historian-Archivist of Montefiore Medical Center, for information about this photograph.

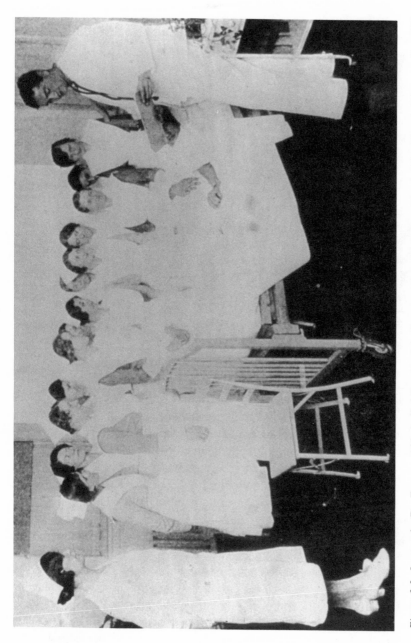

Figure 3.2. Lecture by Dr. Furman, 46th Annual Report of the Trustees of the Montefiore Hospital for Chronic Diseases, Gun Hill Road, New York, 1930. Reprinted with the permission of the Montefiore Medical Center Archives.

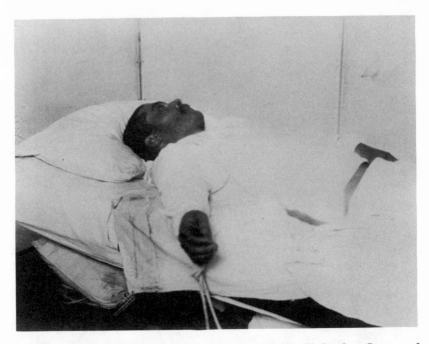

Figure 3.3. Patient with hydrophobia, Bellevue Hospital, New York, 1890. Courtesy of The Edward G. Miner Library, University of Rochester School of Medicine and Dentistry.

that year, or a professional photographer? Who was Pond? Why were certain scenes chosen? All remain unanswered questions. Fortunately the caption for this photograph is quite specific and detailed: "Case of Hydrophobia. A few hours before death. Admited [sic] to Bell. Hospit. July 1890 . . . Bitten by rabid dog 4 weeks before admission." This picture gives us a rare glimpse of rabies treatment in the 1890s. The patient is clearly being restrained by ropes and also probably by an attendant holding his legs. Photographs such as this allow us to observe the application of medical therapies.

Similarly, photographs can document the technologies in a given hospital during a given time period. But assigning a date and place is not always easy or certain. For example, two prints of one photograph show a patient, a nurse (possibly a student), and a male attendant (probably a physician) posed amidst the domestic furnishings of a private hospital room, including a telephone and a trundle bed for use by private duty nurses. One copy of this photograph, dated 1929, is held by the archives of Methodist Hospital, Madison, Wisconsin. The picture was also published in a Madison newspaper in a 1929 article describing the opening of a new wing of Madison General Hospital. Why was the same picture attributed to two different hospitals? An interview with a former employee of Madison General Hospital solved the puzzle. Madison General never used trundle beds, it supplied portable cots.[10] The picture represents a private room at Methodist Hospital. The newspaper probably had this print in its files and included it in articles about Madison General.

Detailed analyses of the influence of changing technology on the idealized operating room can be seen clearly in photographs reproduced in Edward F. Stevens et al., *Modern Hospitals: A Series of Authoritative Articles on Planning Details and Equipment*, Edward F. Stevens, *The American Hospital of the Twentieth Century*, and other contemporary hospital architecture books.[11] However, by following the photographs in the annual reports of one hospital over a series of years, the researcher can often document the time lag between the development of new technologies and procedures and their actual introduction into the institution. For example, comparisons of operating rooms as pictured in the annual reports of Madison General Hospital, Wisconsin, from 1907, 1911, 1919, and 1930 demonstrate the tremendous growth in surgical technology. These changes were apparently instituted with each new addition to the hospital. The photographs illustrate the concern for modern, scientifically up-to-date facilities; we see new equipment, changes in wall and floor materials, and improved lighting.

In addition, the limited captions supplied for these operating-room photographs give some insight into other aspects of the hospital. One picture appeared in the 1919 annual report of Madison General with the caption "The Jackson Operating Room." Then, between 1919 and 1921, the caption for this same operating room picture changed to "The West Operating Room." What did the original title signify?

10. "Open New Madison General Hospital Addition Saturday," *Wisconsin State Journal*, May 23, 1929. Information about this photograph comes from Ms. Sadie Anderson, R.N., who graduated Madison General School of Nursing in 1927 and worked at the hospital for many years after.

11. New York: The American Architect, 1912; New York: Architectural Record Co., 1918.

76   *Rima D. Apple*

What happened between the 1919 and 1921 annual reports? The questions spurred further investigations. Evidently, early in the century the Hospital Association drew up plans for a new hospital and solicited donations. It offered area physicians the opportunity to design and fund the construction of their own operating room. Dr. Reginald H. Jackson, a highly respected Madison surgeon, contributed $3,085 for a private operating room, and the Association agreed that he would have the exclusive use of it.[12] Less than a decade later, according to the hospital, overcrowded conditions made it awkward to reserve one operating room for a single physician. Consequently, Jackson's contract for exclusive use of the room was canceled. The doctor claimed, however, that some unnamed persons had promised the hospital funding if the contract was terminated. At any rate, Jackson severed his relationship with Madison General in a stormy controversy widely reported in the local press.[13]

Occasionally archival holdings allow the historian to compare the "idealized" version of operating rooms like those found in celebratory publications with something closer to daily practice. Moreover, locating a set of photographs that depict the same or a similar procedure in one institution over a span of years can help document changes in actual operating-room setup and practice. Figures 3.4 and 3.5 represent one such instance. Both photographs present surgical practice at Newark City Hospital, separated by approximately three decades. Close inspection could tell us much about developments in surgery as practiced in a large, urban hospital in the late nineteenth and early twentieth centuries.

Though not as plentiful or as accessible as other documents, photographic material is available for study. Some photographs are reproduced in contemporary and historical publications. Institutional histories, annual reports, and other celebratory volumes often include photographic images.[14] Some of these publications provide detailed

12. 12th Annual Report, Madison General Hospital and Training School for Nurses (Madison, Wis., Dec. 31, 1911), 15.
13. "Hospital Board Ends Contract with Jackson," *Madison Democrat*, Oct. 19, 1919; "Jackson Replies to Hospital Head," *Wisconsin State Journal*, Oct. 21, 1919; and "Dr. Jackson in Spirited Reply on Room Letter," *Capital Times*, Oct. 21, 1919. Clippings of these and other articles describing the controversy are located in the scrapbooks of Madison General Hospital Archives.
14. Small photographic images of the over 3,000 historical medical slides held by the

Figure 3.4. Surgical procedure, Newark City Hospital, Newark, N.J., ca. 1882–92. Reprinted with the permission of the George F. Smith Library of the Health Sciences, University of Medicine and Dentistry of New Jersey. PC–2 4/45.

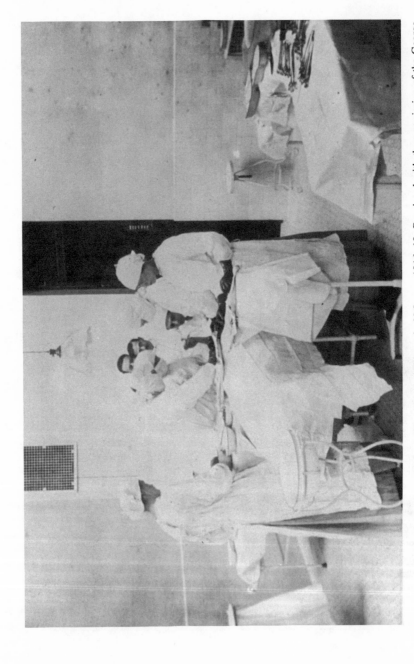

Figure 3.5. Surgical procedure, Newark City Hospital, Newark, N.J., ca. 1916–19. Reprinted with the permission of the George F. Smith Library of the Health Sciences, University of Medicine and Dentistry of New Jersey. PC–2 4/64.

captions for their photographs, carefully integrate photographic images with the text, or explicitly cite photographic illustrations in describing the institution. Others have photographs scattered throughout the text with little identification or explanation. Similarly, articles in the periodical literature and in government health and welfare reports sometimes publish hospital photographs with more or less explanatory material. Today these published sources are most often found in medical, historical, and other libraries. Some hospitals have retained archival copies of their publications, but many did not. The reports of these institutions are frequently lost, although they have sometimes been collected by local and state historical societies or government health departments.[15]

Iconographic and institutional archives hold additional photographic records of hospitals and hospital life. These collections range from specialized archives such as the History of Medicine Division of the National Library of Medicine and university archives to general picture archives such as the Visual and Sound Archives of the State Historical Society of Wisconsin and the Georgia Department of Archives and

---

Slide Archive of Historical Medical Photographs are reproduced in Rima D. Apple, comp., *Illustrated Catalogue of the Slide Archive of Historical Medical Photographs at Stony Brook: Center for Photographic Images of Medicine and Health Care* (Westport, Conn.: Greenwood Press, 1984); many of these are germane to the history of the hospital. Other useful publications include John D. Thompson and Grace Goldin, *The Hospital: A Social and Architectural History* (New Haven: Yale University Press, 1975); Ann Novotny and Carter Smith, eds., *Images of Healing: A Portfolio of American Medical and Pharmaceutical Practice in the 18th, 19th, and Early 20th Centuries* (New York: Macmillan, 1980). For historical studies of individual institutions see publications such as Anthea Hyslop, comp., *The Aim in View: A Pictorial Guide to the History of Ballarat Base Hospital* (Ballarat, Victoria, Australia: Ballarat Base Hospital, 1984); Dorothy Levenson, *Montefiore: The Hospital as Social Instrument, 1884–1984* (New York: Farrar, Straus & Giroux, 1984); Suzanne Hart O'Regan, *The Story of the Theda Clark School of Nursing, 1912–1938: A Pictorial Chronicle* (Amherst, Wis.: Palmer Publications, 1982); and Charles Hazelrigg, comp., "Central State Hospital," *Indiana Medical History Quarterly* 7 (1981): 3–23. Also helpful are publications such as Frederick P. Henry, ed., *Founder's Week Memorial Volume* (Philadelphia: F. A. Davis, The City of Philadelphia, 1909) and *Boston Lying-In Hospital, the 75th Year: The Hospital at 24 McLean Street* (Boston: Boston Lying-In Hospital, 1908.) Photographs from the annual reports of some hospitals may be found in Apple, *Illustrated Catalogue*, which also lists other published sources in its Glossary and Bibliographic Sources.

15. For example, the extant copies of the annual reports from the early years of Madison General Hospital in Wisconsin are located at the State Historical Society of Wisconsin, not the hospital.

History.[16] Directories such as *Picture Sources 4, A Guide to Archives and Manuscripts in the United States*, and the *National Union Catalog: Manuscripts Collections* direct the researcher to photographic holdings in a variety of historical societies, libraries, and similar archives.[17] Unfortunately, these publications cite few archival resources in hospitals and similar institutions.

The *Illustrated Catalogue of the Slide Archive of Historical Medical Photographs at Stony Brook* describes the holdings of some hospital and institutional archives. A list of other likely institutional sources can be generated from the *American Hospital Directory: 1945* and the current *American Hospital Association Guide*.[18] The former provides 1945 statistics for each institution as well as its founding date, allowing the researcher to identify facilities that might hold photographs of historical interest. Though specific institutions have changed over the past four decades, they usually retain a similar name and thus their present status and address can be located in the current *American Hospital Association Guide*. Correspondence with and visits to these hospitals may disclose exciting, previously untapped photographic sources, sometimes in the form of uncatalogued loose prints buried in file cabinets.

Many photographs remain in private hands, either as collectors' items or as mementos, making them difficult for historians to locate and study. Through personal contacts and public announcements, researchers can discover these unexpected photographic caches. For example, in preparation for writing the history of Ballarat Hospital, Anthea Hyslop published inquiries in the local newspaper requesting information about the hospital and soliciting photographs, memorabilia, and the like. Other institutions make such requests before special events, such as the closing of a nursing school, the opening of a new

16. Lists of many of these may be found in Apple, *Illustrated Catalogue*, esp. Glossary and Archival and Institutional Sources.

17. Ernest H. Robl, ed., *Picture Sources 4* (New York: Special Libraries Association, 1983); Philip M. Hamer, ed., *A Guide to Archives and Manuscripts in the United States* (New Haven: Yale University Press, 1961); and Library of Congress, *National Union Catalog: Manuscripts Collections* (Hamden, Conn., 1959–). Additional directories may be found in Apple, *Illustrated Catalogue*, 425.

18. See n. 14 above; *American Hospital Directory: 1945* (Chicago: American Hospital Association, 1945); and *American Hospital Association Guide to the Health Care Field* (Chicago: American Hospital Association, 1972–).

wing, or an anniversary celebration. Employees and patients, both past and present, respond with photographs from their scrapbooks. Though frequently without documentation, these "candid shots" commonly show aspects of hospital life not seen in more formal photographs.

The captions, content, and context of the five photographs reproduced here exemplify the contributions of photographic research to the study of the history of hospitals. Photographic images can tell a story, validate an historiographic claim, or extend a thesis, as well as illustrate a text. Not that photographs alone can, or will, replace other, more traditional sources; these images must be analyzed in conjunction with other primary sources. But the study of photographs can provide significant insights, document changes, and stimulate new avenues of research. Analyses of photographic images give us a better understanding of past views and can help us develop more comprehensive interpretations of that important medical and social institution, the hospital.

4

The Negro Hospital Renaissance: The Black Hospital Movement, 1920–1945

VANESSA NORTHINGTON GAMBLE

In the early 1920s a group of black physicians launched a movement to improve the educational and medical programs of black hospitals. The National Medical Association (NMA), a black medical society, and the National Hospital Association (NHA), an association of black hospitals, feared that the growing importance of accreditation and standardization would lead to the elimination of black hospitals and with it the black doctors' professional existence.[1] Their fears were based on bitter experience. By 1923 the reforms of medical education surrounding and following the influential Flexner Report eliminated five of the seven existing black medical schools.[2] The NHA and the

I would like to thank Morris Vogel, Charles E. Rosenberg, Richard Gillespie, and Ellen Fitzpatrick for their useful comments on earlier drafts of this paper.

1. H. M. Green, "Annual Address of the President of the National Medical Association," *Journal of the National Hospital Association* (hereinafter *JNMA*) 14 (1922): 216.

2. The closed medical colleges were Flint Medical College, New Orleans, Louisiana, in 1910; Leonard Medical College, Raleigh, North Carolina, in 1918; Knoxville Medical College, Knoxville, Tennessee, in 1910; Medical Department of the University of West Tennessee, Memphis, Tennessee, in 1923; and Louisville National Medical College, Louisville, Kentucky, in 1912. Five other black medical colleges existed before the Flexner Report. Lincoln University Medical College, Oxford, Pennsylvania, opened in 1870, but closed in 1876 without graduating any students. Hannibal Medical College, Memphis, opened in 1889, but closed in 1896, also without any graduates. The Medical College of Knoxville operated from 1895 to 1900. The Medical Department of State University opened in Louisville in 1899 and merged with Louisville National Medical College in 1903.

NMA thus hoped to stem the tide of black hospital closings. Their efforts, it was asserted, would improve the status of black hospitals before housecleaning done by outside, and possibly unfriendly, forces swept these institutions away.[3] The physicians realized that their programs would eliminate the prototypical black community hospital—small, proprietary, and without training programs. However, they hoped that their programs would increase the number of first-class hospitals—large, modern facilities with approved training programs.

The activities of the two associations, in concert with philanthropies and government agencies, produced some significant changes in the status of black hospitals by World War II. Indeed, Dr. John A. Kenney, editor-in-chief of the *Journal of the National Medical Association* and executive secretary of the NHA, hailed the transformation of black medical institutions that occurred in the early twentieth century as a "Negro Hospital Renaissance."[4] An examination of the reform movement that inspired Kenney's optimism illuminates not just the development of the American hospital in the 1920s and 1930s, but also the evolution of black social institutions. This essay explores the forces that prompted Dr. Kenney to herald the arrival of a Negro hospital renaissance. It focuses on five questions: What led to an awakening of interest in black medical institutions during the early twentieth century? Who was behind the movement to transform black hospitals? What animated the hospital reformers? How much did they achieve? And what was their legacy?

CATEGORIES OF BLACK HOSPITALS

Any understanding of the character of black hospital reform must be rooted in an analysis of the nature of the hospitals themselves. Black hospitals were of three broad types: segregated, black-controlled, and

---

Chattanooga National Medical College graduated two students before it closed in 1908. For further information on the history of black medical education see James L. Curtis, "Historical Perspectives," in his *Blacks, Medical Schools, and Society* (Ann Arbor: University of Michigan Press, 1971), 1–27; Darlene Clark Hine, "The Pursuit of Professional Equality: Meharry Medical College, 1921–1938, A Case Study," in *New Perspectives on Black Educational History*, ed. Vincent P. Franklin and James D. Anderson (Boston: G. K. Hall, 1978), 173–92; Leonard W. Johnson, "History of the Education of Negro Physicians," *Journal of Medical Education* 42 (1967): 439–46; and Herbert M. Morais, *The History of the Negro in Medicine* (New York: Publishers' Company, 1967).

3. "The National Hospital Association," editorial, *JNMA* 17 (1925): 207.

4. John A. Kenney, "The Negro Hospital Renaissance," *JNMA* 22 (1930): 109–12.

demographically determined. Segregated black hospitals included facilities established by whites to serve blacks. By the turn of the century several such hospitals had been founded. The motives behind their establishment varied. Some founders expressed a genuine, if paternalistic, interest in supplying health care to black people and offering training opportunities to black health professionals. However, white self-interest was also at work. The germ theory of disease, popularized by the end of the nineteenth century, recognized that "germs have no color line."[5] Thus the theory mandated attention to the medical problems of Afro-Americans, especially those whose proximity to whites threatened to spread disease. The white community also established black hospitals to escape the embarrassment of entirely neglecting the black sick without having to take care of them in the same institutions as whites.[6]

These segregated institutions existed predominantly, but not invariably, in the South. Examples included Dixie Hospital and Nurse Training School, Hampton Institute, Virginia, established in 1891; St. Agnes, St. Augustine School, Raleigh, North Carolina, established in 1896; MacVicar, Spelman Seminary, Atlanta, Georgia, established in 1900; and Kansas City (Missouri) General Hospital, No. 2 (Kansas City Colored), established in 1908. Dixie and MacVicar Hospitals were started as adjuncts to two white-run educational institutions for blacks, Hampton Institute and Spelman Seminary, respectively. The existence of nurse training schools at these institutions and the need to give nursing students clinical experience provided the impetus for the establishment of Dixie and MacVicar.[7] MacVicar, however, did not consider the provision of clinical experience to black physicians as worthy of support, and denied these doctors admitting privileges.[8] In contrast, Sara Hunter, a white Episcopal churchwoman who founded

5. "Germs Have No Color Line" served as the slogan for the fundraising campaign in the 1920s to create a center for black medical education at Chicago's Provident Hospital.
6. Julius Rosenwald Fund, *Negro Hospitals: A Compilation of Available Statistics* (Chicago: The Fund, 1931), 19.
7. Patricia E. Sloan, "Commitment to Equality: A View of Early Black Nursing Schools," in *Historical Studies in Nursing*, ed. M. Louise Fitzpatrick (New York: Teachers College Press, 1978), 68–85. For information on the founding of Dixie Hospital see Alice Mabel Bacon, "The Dixie and Its Work," *Southern Workman* 20 (November 1981): 244, and Cora M. Folsom, "The Dixie in the Beginning," *Southern Workman* 55 (March 1926): 121–26.
8. Sloan, "Commitment to Equality," 76.

St. Agnes Hospital, hoped to improve the health care of black people and to offer black physicians a place in which they could hospitalize their patients.[9]

While St. Agnes, Dixie, and MacVicar Hospitals were developed under private auspices, Kansas City Colored was not. It was established by a municipality. The original impetus for the hospital, however, came from the black community. In 1903 black physicians in Kansas City, led by Dr. Thomas C. Unthank, began their efforts to establish a separate municipal hospital because the existing one had very limited facilities for black patients and no black staff.[10] In 1908 the city established a black hospital after it constructed a new municipal hospital and transferred most white patients to the new facility. Black patients and white patients with tuberculosis and other infectious diseases continued to receive care in the old hospital, now called Kansas City General Hospital, No. 2.[11] The clinical facilities of the two hospitals were not equal: the older hospital lacked diagnostic laboratories and radiologic equipment. Initially, black physicians did not have admitting privileges. But in 1911 they received associate staff appointments and thereafter the hospital gradually came under black administrative control. In 1914 a black physician, Dr. W. J. Thompkins, became superintendent of the hospital and a black nurse, Mary K. Hampton-Brown, became superintendent of nurses. By 1924 black people assumed responsibility for all departments in the hospital. However, white physicians from Kansas City Hospital, No. 1, continued to serve as supervisors and consultants.

Black-controlled institutions comprised the second category of black hospitals in early-twentieth-century America. Their founders did not create these hospitals as exclusively black enterprises, but as interracial ones that would not practice racial discrimination. Indeed, white support was crucial for the hospitals' survival. The first black-controlled hospitals included Chicago's Provident Hospital, founded in 1891, and

9. For a history of this hospital see W. Montague Cobb, "Saint Agnes Hospital, Raleigh, North Carolina, 1896–1961," *JNMA* 53 (1961): 439–46.

10. Accounts of the founding and the early history of the hospital can be found in Clyde Reed Bradford, "History of Kansas City General Hospital, Colored Division," *Jackson County Medical Journal* 26 (October 8, 1932): 6–15, and Samuel U. Rodgers, "Kansas City General Hospital No. 2: A Historical Summary," *JNMA* 54 (1961): 523–44.

11. *Annual Report, Board of Hospital and Health for the Year Ending April 14, 1909* (Kansas City, Mo.), 83. I would like to thank Joan E. Lynaugh for this reference.

Philadelphia's Douglass Hospital, founded in 1895. These institutions, established to train nurses and provide clinical opportunities for black physicians, were begun by Dr. Daniel Hale Williams and Dr. Nathan Francis Mossell, respectively.[12] Their professional qualifications equalled those of the elite physicians—white and black—of their time. Both graduated from predominantly white medical schools, Mossell from the University of Pennsylvania in 1882 and Williams from the Chicago Medical College in 1883, and both pursued postgraduate training at a time when it was unusual for the average practitioner of either race to do so. In 1888 Mossell was elected the first black member of the Philadelphia County Medical Society and in 1912 Williams was the only black physician elected to charter membership in the American College of Surgeons (ACS). Both physicians recognized the growing importance of the hospital to the career aspirations of physicians, but despite their credentials, neither was able to obtain hospital admitting privileges until they themselves established hospitals.

The vast majority of the early black-controlled hospitals were proprietary rather than educational institutions. They included Home Infirmary, Clarksville, Tennessee, established in 1906, and Fair Haven Infirmary, Atlanta, Georgia, established in 1909. The physician-owners of these often very small hospitals claimed that they could offer their paying patients "a high type of service along with the courtesy which was lacking in the majority of hospitals where colored patients were admitted."[13] Given their size, equipment, resources, and the training of their owners, it is doubtful whether such institutions

12. Accounts of the founding of Provident Hospital can be found in Helen Buckler, *Daniel Hale Williams: Negro Surgeon*, 2d ed. (New York: Pitman, 1968); W. Montague Cobb, "Daniel Hale Williams, M.D., 1858–1931," *JNMA* 45 (1953): 379–85; Ulysses Grant Dailey, "Daniel Hale Williams: Pioneer Surgeon and Father of Negro Hospitals" (Paper presented at the meeting of the National Hospital Association, Chicago, Ill., August 18, 1941); Henry B. Matthews, "Provident Hospital—Then and Now," *JNMA* 53 (1961): 209–24; and Theresita E. Norris, "An Historical Account of Provident Hospital," (Chicago Medical Society, n.d. [circa 1940]), typescript. Additional information on Mossell and the establishment of Douglass Hospital can be found in W. Montague Cobb, "Nathan Francis Mossell, M.D., 1856–1946," *JNMA* 46 (1954): 118–30; Edward S. Cooper, "Mercy-Douglass Hospital: Historical Perspective," *JNMA* 53 (1961): 1–7; Vanessa Northington Gamble, "Frederick Douglass Memorial Hospital and Training School: The First Ten Years," (December 1979), typescript; and Elliot M. Rudwick, "A Brief History of Mercy-Douglass Hospital in Philadelphia," *Journal of Negro Education* 20 (Winter 1951): 50–66.

13. "Carson's Private Hospital, Washington, D.C.," *JNMA* 22 (1930): 148.

provided patients with superior medical care. However, it is clear that they represented a less onerous option for many black middle-class patients. Despite their resources, these patients were usually placed in municipal hospitals or in the same inferior facilities as poor blacks. Race was even more important than class in determining the nature and quality of early-twentieth-century hospital care.

Changes in population led to the development of the third category of black hospital—those demographically determined. These hospitals were neither established to serve black people nor founded by them. Instead, they progressively evolved into black institutions because of a rise in black populations surrounding the hospitals. The foremost example is Harlem Hospital in New York City, which opened its doors in 1887 long before the black migration uptown. When blacks began to move into Harlem in large numbers, the hospital's admissions reflected the changes in community composition. Hospital reformers largely ignored hospitals in this third category because very few existed during the 1920s and 1930s.

All three types of hospitals were to face similar challenges in the early twentieth century. Their agenda were in fact set by new developments in health-care institutions. In 1919 approximately 118 black hospitals existed, 75 percent in the South.[14] Regardless of sponsorship or evolution, these hospitals were predominantly ill-equipped, small facilities, lacking clinical training programs. Consequently, they were inadequately prepared to survive the changes in scientific medicine, hospital technology, hospital accreditation, and hospital standardization that were taking place. This situation was faced by many American hospitals, but the stakes were extraordinarily high for black institutions. As black medical leaders had warned, the very survival of black health professionals was inextricably linked to the survival of black hospitals.

ROOTS OF THE BLACK HOSPITAL
REFORM MOVEMENT

Most black medical school graduates were barred from training programs at predominantly white institutions. Without programs in

14. This estimate is based on data in "Hospitals and Nurse Training Schools," in *The Negro Year Book and Annual Encyclopedia of the Negro*, ed. Monroe N. Work (Tuskegee Institute, Ala.: Negro Yearbook Co., 1918–19), 424–26.

black institutions, they would have had almost no opportunities for postgraduate training. This threat to the medical profession provided the major impetus for the black hospital reform movement. Black physicians needed hospitals in order to survive professionally and to establish legitimacy in the community. Hospitals provided physicians with a locus in which they could exchange professional knowledge and in which they could have access to expensive hospital-based technologies. In 1920, approximately 3,400 black physicians practiced medicine in the United States.[15] Without access to quality hospitals, leaders of black medical organizations realized that their members would be increasingly out of step with professional developments in modern medicine.

Black physicians also maintained that their lack of hospital privileges placed them at a competitive disadvantage with white physicians in the treatment of black Americans.[16] Physicians of both races cared for black patients. White physicians could promise continuity of professional care upon hospitalization. Their black colleagues could not because they lacked admitting privileges at most facilities and had to relinquish the care of their hospitalized patients to white physicians, even in some segregated black hospitals. This practice undermined confidence in black physicians and contributed to a perception that black physicians were inferior to their white peers. In the case of paying patients, it also adversely affected the physicians' pockets. W. E. B. Du Bois, in his classic study, *The Philadelphia Negro*, described this professional dilemma of black physicians:

> At first it would seem natural for Negroes to patronize Negro merchants, lawyers, and physicians, from a sense of pride and as a protest against race feeling among whites. When however, we come to think further, we can see many hindrances. If a child is sick, the father wants a good physician; he knows plenty of good white physicians; he knows nothing of the skill of the black doctors, for the black doctor has had no opportunity to exercise his skill. Consequently for many years the colored

15. Leonard W. Johnson, "History of the Education of Negro Physicians," 440, and Julius Rosenwald Fund, *Negro Hospitals*, 41. The exact number is not clear. Johnson lists 3,885 and the Rosenwald report lists 3,495.

16. Numa P. G. Adams, "An Interpretation of the Significance of the Homer G. Phillips," *JNMA* 26 (1934): 16, and Lawrence Greeley Brown, "The Hospital Problem of Negro Physicians," *JNMA* 34 (1952): 84.

physician had to sit idly by and see the 40,000 Negroes healed principally by white practitioner.[17]

Physicians who led the black hospital movement maintained that with quality hospitals they could overcome professional handicaps. They also tied their activities to improve their professional opportunities with the general movement to uplift the race. Dr. Algernon B. Jackson, a professor of public health at Howard University, noted that "the successful operation of hospitals among our people is doing much to bring about a higher degree of racial consciousness, racial respect and good will, all of which breed a confidence and faith in the profession which is destined to lead our race to a higher level, socially and economically."[18] Thus, the black hospital movement reflected not only a well-intentioned effort to improve black hospitals and the social status of the race, but a shrewd attempt to protect and promote black professional interests.

Protecting the status of black health professionals was not the only impetus for the black hospital movement; the health needs of the black population also prompted the reformers to act. Racial discrimination restricted the access of black patients to hospitals. Even in the North, they were either denied admission or accommodated—almost universally—in segregated wards. Various segments of the black community including physicians, social scientists, and activists stressed that an inadequate number of hospital beds contributed to the shockingly poor health status of black Americans, especially when compared to whites.[19] In 1920 the tuberculosis rate per 100,000 was 85.7 for whites and 202 for blacks; the pneumonia rate per 100,000 was 97.1 for whites and 145.9 for blacks; and the heart disease rate per 100,000 was 93.1 for whites and 126.4 for blacks.[20] In 1925 the death rate for blacks was 48 percent higher than for whites, and the black infant

17. W. E. B. Du Bois, *The Philadelphia Negro: A Social Study* (Philadelphia: University of Pennsylvania Press, 1899; reprint, New York: Schocken, 1967), 113.

18. Algernon B. Jackson, "Public Health and the Negro," *JNMA* 15 (1923): 258.

19. Charles S. Johnson, "Negro Health in the Light of Vital Statistics," *Proceedings of the National Conference of Social Work* 55 (1928): 173–75; Eugene Kinckle Jones, "Some Fundamental Factors in Regard to the Health of the Negro," *Proceedings of the National Conference of Social Work* 55 (1928): 176–78; Peter Marshall Murray, "Hospital Provision for the Negro Race," *Bulletin of the American Hospital Association* 4 (1930): 37–46.

20. Charles S. Johnson, "Negro Health," 174.

mortality rate exceeded that of whites by 62 percent.[21] Yet, despite these higher morbidity and mortality rates and despite a greater need for health care, blacks had fewer hospital beds available to them than whites. Dr. H. M. Green, president of the NHA, reported in 1928 that one bed existed for every 139 white Americans, but that only one bed existed for every 1,941 black Americans.[22] Green's figures on the number of hospital beds available to blacks may be low, as it is unclear whether they include beds in mixed hospitals. Nonetheless, his central point remains: the number of hospital beds was inadequate to meet the health needs of black people. These realities impressed physicians involved in the hospital movement who hoped that their professional efforts would improve the health status of the race.

Because black hospitals were only one source of hospital care for black patients, with many patients receiving care in mixed hospitals, leaders of the hospital movement had to provide a rationale for community support of these institutions. They noted that mixed hospitals customarily excluded black physicians and often cared for black patients in separate and inferior accommodations. Green argued that quality black hospitals could provide black patients with the best possible care, claiming that mixed hospitals did not have the "heart" of black hospitals.[23] Black hospitals with black staffs offered less hostile environments and were more sensitive to the needs of black patients. Fear and mistrust of the larger society also provided the impetus for the formation of other ethnic hospitals. Catholics, Jews, and Italians also maintained hospitals to meet the particular needs of their communities.

THE MOVEMENT'S VANGUARD—THE NHA AND NMA

The NHA and NMA led the way in spearheading the hospital reform movement and in articulating the concerns of black medical professionals. After a long, unsuccessful effort to integrate the American Medical Association, (AMA) the NMA was founded in 1895 to im-

21. Ibid., 173.
22. H. M. Green, "Hospitals and Public Health Facilities for Negroes," *Proceedings of the National Conference of Social Work* 55 (1928): 179.
23. H. M. Green, *A More or Less Critical Review of the Hospital Situation among Negroes in the United States* (n.d., circa 1930), 4–5.

prove the conditions of black physicians, dentists, and pharmacists with the aim of enabling them to educate the masses about better health and "right" living.[24] Its Committee on Medical Education conducted a survey of the quality of care at black hospitals as early as 1910, but its activities in the hospital field assumed little importance until 1923.[25] In August of that year, members of the NMA founded the National Hospital Association.[26] Any hospital admitting black people was deemed eligible for membership and at the NHA's first meeting, thirty-three black hospitals joined the association.

The stated purpose of the NHA was to ensure proper standards of education and efficiency in black hospitals. Specifically, it hoped to

1. Bring these institutions into one compact body for the good of all
2. Standardize black hospitals
3. Standardize the curricula for the training of black nurses
4. Encourage the establishment of hospitals in areas with sufficient black populations to support them
5. Create internship opportunities for black medical students
6. Conduct an educational and statistical survey of black hospitals[27]

The officers of the NHA viewed standardization of black hospitals as the most crucial issue facing the organization. The association's first president, the ubiquitous Dr. H. M. Green, challenged the 100-bed standard for accreditation used by the ACS and the AMA. The Knoxville physician warned that this policy stood to eliminate approximately 85 percent of the hospitals operated for and by black people.[28] A survey conducted in 1923 by the NMA's Commission of Medical Education and Hospitals proved Green's estimate to be overly optimistic, finding that 93 percent of the 202 black hospitals studied had less than 50 beds.[29]

Since the size of these facilities precluded their accreditation by the

24. John A. Kenney, "Health Problems of the Negro," in his *The Negro in Medicine* (Tuskegee, Ala., 1912), 50.
25. "Report of Committee on Medical Education on Colored Hospitals," *JNMA* 14 (1922): 216.
26. "National Hospital Association," *JNMA* 15 (1923): 286–87.
27. John A. Kenney, "The National Hospital Association," *Southern Workman* 56 (February 1927): 62.
28. H. M. Green, "Annual Address of the President of the National Medical Association," *JNMA* 14 (1922): 216.
29. "National Hospital Association," *JNMA* 15 (1923): 286.

ACS and the AMA, one of the first tasks of the NHA was to establish standards for smaller hospitals. In 1925 the association issued a set of minimum standards for its member hospitals.[30] These standards included criteria on hospital supervision, record keeping, and the operation of nurse training schools. In comparison to standards set six years earlier by the ACS, they were rudimentary, lacking criteria for diagnostic facilities, laboratories, or physician training. Nonetheless, the NHA hoped that its attempts at standardization would forestall the elimination of black hospitals. And they hoped their guidelines would demonstrate to their white colleagues that black physicians could keep abreast of changes in medicine.

As was true in the general medical profession at the time, there was a gap between the ideals of the elite physician and those of the average practitioner. The NHA thus had to convince the vast majority of black medical professionals of the importance of standardization. To achieve this goal, the association provided technical assistance to hospitals, sponsored professional conferences, and produced literature about the proper operation and administration of hospitals. The association also lobbied the major health-care organizations on behalf of its members and urged these organizations to take more active roles in the development of black hospitals.

In August 1927 representatives of the NMA and the NHA appealed to representatives of the AMA, the ACS, and the AHA for funds to conduct a survey of black hospitals. Only the AMA responded favorably and in 1928 its Council on Medical Education and Hospitals appropriated $5,000 for the inquiry. The purpose of the survey was to investigate conditions, to improve the quality of existing institutions, and to plan new hospitals where needed.[31] Conducted by Dr. Algernon B. Jackson, a professor of public health at Howard University, the four-month intensive study involved the inspection of 120 hospitals located primarily in the South.[32] Jackson provided detailed information

30. A list of the National Hospital Association's minimum standards can be found in "National Hospital Association, Minutes of the Third Annual Session," *JNMA* 17 (1925): 231.

31. H. M. Green, "The Hospital Survey," *JNMA* (1929): 13–4; H. M. Green, "President's Address: The National Hospital Association," *JNMA* 19 (1927): 16–21; "Investigation of Negro Hospitals," *Journal of the American Medical Association* 94 (1930): 1375–77.

32. Jackson did not investigate sixty-three hospitals in the North.

on the operation of each institution that he visited and awarded each a grade of A, B, C, or D. Those receiving a D were deemed unworthy of support.

Jackson painted a bleak picture of the facilities. Sixteen (13.3 percent) hospitals received A grades, while twenty-seven (22.5 percent) received D grades. Jackson described conditions in some of the latter hospitals as so poor that "one would hesitate to take a drink of water in them, much less submit to even the most minor surgical operation."[33] He also found the educational programs at most of the nurse training schools to be deplorable. Jackson concluded that the quality and quantity of hospital beds for blacks in the South was inadequate. However, the problem, he said, required a more comprehensive survey. Jackson advised that the better hospitals be supported with financial and educational assistance and that the inferior ones be abolished. His survey also recommended that in general black hospitals should be under black control; but it did not make this an absolute requirement. It is not clear who made the final recommendations of the survey. After Jackson completed his on-site visits, the Council submitted his report for verification to a group of white physicians, "all of whom have had a lifelong contact with the negro [*sic*] and spent a score or more years in medical and hospital service in their midst."[34] The committee then submitted a revised report to the council. The published account of the survey obscured any differences between the two reports.

The NHA also lobbied the AHA for support of the black hospital movement. However, the ties between the two organizations were relatively weak. Although the NHA held affiliate membership with the AHA, the larger organization showed little interest in its black constituency. In 1929 the AHA made a feeble attempt to address the problems of black hospitals when it established an ad hoc Committee on Hospitalization of Colored People, chaired by Chicago physician William H. Walsh.[35] The purpose of the committee was to examine how the AHA could assist the NHA in its efforts. After its investigations, the Walsh committee concluded: "There rests at the door of the American Hospital Association a grave responsibility for colored

33. "Investigation of Negro Hospitals," 1375.
34. Ibid.
35. William H. Walsh, "Report of the Committee on Hospitalization of Colored People," *Transactions of the American Hospital Association* 32 (1930): 53–61.

hospitals, and we believe that more effective efforts should be made by the Association to assist in a difficult undertaking which will require many years for satisfactory accomplishment."[36] It also noted that the lack of a permanent office and a full-time executive secretary severely hampered the work of the NHA. The committee recommended that the AHA assist the NHA in a campaign to secure funds for an executive secretary. It also advised that the committee's work be continued. Despite the modesty of its recommendations the report of the Walsh committee received a lukewarm reception from the AHA. At its September 28, 1931 meeting the board of trustees of the AHA endorsed the general aims of the NHA but failed to make any specific commitments—financial or programmatic—to the NHA or vote to extend the work of the Walsh committee.[37]

The NHA had practical and well-intentioned objectives, but several factors limited its activities and hampered its effectiveness in reforming black hospitals. The association never obtained a full-time administrator or a permanent office. It never received extensive financial support from other organizations or from foundations. The NHA itself lacked the financial and political muscle to implement many of its programs, especially the enforcement of standardization requirements. The association also suffered from the indifference of the majority of black physicians. After visiting Brewster Hospital, a black hospital in Jacksonville, Florida, Dr. Midian O. Bousfield, a prominent leader in the reform movement, commented: "The men in Jacksonville are way behind the times and by no means equal to the demands of such a hospital. . . . I tried to talk to them in the interest of better medicine—better preparation—the National Hospital Association, National Medical Association, Promotion of Specialization, etc. . . . Not a single man in the place knew anything about scholarship and the opportunity for improvement."[38] In 1938 Bousfield, then director of the Negro Health Program of the Julius Rosenwald Fund and a past president of the NMA, characterized the NHA as a conglomerate organization of

---

36. Ibid., 57.

37. American Hospital Association, "Report of the Board of Trustees, 28 September 1931," *Transactions of the American Hospital Association* 32 (1930): 33–38.

38. M. O. Bousfield to P. M. Murray, n.d., Box 76, Peter Marshall Murray Papers, Moorland-Spingarn Library, Howard University.

"inspirational nature" that had made no significant contribution to the improvement of black hospitals.[39]

BLACK HOSPITALS AND WHITE PHILANTHROPY

Certainly, no movement for the elevation of black community hospitals could succeed without the cooperation and financial assistance of the white community. Very few black professionals had the training to administer hospitals or hospital departments. In a 1930 address before the Annual Congress on Medical Education, Medical Licensure, and Hospitals, Dr. Peter Marshall Murray, a prominent black physician, emphasized the necessity of white support:

> The assistance of the broadminded, sympathetic white profession in actual staff responsibilities is not only highly desirable, but, in the present stage of professional development of Negroes, except in a few cities where Negro physicians have enjoyed unusual clinical opportunities, it is absolutely necessary. While in the past, a certain pride might have been justified in pointing to any hospital, no matter how ill equipped or inadequately fitted to meet the health needs of a community, as an example of the Negro's effort to help himself . . . there is to-day [*sic*] no justifiable excuse for such a state of affairs.[40]

Murray assumed the presidency of the NMA in 1932 and became a leading spokesman of the hospital reform movement. He frequently worked with Bousfield to raise funds for black hospitals.

But funds were not readily forthcoming. Indeed, throughout the 1920s and 1930s—a time when government and third-party payments were not yet widely available—all American hospitals grappled with the problem of financing. For black hospitals, however, the problem was particularly severe. Their patients were predominantly poor and could neither afford to pay their hospital bills nor provide the hospitals with charitable assistance. Two philanthropies, the Julius Rosenwald Fund and the Duke Endowment, played central roles in taking up the

39. M. O. Bousfield, "Program for Negro Health," October 9, 1936, Box 76, Julius Rosenwald Fund Archives, Fisk University Library, Nashville, Tenn.
40. Murray, "Hospital Provision for the Negro Race," 44.

slack. These foundations gave substantial grants for operation and construction of black hospitals. Another foundation, the Rockefeller General Education Board, donated funds for educational programs. The foundations worked closely with the NHA and NMA in developing and implementing their plans.

The Chicago-based Julius Rosenwald Fund had been established in 1917 by Julius Rosenwald, president of Sears, Roebuck, and Company, as a clearinghouse for his favorite charities.[41] Until 1927 its work consisted almost exclusively of the construction of rural black schools in the South. In 1928 the Rosenwald Fund reorganized and expanded its interests to include black education and welfare, race relations, medical economics, library service, and social studies. It also maintained a Negro Health Division, which supported programs in professional education, public health, outpatient services, and hospital care.[42] Under the direction of Dr. Midian O. Bousfield, the division assisted projects that would be of educational value in the training of black nurses and physicians and that would demonstrate superiority in race relations. Bousfield also provided the Rosenwald Fund with a direct link to the black medical elite. Between 1927 and 1936 the foundation gave over $550,000 to twelve black hospitals and to two units at mixed hospitals.[43] These grants included funds for equipment, medical and nursing staff development, and hospital construction and renovation.

In contrast to the Rosenwald Fund, the Duke Endowment did not have a specific black health program; but it maintained a hospital section that defrayed the operating costs and capital expenses of any nonprofit hospital in North and South Carolina that it judged to be properly operated.[44] The endowment was formed in 1924. In addition

41. For general histories of the philanthropy and its founder see Edwin R. Embree and Julia Waxman, *Investment in People: The Story of the Julius Rosenwald Fund* (New York: Harper, 1949), and M. R. Werner, *Julius Rosenwald: The Life of a Practical Humanitarian* (New York: Harper, 1939).

42. For descriptions of the Negro Health Program see Bousfield, "Program for Negro Health," and Julius Rosenwald Fund, *Negro Hospitals*, 1–5.

43. Edwin R. Embree, *Julilus Rosenwald Fund: Review of Two Decades, 1917–1936* (Chicago: The Fund, 1936), 36.

44. For descriptions of the hospital program of the endowment see George P. Harris, "The Work of the Duke Endowment with South Carolina Hospitals," *Journal of the South Carolina Medical Association* 38 (1942): 282–84; W. S. Rankin, "The Interest of the Duke Endowment in Medical Education," *Journal of American Medical Association* 92 (1929): 1274; W. S. Rankin, "The Hospital Program of the Duke Endowment," Box 6, Duke Endowment Archives (hereinafter DE Archives), Duke University Library, Durham, N.C.

to hospitals, it assisted schools, orphanages, and Methodist churches in the Carolinas. Its support of black hospitals stemmed from the Duke family's long-standing interest in Durham's Lincoln Hospital, founded in 1901 in appreciation of the loyalty of slaves during the Civil War.[45] The endowment's assistance to these facilities had a pragmatic basis. It recognized that improvements in public health would require the provision of hospital facilities for both white and black citizens. While it acknowledged and even supported the establishment of a few black district hospitals for use as training centers, the Duke Endowment believed that black hospitals unnecessarily duplicated existing hospital facilities, and encouraged instead the development of black units and wards in mixed hospitals.[46] Nonetheless, foundation guidelines led the endowment to donate $1.2 million for operating expenses to twenty-two black nonprofit general hospitals in North and South Carolina and $130,000 for capital expenses to seven of these institutions between 1925 and 1939.[47]

These appropriations provided critical financial support for the funded hospitals: between 1930 and 1937 Duke subsidies comprised 55 percent of the charitable contributions that the hospitals received for operating costs.[48] Ironically, in opposition to its stated policy, the Duke Endowment's financial support enabled many black general hospitals in the Carolinas to survive and enabled some institutions to receive accreditation from the ACS and the AMA.

The involvement of the General Education Board (GEB), a Rockefeller philanthropy, in the black hospital field evolved out of its interest in the overall improvement of black education. The GEB was estab-

For a discussion of the endowment's work in black hospitals see Vanessa Northington Gamble, "The Duke Endowment's Black Hospital Policy, 1924–1939" (Paper presented at the meeting of the Southern Historical Association, November 1982).

45. "One First in Which We My [sic] Take Justifiable Pride," *The Health Bulletin* (North Carolina State Board of Health) 45 (March 1930): 6.

46. The Duke Endowment, *The Annual Report of the Hospital Section, 1937* (Charlotte: The Endowment, 1938), 24.

47. George P. Harris, "Record Keeping Procedures in the Small General Hospitals," Box 181 (Paper presented at Tri-State Conference of Hospital Administrators, Lincoln Hospital, Durham, N.C., October 24–25, 1940), DE Archives.

48. See tables, Operating Account Contributions by Principal Sources, included in the annual reports of the hospital section from 1930 to 1937. Black hospitals were more dependent on the endowment than were other hospitals. Between 1930 and 1937, white hospitals received 39 percent of their operating account contributions from the Duke Endowment while mixed hospitals received 36 percent.

lished in 1903 by John D. Rockefeller "to promote education within the United States of America without distinction of race, sex, or creed."[49] Among its major activities were the reform of American colleges and universities, the improvement of education in the South, and the provision of adequate educational opportunities to Afro-Americans. The GEB program in black education encompassed all educational levels, granting frunds to improve teaching at black public schools in the South, to provide endowments at black colleges such as Fisk University in Nashville and Morehouse College in Atlanta, and to establish teaching fellowships for black professors. One of the GEB's primary interests was black medical education. It spent substantial sums to improve the medical curricula, upgrade facilities, and establish clinical fellowships for teachers at Howard and Meharry, the only black medical schools that existed after 1923.[50] The GEB did not provide grants for operating and capital expenses; its interests were focused exclusively on educational projects. For example, it funded the development of a postgraduate refresher course for black physicians at Richmond's St. Philip's Hospital, a black hospital operated by the Medical College of Virginia.

Despite their divergent interests, all three foundations worked together to improve black hospitals. In the Carolinas, the Julius Rosenwald Fund worked solely through the Duke Endowment and assisted only those projects that had the endowment's endorsement.[51] The Rosenwald Fund hoped that its efforts would supplement those of the Duke Endowment in the Carolinas because the endowment could not directly fund outpatient services and public health work. Between 1928 and 1939 the two foundations jointly financed projects at five black hospitals. These included the construction of Good Shepherd Hospital in New Bern, North Carolina; hospital staff reorganization at Lincoln Hospital, Durham, North Carolina; and the remodeling and building of facilities at St. Agnes Hospital, Raleigh, North Carolina, L. Richardson Memorial Hospital, Greensboro, North Carolina; and Good

49. *General Education Board: Review and Final Report, 1902–1964* (New York: The Board, 1964), 3. For a general history of the GEB see Raymond B. Fosdick, *Adventure in Giving: The Story of the General Education Board* (New York: Harper, 1962).

50. For a history of the General Education Board's activities at Meharry Medical College see Hine, "The Pursuit of Professional Equality."

51. Julius Rosenwald Fund, Trustee Minutes, November 16, 1929, Addenda, Box 2, Julius Rosenwald Papers, University of Chicago Library, Chicago, Ill.

Samaritan Hospital, Charlotte, North Carolina. The foundation also cooperated in offering technical assistance to the hospitals.

Together the Rosenwald Fund and the GEB backed the black hospital movement's most widely heralded project, the 1928 affiliation of Provident Hospital with the University of Chicago.[52] Provident Hospital, a 58-bed facility, was one of the best black hospitals in the United States, approved for internship training by the AMA and accredited by the ACS. It also had a nurse training school and biracial community support.

But this premier black hospital had many problems. Its financial situation was precarious, its physical plant run-down, and its medical service so deteriorated that one of Chicago's largest employers, Armour and Company, threatened to send its black employees elsewhere.[53] Provident had no medical school affiliation and its medical staff could not keep abreast of the latest medical developments. In the spring of 1928 representatives of Provident Hospital proposed that the hospital affiliate with the University of Chicago. The university proved receptive to the proposal and agreed to the plan.

The association was very significant because it represented a new strategy for black hospital reform, namely affiliation with a white university. Supporters of the Provident Hospital project hoped to create the foremost center for black medical education in the United States. They also sought to provide black professionals with at least one clinical program that equaled those available to their white colleagues. The project received enthusiastic praise from the NMA. Julius Rosenwald himself hailed it as one of the most important steps in the progress of the black race since the Emancipation Proclamation.[54] But despite this early optimism, the project ended in 1944, when the GEB withdrew its financial support.

Several factors contributed to the project's demise, including the growing indifference of the University of Chicago, financial problems and mismanagement at Provident Hospital, and the developing per-

52. The history of this project is analyzed in Vanessa Northington Gamble, "The Provident Hospital Project: An Experiment in Black Medical Education" (Paper presented at the meeting of the American Association for the History of Medicine, May 1982).

53. H. G. Ellerd to George Arthur, February 21, 1929, Box 242, Julius Rosenwald Fund Archives.

54. Werner, *Julius Rosenwald*, 274.

ception of the project as Jim Crowism by Chicago's black community. The divergent goals of the Julius Rosenwald Fund and the GEB also played a significant role in the failed affiliation. The GEB saw the project as an educational endeavor, the Rosenwald Fund saw it as an educational *and* hospital service endeavor. The GEB decided to withdraw its funds after the project did not live up to its educational expectations—the affiliation had not attracted increased numbers of black medical students to the Provident program. Between 1931 and 1938 only seven black students graduated. Provident Hospital also had difficulty finding black interns, and by 1938 began to recruit white foreign doctors. Apparently the deans at Howard and Meharry did not hold the clinical program at Provident in high regard.[55] Thus, the GEB considered the project an educational failure. On the other hand, the interest of the Rosenwald Fund in the project continued because, as even the GEB acknowledged, the medical services at the hospital had improved with the affiliation. But without the financial support of the GEB, the project was doomed.

GOVERNMENT SUPPORT OF BLACK HOSPITALS

In addition to philanthropic contributions, local governments funded programs to meet the health needs of their black citizens. In some localities, such as Kansas City and St. Louis, political pressure prompted the municipalities to act. The black community argued that as taxpayers they should not be excluded as professionals or patients from publicly financed facilities. The NMA and the NHA aimed especially harsh criticism at municipal hospitals that admitted black patients, but excluded black physicians.[56] Although Kansas City and St. Louis both had black municipal hospitals prior to the 1920s, these facilities developed out of old, run-down physical plants. In the 1920s the black communities of both cities applied political pressure to establish modern facilities, and a new

55. E. E. Embree and R. A. Lambert, telephone interview, April 12, 1938, Box 699, General Education Board Papers, Rockefeller Archive Center, Tarrytown, N.Y.
56. Midian O. Bousfield, "Presidential Address," *JNMA* 26 (1934): 155; Murray, "Hospital Provision for the Negro Race," 44.

black municipal hospital opened in Kansas City in 1930 and in St. Louis in 1937.[57]

Even in places where state-sanctioned racism prohibited black suffrage, local governments (perhaps cognizant of the color blindness of disease) agreed to construct black hospitals, which typically consisted of separate units in the existing public hospitals. For example, when Spartanburg General Hospital opened in 1921 in Spartanburg, South Carolina, it had no facilities for blacks. With the assistance of the Duke Endowment and the Rosenwald Fund, by 1930 the hospital had constructed a separate unit for black patients and physicians.[58]

The federal government also contributed to the black hospital movement. Under the auspices of the Department of the Interior it continued its support of Freedman's Hospital in Washington, D.C. By 1939 this federal facility had grown to 322 beds and provided one of the few approved internships for black physicians.[59] In addition to supporting Freedmen's Hospital, in 1923 the federal government opened a hospital in Tuskegee, Alabama for black veterans.[60] After World War I the nearly 400,000 black people who had served in the American armed forces were barred from most veterans hospitals. Black organizations protested this discrimination and in 1921 the Harding administration decided to build a federal hospital for black veterans. The decision eventually created a storm of controversy that centered on whether the hospital would be operated by whites or blacks. Racists in Alabama,

57. For accounts of the black municipal hospital in Kansas City see Bradford, "History of Kansas City General Hospital," and Rodgers, "Kansas City General Hospital." For histories of the hospital in St. Louis see Homer G. Phillips Hospital, *The History and Development of Homer G. Phillips Hospital* (St. Louis, Mo.: 1945), and H. Philip Venable, "The History of Homer G. Phillips Hospital," *JNMA* 53 (1961): 541–51.

58. For a discussion of this cooperative project see George P. Harris, "Memo: Spartanburg General Hospital," October 17, 1930, Box 184, DE Archives.

59. "Hospitals Registered by the American Medical Association," *Journal of the American Hospital Association* 114 (March 30, 1940): 1195–1258.

60. The founding of this hospital and the subsequent controversy are extensively discussed in Pete Daniel, "Black Power in the 1920s: The Case of Tuskegee Veterans' Hospital," *Journal of Southern History* 36 (1970): 368–88; Allan W. Ryff, "The Tuskegee Hospital Controversy, 1921–1924" (Master's thesis, University of Delaware, 1970); and Raymond Wolters, "Major Moton Defeats the Klan: The Case of the Tuskegee Veterans' Hospital," in his *The New Negro on Campus: Black College Rebellions in the 1920s* (Princeton: Princeton University Press, 1975), 137–91.

led by the Ku Klux Klan, did not want a black-operated federal institution in the heart of Dixie. The black community, particularly the NMA and the National Association for the Advancement of Colored People (NAACP), argued that blacks should be in charge of a facility built for the care of their race. President Harding supported black control of the facility because he did not want to alienate black voters and because of his personal racial ideology.[61] He believed that blacks should develop leaders capable of heading a separate black society. Yet when the hospital opened in May 1923 whites comprised the entire professional staff. The hospital did employ black nursemaids, however, since Alabama law forbade white nurses to touch black patients.[62] Subsequently, the Harding administration made a commitment to eventual black operation of the hospital and in July 1924 the dreams of the NMA and NAACP became a reality.

THE RISE OF INTEGRATIONISM

The necessity of separate facilities for black people was at the heart of the black hospital movement's ideology. The NMA and NHA adopted accommodationism as their strategy for black social and economic advancement. This political philosophy had been popularized by Booker T. Washington and emphasized black self-reliance, the development of black social institutions, and the avoidance of political activism on the issue of social equality and institutional integration. The NMA and NHA claimed that their programs represented a practical response to the racial realities of American life in the 1920s and 1930s.[63] While they did not condone segregation and its concomitant ideology of white superiority, the leaders of the black hospital movement believed that separate institutions were necessary because integration was a slow process and the advancement of the race could not afford to wait for its eventual development.

61. Wolters, "Major Moton Defeats the Klan," 160.
62. Ibid., 159.
63. John A. Kenney, "Why the Community Hospital?" in *Historical Sketch of the Community Hospital* (Newark, N.J.: The Hospital, 1939), 5; W. H. Miller, "What Is Ours, We Should Conserve," *JNMA* 21 (1929): 114–16; "Why a National Hospital Association?" *JNMA* 18 (1926): 138–39.

By World War II this ideology came under increased fire from a growing and uncompromising group of integrationists, who rejected the establishment of segregated institutions and advocated instead the complete equality of black people in American society. Tensions between integrationists and accommodationists had in fact developed in the hospital field during the 1920s and 1930s. In Cleveland, their disputes led to the abandonment of plans to construct a black hospital in 1927 and split New York City's black medical society into two organizations in 1930.[64] Indeed, the integrationists made some tentative, but important, strides in this era. Increasing numbers of publicly financed hospitals, for example Harlem and Boston City Hospitals, began to add a few black physicians to their staffs. The premier example was the reorganization of New York City's Sydenham Hospital as an interracial hospital. In December 1943 Sydenham lifted all racial barriers and added blacks to positions on the board of trustees and the medical staff.[65]

The black hospital movement had changed the black hospital by World War II, mostly as a result of the combined efforts of the NMA, the NHA, philanthropies, and government agencies. But there was no Negro hospital renaissance as Dr. John A. Kenney had enthusiastically promised in 1930. An analysis of the data plainly reveals that Kenney's assessment was overly optimistic. In 1923 approximately 202 black hospitals were in operation. Only 6 had internship programs and none had a residency program.[66] Of the approximately 169 black hospitals that existed in 1929, the AMA approved 14 for internship training and 2 for residencies; the ACS approved 17 for general accreditation.[67] By 1944 the number of hospitals that admitted black patients exclusively had decreased

64. For an analysis of the Cleveland controversy see William Giffin, "The Mercy Hospital Controversy among Cleveland's Afro-American Civic Leaders, 1927," *Journal of Negro History* 61 (1976): 327–50. For information on the professional split in New York City see Louis T. Wright, "Health Problems of the Negro," *Interracial Review* 8 (January 1935): 6–8.

65. "Reorganized Sydenham Hospital Has Interracial Board and Staff," *Modern Hospital* 62 (February 1944): 120.

66. "National Hospital Association," *JNMA* 15 (1923): 286.

67. Julius Rosenwald Fund, *Negro Hospitals*, 16. The exact number of black hospitals in 1929 is unknown. Dr. Algernon B. Jackson surveyed 120 and the Rosenwald study reported 122. Only 73 institutions appeared on both lists. See *Negro Hospitals*, 13.

from 202 to 124.[68] The AMA now approved 9 of the facilities for internships and 7 for residencies; the ACS fully approved 23 and provisionally approved 3, an undistinguished record at best. In addition, 2 hospitals had approval for graduate training in surgery or a surgical specialty. It is important to note that all the hospitals with accreditation had external sources of support. Although the overall number of black hospitals that were recognized by accrediting agencies had increased by 1944, the great majority of the facilities still remained unaccredited. Moreover, the quality of some approved hospitals was suspect. Representatives of the AMA's Council on Medical Education and Hospitals freely admitted that a number of these hospitals would not have been approved except for the need to supply at least some internship opportunities for black physicians.[69] The council's approval reflected the accepted practice of educating and treating black people in separate, and not necessarily equal, facilities.

The decrease in the total number of hospitals between 1923 and 1944 resulted primarily from the closing of small, poorly equipped facilities. These facilities, for the most part, had severely limited financial resources and the depression hastened their demise. It is not clear why the number of approved internships decreased from fourteen to nine between 1928 and 1944. One explanation may be that by 1944 the need to provide internship positions for black medical school graduates was less urgent because there were fewer black medical school graduates. Between 1927 and 1938 the number decreased by 50 percent—from 120 to 60—primarily as a result of the depression.[70]

The Negro Hospital Renaissance envisioned by Dr. Kenney was limited to a few hospitals. By World War II the majority of black hospitals remained small, poorly financed, and ill-equipped. The limits of the black hospital movement can be explained by a number of factors. Among the most important were the impotence of the NMA and the NHA, the indifference of the majority of black physicians, the

68. Eugene H. Bradley, "Health, Hospitals, and the Negro," *Modern Hospital* 65 (August 1945): 43.

69. Julius Rosenwald Fund, *Negro Hospitals*, 15.

70. John W. Lawlah, "How the Facilities of Our Medical Schools Could Be Enlarged to Meet the Prospective Shortage of Negro Doctors," *JNMA* 35 (1943): 28.

less than enthusiastic support of the major health-care organizations, and the rise of integrationism. It is difficult to conceive of the black hospital movement as a renaissance; its limitations overshadowed many of the movement's accomplishments. Nonetheless, the reform movement forestalled the feared extinction of the black hospital in the face of mounting accreditation pressure, and enabled the black medical profession to survive at a time when its existence was surely endangered.

Part II

COMMUNITIES IN THE AMERICAN HOSPITAL, 1900–1970

5

Machines and Medicine: Technology Transforms the American Hospital

JOEL D. HOWELL

American hospitals were radically transformed from the 1880s through the 1920s. Originally facilities for long-term care of the chronically ill, hospitals gradually became scientific appearing facilities for acute intervention. Their size and number increased dramatically, and they began to attract paying, middle-class patients. At the same time, doctors began to exercise more autonomy on the wards. While most recent studies emphasize the administrative structure of the hospital and its relationship with the community, none systematically examine the content of medical practice within the changing hospital.[1]

I thank Barbara Gastel, Janet Golden, and Lester King for reading and commenting on this essay. Caroline Morris provided invaluable assistance in using the Pennsylvania Hospital Archives. Preparation of this essay was supported in part by the Henry J. Kaiser Family Foundation, Menlo Park, California. Portions of this article were published in a preliminary form by Joel D. Howell, "Early Use of X-ray Machines and Electrocardiographs at the Pennsylvania Hospital: 1897–1927," *Journal of the American Medical Association* 255 (1986): 2320–23.

1. Morris J. Vogel, *The Invention of the Modern Hospital: Boston, 1870–1930* (Chicago: University of Chicago Press, 1980); Charles E. Rosenberg, *The Care of Strangers: The Rise of America's Hospital System* (New York: Basic Books, 1987); David Rosner, *A Once Charitable Enterprise: Hospitals and Health Care in Brooklyn and New York, 1885–1915* (Cambridge: Cambridge University Press, 1982).

Like the hospital, medical practice also underwent a dramatic transformation between 1880 and 1930, and medical technology came to play an important, perhaps even central, role.[2] Diagnostic laboratories gave physicians the ability to confidently identify specific microbial diseases. Anesthesiology and asepsis encouraged surgeons to invade the body and to repair hernias, remove appendixes, and snare tonsils.[3] New medical technology, the most important being the X ray and the electrocardiogram (ECG), allowed physicians to peer inside the human body and to monitor precisely its function.

This technology enabled the physician to make "objective" measurements and diagnoses, and thus to take on, in part, the role of scientist. During these critical decades the authority of many professions became firmly established, including education, engineering, and medicine.[4] It is an arguable point that much of medicine's current high standing derives from its identification with science and technology. Thus, it is important to document the relationship between the growth of technology and the rise of medicine's status during the early twentieth century. Medical specialties also started to become more clearly defined, in part by the use of new and complex instruments.[5]

Machines and medicine had much to do with each other during the early twentieth century. This essay is a case study of how technology became an integral part of medicine at Pennsylvania Hospital, located in Philadelphia. Though not an elite academic hospital, it was a stable,

2. Stanley Joel Reiser, *Medicine and the Reign of Technology* (Cambridge: Cambridge University Press, 1978), and Audrey B. Davis, *Medicine and Its Technology: An Introduction to the History of Medical Instrumentation* (Westport, Conn.: Greenwood Press, 1981). Edward Shorter has perceptively discussed the impact this change had on doctor-patient relationships in *Bedside Manners: The Troubled History of Doctors and Patients* (New York: Simon and Schuster, 1985).

3. For example, at Pennsylvania Hospital the most frequently performed operation in 1895 was excision of cervical adenitis, which was performed twenty-five times. Thirty years later, surgeons performed 1,356 tonsillectomy and adenectomy operations, removed 234 appendixes, and repaired 98 hernias. Note not only the change in the type of operation performed, but also the dramatic increase in the absolute number of operations.

4. Robert H. Wiebe, *The Search for Order, 1877–1920* (New York: Hill and Wang, 1967), and Burton J. Bledstein, *The Culture of Professionalism: The Middle Class and the Development of Higher Education in America* (New York: W. W. Norton, 1976).

5. George Rosen, *The Specialization of Medicine with Particular Reference to Ophthalmology* (New York: Froben Press, 1944), and Rosemary Stevens, *American Medicine and the Public Interest* (New Haven: Yale University Press, 1971).

well-respected, and relatively well-funded institution. Physicians carried on relatively little clinical research there, although in this respect Pennsylvania Hospital is probably representative of most American hospitals.

A few definitions are in order. I consider only machines that required special skills to operate, as determined by people with some medical training, initially physicians.[6] This is, to be sure, an arbitrary and somewhat presentist definition of medical machines. However, the increasing autonomy of physicians within the hospital during this period justifies such an approach. Physicians increasingly decided which tools were purchased, who used them, and when. They used some instruments, such as the microscope, primarily in diagnostic laboratories. However, these tools were applied only to specimens from the patient's body—his blood, or sputum, or urine—not to the person himself. I discuss laboratory-based tools only insofar as changes in the presentation of information from the diagnostic laboratory correlate with and provide supporting evidence for a more general transformation in the way information was presented in the patient record.

Three distinct questions are addressed. First, I assess the role of medical technology in the rise of the modern hospital and its transformation into, by the third decade of the twentieth century, something we might recognize as an early version of the familiar high-technology, machine-oriented institution we now call a hospital. Second, I explore how the use of a machine is determined. Specifically, I ask if the concept of autonomous technology, the idea that machines—purely by their physical characteristics—determine their own application within a social system, is an accurate and/or useful concept when applied to hospital-based medical machines.[7] Third, I evaluate the value of

6. Although technological developments such as the automobile and the assembly line dramatically shaped American medicine in the early twentieth century, this chapter discusses only technology that was used within the hospital. The use of machines within the hospital's laundry or kitchen is not examined, although such machines would probably leap first to the mind of a sanitation-minded, turn-of-the-century hospital superintendent who was asked about machines in his institution. I focus on the inpatient use of technology, and therefore do not discuss therapeutic use of the X ray, primarily an outpatient procedure. Nancy Knight is preparing a Ph.D. thesis at Duke University on this subject.

7. Langdon Winner, *Autonomous Technology: Technics-out-of-Control as a Theme in Political Thought* (Cambridge: MIT Press, 1977).

patient-care records for historical analysis of medical technology use. Published literature, such as journals or books, forms the basis for most previous studies of medical technology. While published sources are essential for assigning the priority of various inventions and applications, they tell us precious little about actual medical practice. Erwin Ackerknecht's plea for a "behaviorist approach" to the history of medicine has been far more often quoted than followed.[8]

In addition to telling us about the behavior of health-care providers, patient records themselves are physical artifacts, revealing how information was produced and transmitted in the early-twentieth-century hospital. As Ludwik Fleck has demonstrated, medical observations reflect the larger society within which they are produced.[9] Similarly, the form of the patient record reflects what those who produced it thought machines and their information meant. Although early-twentieth-century machines appeared to produce unequivocally objective data, on close inspection the construction of reality based on such "hard data" was no less socially defined than the earlier, "soft" sensory information.[10]

This study is based primarily on a systematic sampling of Pennsylvania Hospital patient records from 1897 to 1927.[11] In 1897 the hospital

8. Erwin H. Ackerknecht, "A Plea for a 'Behaviorist' Approach in Writing the History of Medicine," *Journal of the History of Medicine and Allied Sciences* 22 (1967): 211–14. For an essay so frequently referred to, this plea has been cited surprisingly infrequently, perhaps because its advice has been so seldom followed. *Social Science Citation Index* lists only seven citations. Of these, four were published between 1980 and 1984, so perhaps the recent trend is toward a more behaviorist approach. Two recent studies have used hospital patient records to study decision making in nineteenth-century therapeutics. Martin S. Pernick, in *A Calculus of Suffering: Pain, Professionalism, and Anesthesia in Nineteenth-Century America* (New York: Columbia University Press, 1985), shows how physicians' choices of which patients received anesthesia was as much social as scientific. John Harley Warner, in *The Therapeutic Perspective: Medical Practice, Knowledge, and Identity in America, 1820–1885* (Cambridge: Harvard University Press, 1986), discusses how prescribing practices were informed both by therapeutic ideas and professional values.

9. Ludwik Fleck, *The Genesis and Development of a Scientific Fact* (1935; reprint, Chicago: University of Chicago Press, 1979).

10. Joel D. Howell, "Early Perceptions of the Electrocardiogram: From Arrhythmia to Infarction," *Bulletin of the History of Medicine* 58 (1984): 88–89, and Joel D. Howell, "Machines' Meanings: British and American Use of Medical Technology, 1880–1930" (Ph.D. diss., University of Pennsylvania, 1987).

11. Unless otherwise noted, information specific to Pennsylvania Hospital comes from that hospital's patient records, Minutes of the Board of Managers, and Annual Reports,

purchased its first X-ray machine. Thirty years later it adopted a new system for filing case records.[12] I examined records at five-year intervals. For each study year I examined in detail the first 300 records starting with a bound volume from December or January, and scanned the subsequent 150–300 admissions looking specifically for use of technology. Total yearly patient admissions over the period ranged from 2,535 to 5,904.

THE NEWEST TECHNOLOGY AT AMERICA'S OLDEST HOSPITAL

Roentgen's description of X rays late in 1895 shocked and amazed the Western world. To be able to see within the human body had a profound impact on both the lay and professional communities. In 1897 Pennsylvania Hospital, like many other American hospitals, purchased an X-ray machine—the symbol of advanced, scientific medicine.[13] However, despite the widespread attention given this amazing new tool, for at least a decade following its purchase the machine played little or no role in patient care.

Soon after its invention the X ray was widely described in the medical literature as being useful for diagnosing abnormal conditions of bones, such as fractures. However, one should not mistake descriptions in medical literature for application in medical practice. Despite the fact that trauma accounted for four of the five most common surgical diagnoses, I found no mention of X-ray use for a hospitalized patient in 1897.[14]

---

all of which are located at the Pennsylvania Hospital Archives, 9th and Spruce Streets, Philadelphia, Pa.

12. H. Auchincloss, "Unit History System," *Medical and Surgical Report of the Presbyterian Hospital in the City of New York* 10 (1918): 30–72. Identification of consecutive records is far more difficult under this system of storing records.

13. Two other major Philadelphia hospitals, the Hospital of the University of Pennsylvania and Philadelphia General, purchased their machines in 1896 and 1899, respectively. See George E. Pfahler, "Fifty Years of Trials and Tribulations in Radiology," in *The American Roentgen Ray Society, 1900–1950: Commemorating the Golden Anniversary of the Society* (Springfield, Ill.: Charles C. Thomas, 1950), 15–24, and Lynne Allen Leopold, *Radiology at the University of Pennsylvania, 1890–1975* (Philadelphia: University of Pennsylvania for the Department of Radiology, 1981), 3–18.

14. Those five diagnoses were contusion of extremities, simple fracture of tibia and fibula, ankle sprain, adenitis, and lacerated extremities.

Five years after its arrival, in 1902, the X-ray machine was rarely used, and then out of curiosity rather than for patient care. In one instance, an unfortunate nine-year-old boy with cyanotic congenital heart disease had X rays taken of his enlarged heart and of his deformed, "spatula like" fingers.[15] The examination was performed to see if the finger deformity was bone (it was not) and to see how the heart appeared with the new instrument. The X-ray image had no impact on the patient's therapy or prognosis, nor was it taken as part of any clinical research. Rather, the machine was used to answer a simple structural question: What was the nature of the deformed fingers? A more subtle 1902 example of the X ray's use for curiosity, not patient care, illustrates the value of clinical records. A gentleman was admitted to the hospital complaining of "inability to walk after being run over by a horse."[16] A roentgenogram revealed that his leg was broken. This was not, however, an early diagnosis of fracture by X ray, at least not in any clinically significant sense. The plate was exposed only after two and a half weeks of uncomplicated hospitalization, during which time the patient had been treated for a broken leg. The X ray was taken out of interest, not for improving patient care. Even a decade later, in 1912, X-ray examination was still quite an unusual event for the hospitalized patient. Patients with broken bones severe enough to require surgery usually did not have an X ray taken before going to the operating room for repair.[17] The occasional use of the X ray took place in cases involving fractures, kidney stones, or foreign bodies.

Who was creating these images? From 1897 to 1909 the chief resident operated the X-ray machine, in addition to running the operating room, sterilizing room, and photography room, and being responsible for the maintenance and care of "all apparatus and instruments." The position of chief resident had only been created and defined in 1897.[18] Clearly, the board of managers did not anticipate that medical instrumentation would occupy a large part of the chief resident's day. X-ray equipment care and use eventually assumed more of the chief resident's time, and in both 1910 and 1911 the former chief resident

15. Pennsylvania Hospital Case Records (henceforth, PHCR) 96 (1902): 3300.
16. PHCR 96 (1902): 3277.
17. See, for example, PHCR 196 (1912): 3161.
18. Minutes of the Board of Managers, November 11, 1897.

stayed on for an extra year specifically to run the X-ray machine. The first, Walter Estell Lee, promptly declared the old equipment obsolete and insisted on the purchase of $940 worth of new X-ray machinery.[19] Lee went on to a career as professor of surgery at the University of Pennsylvania, where he used his early familiarity with X rays in several radiological studies of pulmonary atelectasis. His successor, Charles Montgomery, negotiated, with some difficulty, a pay raise from $25 to $50 per month.[20]

The year 1912 marked a critical turning point in the operation of the X-ray machine. The responsibility for running the machine was shifted from a series of chief residents to a physician who devoted his career to roentgenology. In 1911 David Bowen was appointed radiographer at Pennsylvania Hospital.[21] The following year an X-ray department was established, and Bowen assumed the position of radiographer-in-charge. Bowen, an 1894 graduate of Jefferson Medical College, started his career as a country general practitioner. In 1906 he came across some discarded X-ray equipment in Rome, New York, which he was able to repair and use. The following year he studied roentgenology with Sidney Lange for two weeks in Cincinnati and attended the annual meeting of the new American Roentgen Ray Society. From 1907 onward Bowen attempted to limit his practice to taking and interpreting radiographs. He received further training from 1911 through 1920 as an assistant to Willis Manges, in the Jefferson Hospital Radiology Department.

Whereas the earlier appointments at Pennsylvania Hospital lasted only one year, Bowen remained in his position into the 1930s. By 1913 his title was changed to the slightly more formal "Roentgenol-

19. Herbert Reid Hawthorne, "Memoir of Walter Estell Lee," *Transactions and Studies of the College of Physicians* 20 (1952): 159–60.

20. Minutes of the Board of Managers, April 25, 1911.

21. Ralph S. Bromer, "Memoir of David Ralph Bowen, M.D.," *Transactions and Studies of the College of Physicians* 8 (1940): 132–34, and George E. Pfahler, "The Early History of Roentgenology in Philadelphia: The History of the Philadelphia Roentgen Ray Society (1905–1920), Part 1: 1899–1920," *American Journal of Roentgenology* 75 (1956): 14–22. Two of Bowen's papers are "Roentgen Examination of the Sphenoidal Sinus: Presenting a Vertical Technique," *American Journal of Roentgenology* 12 (1914): 449–59, and "Acute Massive Collapse (Atelectasis) of the Lung," *American Journal of Roentgenology and Radium Therapy* 21 (1929): 101–41. The latter was presented in 1928 at the Second International Congress of Radiology in Stockholm, Sweden.

ogist," in honor of the X-ray's inventor, and perhaps prompted by Bowen's election as secretary of the Philadelphia Roentgen Ray Society. In 1919 Bowen was elected president of the American Roentgen Ray Society, thus holding an official position in two early specialty groups. The Philadelphia society, originally constituted in 1905, heard presentations on radiological topics, often in joint session with other medical societies. In 1913 they instituted a postgraduate course of instruction in roentgenology, the first formal specialty training for radiologists in the United States. This one-month course included clinical instruction at Pennsylvania Hospital under Bowen's supervision. During his career Bowen published several articles and was an editor of the *American Journal of Roentgenology and Radium Therapy*. From 1907 he was, as we now define the term, a specialist, and an active member of the group of early radiologists who practiced and taught in Philadelphia.

The terms of Bowen's employment differed significantly from those of his predecessors in ways that marked a qualitative change in the relationship between the physician, the machine, and the hospital. In return for devoting 50 percent of his time to the X-ray department, Bowen received an annual salary of $1,500. In addition, his income included 75 percent of all fees generated by taking X rays of paying patients; the hospital retained 25 percent. This agreement reflected the growing number of patients who paid for some part of their hospital care. At the same time as Bowen's 1911 appointment, contributions from an anonymous donor allowed the hospital to purchase $6,500 worth of new X-ray equipment, a sharp increase in their capital investment in diagnostic machinery and perhaps also an indication of lay interest in X rays.

Hospitals were becoming complex institutions, and X-ray machines added to that complexity. First, the machines required special training to operate. No longer could a single superintendent confidently assert control over every decision about how his hospital was run. The decision to establish a separate X-ray unit, run by a physician with special technical skills, reflected the increased complexity of the structure of American business.[22] Second, the X-ray machine generated formal

22. Alfred D. Chandler, *The Visible Hand: The Managerial Revolution in American Business* (Cambridge: Harvard University Press, 1977).

reimbursement for services performed within the hospital using hospital equipment, and thereby added to levels of authority and accounting within an increasingly more complicated institution.

Like the administrators of most voluntary hospitals of this period, the board of managers of Pennsylvania Hospital became increasingly concerned with financial matters. Because the X ray symbolized the exact, scientific nature of medicine it was seen as one way to attract more private, paying patients. X rays were ever more conspicuous in annual reports of this period, which were sent not only to potential contributors but also to potential patients. Indeed, the number of patients examined by X ray rose steadily, and in 1916 a part-time nurse was assigned to the X-ray department.

Physicians requested X-ray examinations more frequently. By 1917, the X ray had become a routine diagnostic test for patients with kidney stones or limb fractures. Those with suspected broken legs often had examinations performed on admission, not 2 1/2 weeks later, as had been the case in 1902. Physicians made specific diagnoses of tuberculosis, renal stones, and fractures solely on the basis of radiological evidence. Although the X ray was used more often after patients entered the hospital, none were admitted specifically for an X-ray examination.

In 1917 the United States formally entered World War I. This conflict encouraged X-ray use in two ways. Several American hospitals established units overseas, and dozens of nurses and physicians from Pennsylvania Hospital staffed Base Hospital No. 10, in France. While caring for an unprecedented flow of casualties, these nurses and physicians daily witnessed the value of X rays in detecting the presence of fractures and foreign bodies.[23]

Even before the United States entered the war, World War I stimulated technical advances in X-ray technique. X-ray pictures were originally taken on glass plates imported from Belgium. After 1914 these plates became difficult to obtain, and manufacturers were forced to use film for X-ray pictures. Additional incentive for developing another medium to record the X-ray image came from the use of portable X-ray units near the battlefield. Such machines were less powerful than stationary ones, and required faster film to take high

23. *History of the Pennsylvania Hospital Unit (Base Hospital No. 10, U.S.A.) in the Great War* (New York: Paul B. Hoeber, 1921).

quality pictures. Thus, World War I led to both improved portable units and the use of faster film.[24] Both advances were rapidly incorporated into civilian use.

After World War I the Pennsylvania Hospital X-ray department expanded rapidly. A new physician was employed as assistant radiologist in 1919. Bowen became the full-time radiographer in 1920, a year in which 4,005 patients were examined by X ray. A portable X-ray unit was purchased in 1920, in part because the board of managers anticipated the need to take X-ray pictures of patients in their homes. The gradual shift of medical care from the home into the hospital lasted several decades; it was by no means complete even by 1920. The board of managers of Pennsylvania Hospital still anticipated that some people would elect not to visit the hospital for their medical care. Also, the decision to purchase an expensive piece of machinery to be used by physicians outside the hospital may be indicative of changing relationships between physician and hospital. While the board may have anticipated that the symbolic value of the latest and best equipment would eventually encourage middle-class patients to enter the hospital, the purchase of a portable X-ray machine may also reflect the growing power of physicians to demand that new technology be made available for their use both in and out of the hospital.

X RAYS, ECGS, AND THE HOSPITAL AS A
DIAGNOSTIC CENTER

The second major diagnostic technology introduced into Pennsylvania Hospital was the ECG. Unlike the dramatic discovery of the X ray, the development of the ECG followed many earlier attempts to record the electrical action of the human heart.[25] After Einthoven described the ECG machine in 1902, hospitals did not rush out to buy one as rapidly as they did X-ray machines. For the decade before

24. Arthur W. Fuchs, "Radiographic Recording Media and Screens," in *The Science of Radiology*, ed. Otto Glasser (Springfield, Ill.: Charles C. Thomas, 1933), 104–5.
25. George E. Burch and Nicholas P. DePasquale, *A History of Electrocardiography* (Chicago: Year Book Medical Publishers, 1964), and John Burnett, "The Origins of the Electrocardiograph as a Clinical Instrument," *Medical History*, Supplement no. 5 (1985): 53–76.

Pennsylvania Hospital purchased an ECG machine in 1921, the occasional patient who required an ECG was sent elsewhere to have a
tracing made. When an ECG was purchased, arrangements were modeled on those for the X ray. The board of managers quickly approved
the same 75 percent/25 percent split of fees for the "electrocardiog-
rapher" as they had earlier for the radiographer. Electrocardiograph
reports appeared on patients' charts within the year, usually on patients
with irregular heartbeats. A separate room was set aside to house the
ECG machine.

By 1927, although not as widely accepted as the X ray, the ECG
was well on its way to becoming a routine part of patient care. The
machine was used intensively enough to require that a part-time
technician be employed by the ECG laboratory. Attention and
money was directed to heart disease; a special heart clinic attracted
large numbers of patients, and a fellowship in cardiac disease was
established.

The X-ray department, like the ECG, was rapidly expanding. It
performed 6,621 examinations during 1927 in a new, twelve-room,
$21,000 suite that had been the featured topic in the 1925 annual report.
The department also boasted a stereo unit to examine the lungs, reports
within the same day for 95 percent of cases, and, with three trans-
formers, the ability to handle even emergency cases. Exams for possible fractures were done at admission, even when there was low
suspicion that a fracture was actually present. For almost every case
diagnosed as a fracture an X ray was taken.

But in 1927 there was an even more significant transformation
than the increased number of patients receiving an X ray or ECG.
For the first time, patients entered the hospital specifically for
study. This new indication for hospital admission marks a distinct
qualitative shift in its use. The nineteenth-century hospital had been
a home for the long-term care of the chronically ill, and gradually
became a turn-of-the-century institution for acute management of
accident cases as the community became increasingly hard-pressed
to care for the sick at home. Only in 1927 did Pennsylvania Hospital start to function as a repository for complex diagnostic machinery. Why did this function not emerge until thirty years after the
hospital originally bought an X-ray machine?

HOSPITAL ORGANIZATION AND THE USE OF
MEDICAL TECHNOLOGY

One explanation, appealing in its simplicity, might be that technical improvements in diagnostic tools led directly to greater clinical utility. Clearly, a combination of new tubes, improved power supplies, and a moving grid improved the quality of X-ray pictures and made the X ray a more useful clinical tool.[26] Comparison with the ECG reveals a somewhat different story. Early ECG machines produced tracings of quality comparable to the best obtained today, albeit with considerably more difficulty. However, the ECG, unlike the X ray, was of little clinical value in the 1920s.[27] Its rapid integration into patient care by 1927 cannot be explained simply by assuming that technical improvement with resulting clinical utility dictated a machine's use.

In 1897, when the hospital purchased its first X-ray machine, there was no structure into which such a diagnostic tool could fit. There were no physicians performing tests for fees, there were no forms for reporting results of any kind. A decade later, in 1912, the hospital employed a physician specifically to take X rays. A growing base of private patients allowed this specialist to substantially augment his income by retaining 75 percent of all fees. By 1921, the X ray had become an accepted part of the hospital routine. When the board of managers purchased an ECG machine in that year, they could easily adopt the same institutional procedures for the ECG that had been developed for the X ray. With a mechanism for sharing reimbursement with the physician-operator as well as a format for reporting test results from special units already in place, the hospital could incorporate a new technology with relative ease. By 1921, the hospital's experience with the X ray, as well as the ideology that made it desirable to take precise, quantitative measurements with machines, provided a structure into which the ECG could be easily inserted.

Chart 5.1 demonstrates the differences between acceptance of the X

26. Ruth Brecher and Edward M. Brecher, *The Rays: A History of Radiology in the United States and Canada* (Baltimore: Williams and Wilkins, 1969).
27. Howell, "Early Perceptions," 89.

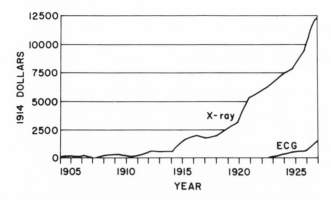

Chart 5.1. Pennsylvania Hospital X-ray and ECG receipts, expressed in constant 1914 dollars, 1905–1927. From Pennsylvania Hospital Annual Reports.

ray and the ECG. Annual X-ray and ECG receipts are displayed in constant 1914 dollars.[28] Both Chart 5.1 and patient records reveal a substantial delay between the purchase of the X-ray machine in 1897 and its widespread application by the late 1920s. In contrast, the ECG, a less clinically valuable tool, found almost immediate acceptance after 1921. Receipts for X rays rose sharply in 1914, following the appointment of a half-time radiographer. After 1919, when the radiographer became a full-time employee and hired an assistant, receipts rose again. But more than organizational routines, financial reimbursement schemes, or standard operating procedures encouraged the introduction of machines. The ideological context in which the hospital incorporated the ECG and X ray became particularly receptive to the information these machines produced as the practice of medicine became more complex, more quantitative, and more "scientific"—a change reflected in the form of hospital records.

THE TRANSFORMATION OF THE HOSPITAL RECORD

The way information was reported within the hospital underwent a dramatic change from 1897 to 1927, when quantitative results of di-

28. The increase in receipts is similar to that for the number of exams performed, although exact data on the exam totals are not available.

agnostic tests were reported on separate, standardized forms. These forms often depicted the information with graphs, and physicians' increasing familiarity with visual, graphic, and quantitative reports produced by special units of the increasingly bureaucratic hospital in turn promoted the use of medical machines. Test results went from being handwritten by the intern, to being laid into the chart in a patchwork fashion, to finally being typed on a separate sheet of paper and signed by a specialist.

In 1897 patient charts contained no pictures, no separate forms, few numbers, and no graphs save the temperature chart. Patient records were strikingly brief. People stayed for as long as three months with only a dozen or so lines written in the chart.[29] Figure 5.1 shows a typical record. In 1902, this unfortunate man's leg was broken by a trolley car. The house officer wrote the entire case record by hand, including results of the urinalysis, the most commonly performed laboratory test. Note that diagnosis and treatment of the fracture proceeded without use of the X-ray machine. Most other test results of this period share two characteristics of the urinalysis report shown here; they are not signed, and they are unstructured—no form defines a particular item as part of the test results. The handwritten urinalysis includes no specific series of tests, nor does it formally indicate who examined the urine, although one may, with reasonable confidence, assume that it was the intern. There is no hint in this record of special units within the hospital.

In 1902, however, the newly formed Ayer Clinical Laboratory introduced a general printed form for reporting test results.[30] This form left a blank space for both the specimen and the result, and could be used for any examination. Each form was signed by the laboratory director, Simon Flexner. Thus, the first initiative for placing special forms into the case record came from one of the special units of the hospital.

In 1912 urinalysis results appeared on a small, printed slip of paper filled out by the intern and laid into the chart, as shown in figure 5.2.

---

29. Many hospital patients had broken limbs, which made it difficult for them to move about and take care of themselves, and may explain lengthy hospitalizations for those who could not be cared for at home.

30. Edward T. Morman, "Clinical Pathology in America, 1865–1915: Philadelphia as a Test Case," *Bulletin of the History of Medicine* 58 (1984): 198–214.

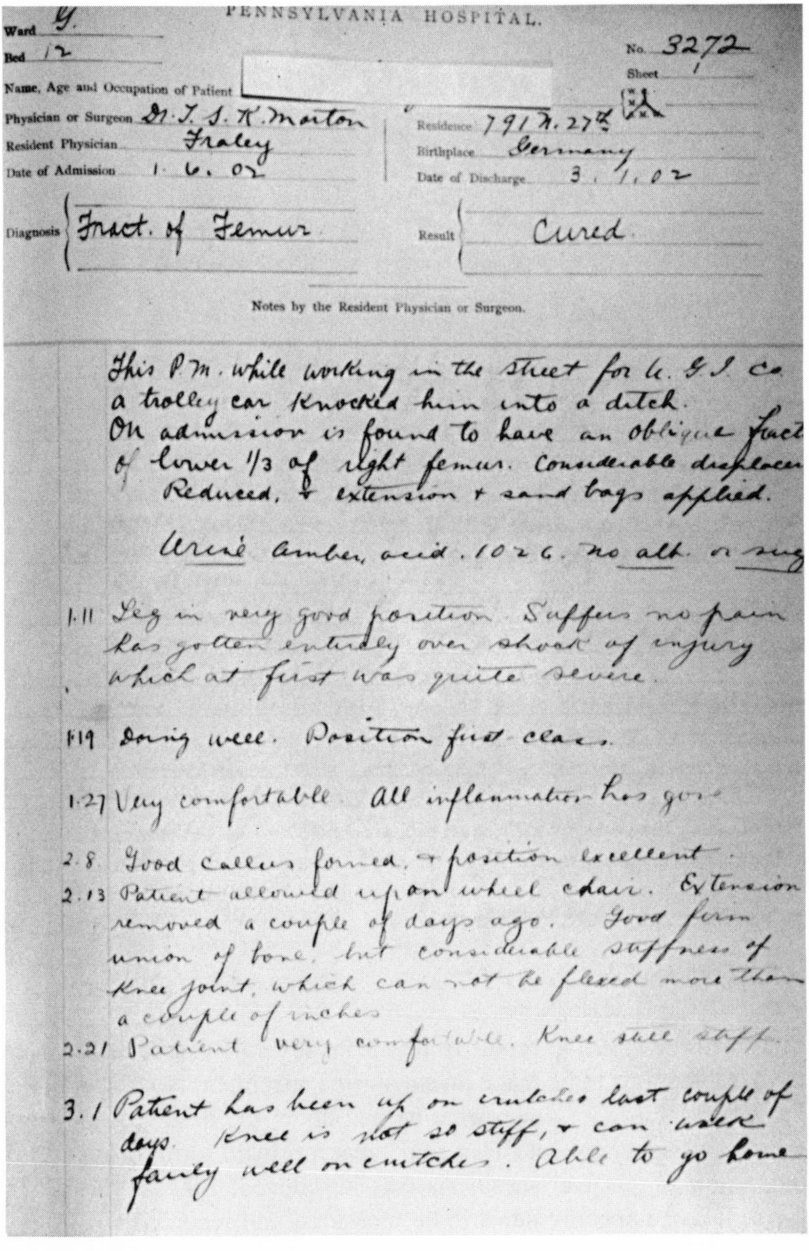

Ward _y._

Bed _12_

No. _3272_

Sheet _1_

Name, Age and Occupation of Patient _____

Physician or Surgeon _Dr. T. S. K. Morton_

Residence _791 N. 27th_

Resident Physician _Fraley_

Birthplace _Germany_

Date of Admission _1. 6. 02_

Date of Discharge _3. 1. 02_

Diagnosis { _Fract. of Femur_

Result { _Cured._

Notes by the Resident Physician or Surgeon.

This P.M. while working in the street for U. G. I. Co. a trolley car knocked him into a ditch. On admission is found to have an oblique fract of lower 1/3 of right femur. Considerable displacement. Reduced, & extension + sand bags applied.

Urine amber, acid. 1026. no alb. or sug

1.11 Leg in very good position. Suffers no pain has gotten entirely over shock of injury which at first was quite severe.

1.19 Doing well. Position first class.

1.27 Very comfortable. All inflammation has gone

2.8 Good callus formed, & position excellent.

2.13 Patient allowed up on wheel chair. Extension removed a couple of days ago. Good firm union of bone, but considerable stiffness of knee joint, which can not be flexed more than a couple of inches.

2.21 Patient very comfortable. Knee still stiff.

3.1 Patient has been up on crutches last couple of days. Knee is not so stiff, & can walk fairly well on crutches. Able to go home

Figure 5.1. Typical case record from 1902, showing care of patient with broken leg. *Pennsylvania Hospital Clinical Records* 96 (1902): 3272.

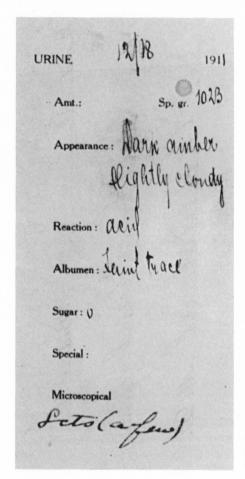

Figure 5.2. Urinalysis form introduced in 1912. *Pennsylvania Hospital
Clinical Records* 196 (1912): 3165.

The form, designed to report results from several specific tests, listed
the examinations to be made on each urine specimen. No longer could
the intern simply jot down what he had done; the design of the form
made omissions obvious. That same year a printed form for recording
the course of surgical anesthesia was introduced. Like the urinalysis
form, it listed specific items to be measured and recorded.

Also in 1912, physicians at Pennsylvania Hospital began to display
information in an increasingly visual manner, perhaps an indication of

the X-ray machine's influence on the way they thought about their patients' bodies and diseases. House officers started to illustrate their physical exams by drawing pictures of the patient's body.[31] Figure 5.3 depicts one intern's diagrammatic representation of the physical findings for a patient with pneumonia. He noted on his drawing a combination of characteristics that demonstrated that the right lung's lower section was infected and partially solidified. Such illustrations were consonant with the X-ray's visual, anatomic display of information, and served to communicate evidence based on sensory findings to the growing number of people involved in patient care.

Five years later, in 1919, most laboratory results were summarized on a single, full-size sheet as shown in figure 5.4, rather than scattered on the earlier patchwork of pieces of paper pasted into the record. Urinalysis and blood exams were included, with several defined components listed. On the reverse side pathological findings could be noted. Also, instead of handwritten X-ray reports entered into the chart by the intern, a formal, official reading was now reported on a separate, standard form, signed by the radiologist, Dr. Bowen.

In the same year the American College of Surgeons (ACS), prompted by its inability to accurately evaluate candidates for admission, began promoting hospital standardization.[32] Standardization meant to the ACS, among other things, standardized forms, and it soon published examples of what it considered acceptable record keeping. Like Abraham Flexner and his famed 1910 report to the Carnegie Foundation, the ACS has often been hailed as the prime mover of a drastic change in American medicine. However, Pennsylvania Hospital had already standardized much of its record-keeping system by 1917. If this was the case at other hospitals as well, and there is no indication that Pennsylvania Hospital was a particular trailblazer in the standardization movement, then the ACS report may have been more a reflection of a transformation already well under way than a force for change. A

31. Such drawings are found in the mid-nineteenth century at the Massachusetts General Hospital (Martin Pernick, personal communication).

32. "Conference on Hospital Standardization," *Bulletin of the American College of Surgeons* 3 (1917): 1–53, and Stanley Joel Reiser, "Creating Form out of Mass: The Development of the Medical Record," in *Transformation and Tradition in the Sciences*, ed. Everett Mendelsohn (Cambridge: Cambridge University Press, 1984), 303–16.

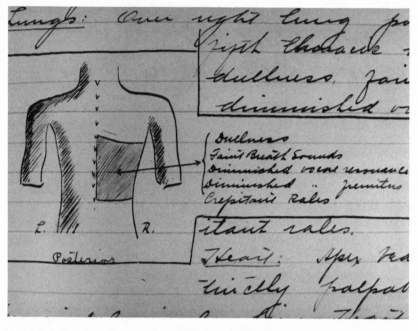

Figure 5.3. Drawing of a lung examination of a nine-year-old schoolgirl with pneumonia. *Pennsylvania Hospital Clinical Records* 196 (1912): 3165.

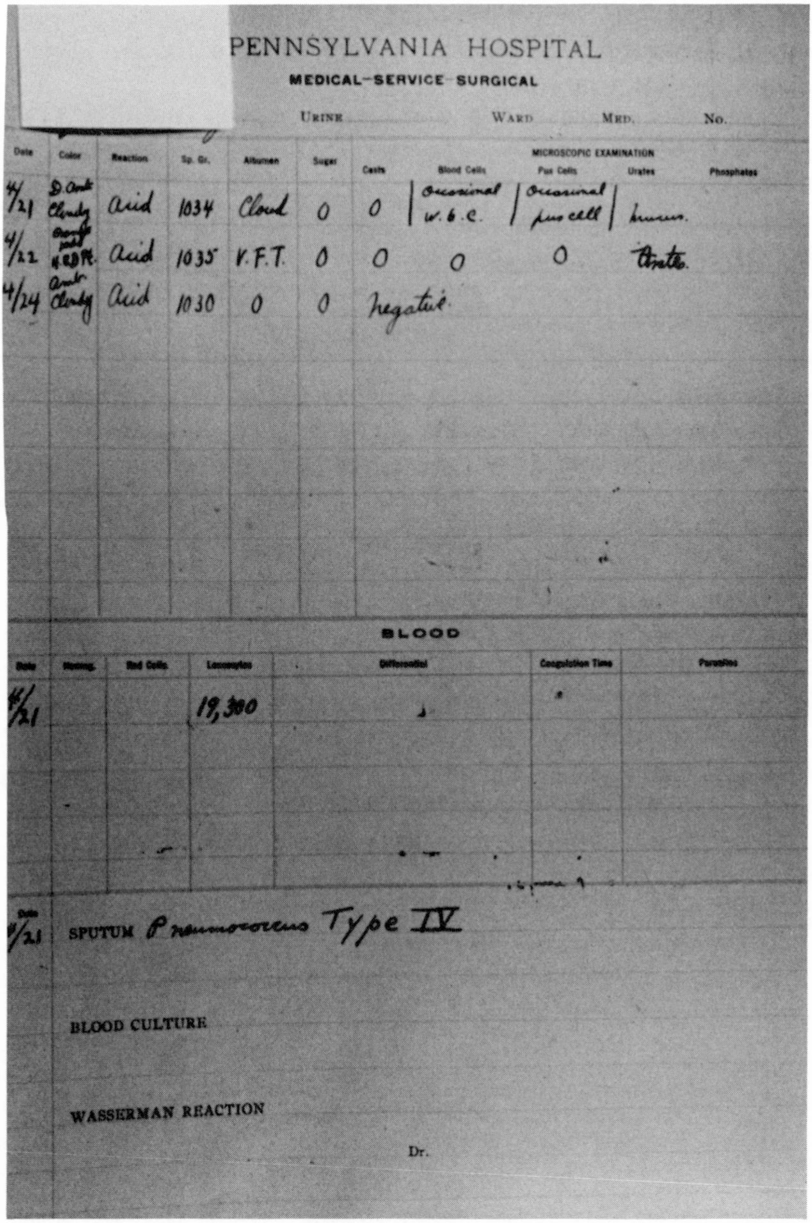

Date	Color	Reaction	Sp. Gr.	Albumen	Sugar	MICROSCOPIC EXAMINATION				
						Casts	Blood Cells	Pus Cells	Urates	Phosphates
4/21	D. amb Cloudy	acid	1034	Cloud	0	0	Occasional w.b.c.	Occasional pus cell	kurus.	
4/22	orange red ppt.	acid	1035	V.F.T.	0	0	0		0	Urate.
4/24	amber Cloudy	acid	1030	0	0	negative				

BLOOD

Date	Hgmg.	Red Cells	Leucocytes		Differential	Coagulation Time	Parasites
4/21			19,300				

Date		
4/21	SPUTUM	P. neumococcus Type IV
	BLOOD CULTURE	
	WASSERMAN REACTION	

Dr.

Figure 5.4. Sheet used to summarize laboratory information for a twenty-nine-year-old housewife who underwent a hysterectomy for a fibroid uterus. *Pennsylvania Hospital Clinical Records* 396 (1917): 3198.

similar reinterpretation has been widely accepted for the Flexner Report.[33]

Standardization and quantification proceeded apace after 1917. ECG reports written in precise, numerical terms appeared on patients' charts by 1922. These reports included the actual physical, graphic information produced by the machine—the ECG tracing itself was laid into the chart. Records from 1922 also included hand-drawn diet charts recording diabetic patients' intake of fat, protein, and carbohydrates in grams. For reporting results from gastrointestinal X rays, the radiology department introduced the standardized form shown in figure 5.5, on which the interpreting physician needed only to circle the appropriate description for each anatomic portion of the examination. Because there were only a few possible descriptions, standardized responses were easily achieved. Even the visual display of anatomic information became standardized, as an inked stamp of the thorax replaced the intern's hand-drawn effort.

The hospital record became progressively more visual and quantitative. By 1927 house officers charted cardiac murmurs visually, with a graphic representation of what they heard in addition to a written description. The size of the heart was also noted with precise, quantitative measurements on the standardized stamp of the patient's body. Figure 5.6 shows yet another graph, a chart with colored bars used to indicate both visually and quantitatively the fluid intake and output of a patient with kidney disease. The hand-drawn diet chart used for diabetic patients in 1922 had become, by 1927, a formal, standardized printed form.

This transformation of the hospital chart from the handwritten record of a single intern to a complex collection of specialists' reports led to a new system of medical record keeping.[34] The older bound volumes,

33. Robert P. Hudson, "Abraham Flexner in Perspective: American Medical Education 1865–1910," *Bulletin of the History of Medicine* 46 (1972): 545–61; Carleton B. Chapman, "The Flexner Report by Abraham Flexner," *Daedalus* 103 (1974): 105–17; Howard Berliner, "A Larger Perspective on the Flexner Report," *International Journal of Health Sciences* 5 (1975): 573–92; and Kenneth M. Ludmerer, "Reform at Harvard Medical School, 1869–1909," *Bulletin of the History of Medicine* 55 (1981): 343–70 and *Learning to Heal: The Development of American Medical Education* (New York: Basic Books, 1985).

34. Auchincloss, "Unit History System"; M. M. Davis, "Records," ch. 18 in *Clinics, Hospitals, and Health Centers* (New York: Harper, 1927), 238–69; and Dorothy L. Kurtz,

PENNSYLVANIA HOSPITAL
X-Ray Department

No. 6664

Ward D

GASTRO-INTESTINAL REPORT

Name

Date 3-20-22   Age   28   Dr.   Gibbon/Cadwall

Provisional Diagnosis   Gastric ulcer

Final Diagnosis   Oper.   Clin.   Path

Duration of Illness

Previous Operation, if any

27739

X-Ray Findings There is the possibility of a lesion in the 1st portion of the duodenum. I
am, however, unable to make this diagnosis positively.   / Bowen

Esophagus

Outline.. ....Normal   Constricted   Dilated   Irregular

Delay at ....1st   2nd   3rd Part

Stomach

Position................Medium'   High   Low   Right   Left

Peristalsis ....Normal   Vigorous   Deep   Irregular   Sluggish   Absent

Tonus.................Normal   Atonic   Hypertonic

Tender Points at.......Sphincter   Cardia   L-Curvature G.Curvature

Mobility................Free   Slightly Fixed Fixed

Filling Defects..........Cardia   Media   Antrum

Incisura.................Present   Absent

Outline.................Regular   Irregular   Projections from

Sphincter..............Seen   Not Seen   Regular   Irregular

Residue........4 1/2 Hours   None   Small   Medium   Large

Duodenum

Filling ....Normal   Absent   Irregular

Delay at..............1st   2d   3rd part

Position...............Normal   Oblique   High   Low

Tender Points.........Present   Absent

Ileum

Position..............Normal   High   Low   Kinked

Mobility...............Free   Slightly Fixed Fixed

Residue..............At ....hours

Head of Bismuth Column, Ileum   Cecum   Hepatic   Trans.   Splenic   Sigmoid   Rectum
                                                                               24 hrs

Colon negative

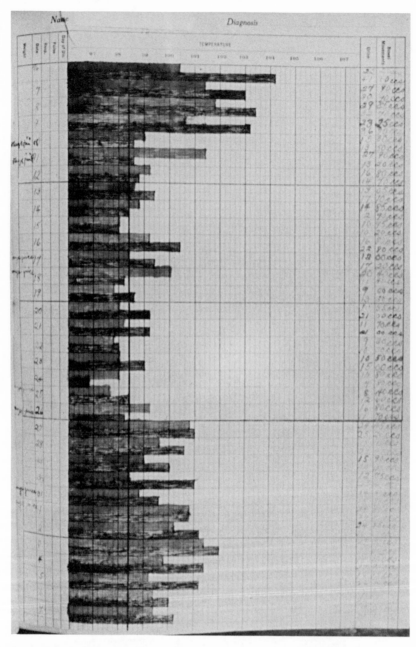

Figure 5.6. Graph showing fluid intake and urine output for a seventeen-year-old schoolboy with nephritis. *Pennsylvania Hospital Clinical Records* 1036 (1927): 4253.

logical when the case record consisted of one or two sheets, became unworkable when the records included charts, graphs, and multiple forms. Each large volume held fewer and fewer patients' records. Repeated admissions required the reader to refer back and forth in the ever-larger books. New outpatient clinics and social service departments created separate records and more problems; a single patient's record might be split into three parts, each in a different department. With the unit file system each patient was assigned a unique number and a single file into which all records were placed. The new system made it easy to collect and compare the records of patients with similar characteristics and diseases, and may have been an important impetus for clinical research.

The use of forms to report diagnostic test results standardized the language used to describe findings, and thereby standardized the information passed on to those caring for the patient. This was explicitly true for gastrointestinal X rays; to produce the report a radiologist needed only to select which phrase to use. The language was also implicitly limited, as physicians interpreting each test came to report findings routinely in a particular way. In both instances standardized forms constrained the possible results that a test could provide. In so doing, systemization aided clinical research by making it easier to follow findings on a single patient over time and by facilitating quantitative comparisons between patients. Standardized reporting also improved communication between diagnostic units and treating physicians.

The widespread use of standardized forms both reflected and encouraged medical specialization.[35] Forms emphasized the increasingly specialized nature of the knowledge produced by machines, and, when signed by the director of a particular unit, reinforced the need for specially trained experts to interpret the results. They also symbolized the scientific nature of early-twentieth-century medicine. The exact meaning of "scientific" is difficult to define precisely, but it is probably reflected in at least two ways by the early use of medical machines

Unit Medical Records in Hospital and Clinic (New York: Columbia University Press, 1943).

35. Stevens, *American Medicine*, and Lester S. King, *American Medicine Comes of Age: 1840–1920* (Chicago: American Medical Association, 1985).

and standardized forms. Graphs, first used widely in the mid-nineteenth century by physiologists, had by the early twentieth century become associated with science by professionals and lay people alike. Graphic forms made particularly explicit the exact, quantitative, "objective" nature of information provided by medical technology such as the X ray and ECG. Also, the standardization of forms (and of anatomical stamps) implicitly served to standardize patients as well, in the same way that the natural sciences attempted to devise reproducible experiments. All patients' thoraxes, despite their obviously different sizes and shapes, were represented by a single stamp. Likewise, recording the daily amount of urine excreted by a patient or his food intake was very different from listening to symptoms or making general assertions about diet. This change in the perception of the patient was consistent with the scientific ideology of controlled, reproducible experiments. Viewing test results in only a few, sharply defined ways deflected attention from differences between individual patients and focused instead on similarities in the particular organs under investigation. Thus, people started to become organs, and symptoms diseases.

TECHNOLOGY AND MEDICINE

The placement of X-ray machines in hospitals has been used to explain, in part, the rapid growth of hospitals in the early twentieth century.[36] This study suggests the importance of other factors. Although Pennsylvania Hospital purchased its first X-ray machine in 1897, it took three decades for such technology to draw patients into the hospital. The mere existence of diagnostic technology did not dictate how or where it would be used; both hospital and machine had to change before the X-ray or any other machine could significantly influence the utilization of hospital care. At least in this instance, health-care technology was not autonomous.

Historical analysis should give us pause as we attempt to predict, using unequivocally rational and logical criteria, just how machines new in 1984, such as position emission tomography scanners and

36. Henry E. Sigerist, "An Outline of the Development of the Hospital," *Bulletin of the History of Medicine* 4 (1936): 573–81.

magnetic resonance imaging devices, will be applied. The X ray was first used in an exploratory, experimental fashion, and pictures were taken of patients with many different conditions. Only after the social system in which it was applied had changed did specific indications for its application become accepted. The lesson of this study for contemporary technology assessment is that changes in both organizational and conceptual systems are critically important in determining how technology is used, albeit difficult to predict.

My conclusions are based on examination of patient records, which reveal which patients underwent an X-ray or other diagnostic procedure, when in their hospital stay a given technology was applied, and how that information was presented. Historical studies of medical technology that fail to examine patient records may fall prey to a methodological trap. By the end of 1896, over 1,044 articles and 49 books had been written about the new X rays,[37] yet it was three decades before the machine become widely used at Pennsylvania Hospital. To assume, explicitly or implicitly, that published papers accurately reflected medical practice is very likely to lead to erroneous conclusions.

However, by using hospital patient records as the primary source of information about the way machines were used, I am restricted to what physicians and nurses chose to record. Presumably, but not necessarily, they noted when X rays were taken before standardized reporting became common around 1917. This study is also limited to a single institution, and any conclusions must be regarded as tentative until records of others have been studied. But my findings correlate well with *vade mecum* knowledge of the period, as well as with the annual reports of similar institutions. Comparative studies are necessary to evaluate the impact of research on X-ray and ECG use, as well as to delineate any regional differences in the introduction of medical technology.

Technology is a ubiquitous feature of twentieth-century American medicine, and its proper role in medical practice is widely and vigorously debated. To understand how new technology can best be used in contemporary medical practice we must understand the process by

37. Otto Glasser, *William Conrad Roentgen and the Early History of the Roentgen Rays* (Springfield, Ill.: Charles C. Thomas, 1934).

which earlier technology came into prominence. This historical case study emphasizes the importance of institutional structure and presentation of information in determining how physicians will apply a new machine. Technology has indeed transformed the American hospital. But before medical technology could be incorporated into hospital medicine, the hospital itself had to be transformed into an institution more hospitable to the role of machines in medicine.

6

A Legitimate Relationship: Nursing, Hospitals, and Science in the Twentieth Century

At an American Hospital Association (AHA) meeting in 1932, president Paul Keller argued against a nursing report that criticized hospitals for exploiting their student nurses. Searching for language that might really explain the hospital-nursing relationship, Keller declared that nursing was "the one and only legitimate daughter of hospitals."[1] While we might debate this view of nursing's lineage (it could be argued that nursing's legitimate daughter is the hospital), legitimacy in this relationship has been a crucial issue. Over much of the twentieth century American nurses have sought, through professional associations and informal work groups, to establish a basis for their authority separate from physician and hospital control. In attempting to legitimate their right to autonomy as individual workers or as a profession, nurses have struggled against both health-care institutions and the cultural meaning of nursing itself.[2]

I am grateful for the interviews granted by Ellen Baer, Florence Downs, Ellen Fuller, and above all, Virginia Henderson. Susan Bell, Joan Lynaugh, and Karen Buhler-Wilkerson were more than helpful in guiding me through the material and answering my endless questions. Russell Maulitz and Joel Howell shared clues to the medical parallels. Allan Brandt, Janet Golden, Diana Long, and Ellen More provided criticism of an earlier draft.

1. Paul Keller, "The Grading Committee and Quality Nursing," *Transactions of the American Hospital Association* (1932): 745.
2. This article is part of my larger work on the evolution of the hospital-nursing rela-

This article examines the efforts of a group of twentieth-century nursing educators to lay claim to a transformed definition of nursing and a new kind of nursing education. I argue that these educators appealed to differing conceptions of science in an attempt to legitimate nursing's struggle for freedom from hospital control. But in the general culture it was assumed that the nurse's enduring authority should come from gender, not science; her place of work the bedside or hospital, not the laboratory.[3] Hospitals, in turn, demanded that nursing provide them with a workforce, not a research team. Physicians primarily wanted assistants, not colleagues. Working nurses often wanted reasonable hours, not more education, and nursing educators believed in science, but could not agree on its meaning.[4] Establishing a relationship to science thus became a complicated, yet necessary task for nursing. It also proved to be a troubling basis for either legitimacy or a change in "daughter" status.

The difficulties began with Florence Nightingale and her model for nursing reform. Nightingale envisioned nursing as an art, rather than a science, which required systematic education and structured practical work. Her ideas for a transformed nursing linked medical and public health notions to her class and religious beliefs. Her mid-nineteenth-century sanitarian's genius served "moral understandings of disease causation," and notions of disease specificity and germ theory did not fit her moral categories.[5] Disease was, for her, a sign of personal disorder; filth and "excrementitious matter," the dangers that kept the

---

tionship; see Susan Reverby, *Ordered to Care: The Dilemma of American Nursing* (New York: Cambridge University Press, 1987). See also Barbara Melosh, *"The Physician's Hand": Work, Culture and Conflict in American Nursing* (Philadelphia: Temple University Press, 1982), and JoAnn Ashley, *Hospitals, Paternalism, and the Role of the Nurse* (New York: Teachers College Press, 1976).

3. See Melosh, *"The Physician's Hand"*; Leo W. Simmons, "Images of the Nurse: Theory and Studies," in *Nursing Research: A Survey and Assessment*, ed. Leo W. Simmons and Virginia Henderson (New York: Appleton-Century-Crofts, 1964), 167–223, and Anne Hudson Jones, ed., *Images of Nursing in History, Art, and Literature* (Philadelphia: University of Pennsylvania Press, 1986).

4. For a discussion of the theoretical question of the relationship between "institutional forms and congitive processes" in the creation of science, see Everett Mendelsohn, "The Social Construction of Scientific Knowledge," in *The Social Production of Scientific Knowledge*, ed. Everett Mendelsohn, Peter Weingart, and Richard Whitley (Dordrecht, Holland, and Boston: D. Reidel, 1977), 3–26.

5. Charles Rosenberg, "Florence Nightingale on Contagion: The Hospital as Moral Universe," in *Healing and History*, ed. Charles E. Rosenberg (New York: Science History Publications, 1979), 124.

patient from recovery. Thus the proper "hospital morale" had to be created in institutions to allow for the natural restorative processes to occur. The creation of such morale—broadly defined as clean drains, sewers, and proper ventilation as well as appropriately fed, cleaned, and disciplined patients—was to be the task of the trained nurse.[6]

Accepting the Victorian idea of separate spheres, she thought women had to be trained to nurse through a disciplined honing of their womanly virtues. She stressed character development, the laws of health, and strict adherence to orders passed through the female hierarchy. Medical therapeutics and "curing" seemed of less importance, and she willingly gave this realm to the physicians. Character and caring, the arenas she did think of great import, were assigned to the trained nurse.[7]

Unwittingly, Nightingale's sanitarian ideas and her beliefs about womanhood provided some of the ideological justification for many of the dilemmas that faced American nursing by 1900. Having fought physician and trustee prejudice against the training of nurses in hospitals in the last quarter of the nineteenth century, American nursing reformers succeeded only too well in the early twentieth. Between 1890 and 1920 the number of nursing schools jumped from 35 to 1,775 and the number of trained nurses from 16 per 100,000 population to 141.[8] Administrators quickly discovered that the opening of a nursing school provided their hospitals, with a young, disciplined, and cheap labor force in exchange for "training." The exigencies of nursing acutely ill or surgical patients continually required, however, the sacrifice of a coherent educational program.

The emphasis on statistical data, comparative mortality rates, and objective testing so central to Nightingale's powerful reformer's outlook are absent from early American nursing education and its textbooks. The "too-muchness," as one nursing educator labeled it, of nursing texts and the "old haphazard way of acquiring instruction by note-taking" thwarted the curious nursing student's critical thinking.[9]

6. Florence Nightingale, *Notes on Nursing* (New York: D. Appleton, 1861), 80, and *Notes on Hospitals*, 3d rev. ed. (London: Longmans, Green, 1863), 17.

7. For further discussion see Reverby, *Ordered to Care*, ch. 3.

8. Committee on the Grading of Nursing Schools, *Nurses, Patients, and Pocketbooks* (New York: The Committee, 1928), 36–37.

9. See Florence Nightingale, *Notes on Hospitals and Introductory Notes on Lying-In Institutions: Together with a Proposal for Organising an Institution for Training Midwives and Midwifery Nurses* (London: Longmans, Green, 1871), and Isabel Stewart, *The Edu-*

Didactic, repetitive, watered-down medical lectures by physicians or older nurses were often provided to the nursing students after they finished ten to twelve hours of ward work.

Ushered onto the wards as timid probationers, students had little time to learn either an objective testing of alternative procedures or the scientific theories underlying nursing care. Training focused on the "one right way" of doing procedures in hopes that following specific rules would cause the least damage to patients from ill-prepared students. Particular adherence to the historically enshrined methods of each nursing school was emphasized. If a student's interest survived her texts and lectures, it was surely rebuked on the wards by student head nurses or the superintendent bent on getting the work done.

Students were not encouraged or even allowed to think objectively about procedures. Few schools gave even a basic science course before the beginning of ward work. Such preliminary or preparatory studies were first introduced at the training school at Waltham in 1895, then at Johns Hopkins in 1901. Ten years later only eighty-six schools had some version of a basic course in their curriculum. Standards varied widely and often did not even reach the level of a high school science course.[10]

The emphasis on discipline, order, and practical skills thus underlay the rationalization and abuse of student labor. Because the workforce was almost entirely women, altruism, sacrifice, and submission were expected, indeed demanded. Exploitation was inevitable in a field where, until the early 1900s, there were no accepted standards for how much work an average student should do, how many patients she could successfully care for, or the mechanisms through which to enforce such standards. In this kind of environment nurses were trained, but they were not educated.

---

cation of Nurses (New York: Macmillan, 1948; reprint, New York: Garland, 1985). On the problem with texts, see Charlotte Aikens, *Primary Studies for Nurses: A Text-book for the First Year Pupil Nurses*, 3d ed. (Philadelphia: W. B. Saunders, 1915).

10. See M. Adelaide Nutting, *A Sound Economic Basis for Schools of Nursing* (New York: G. P. Putnams, 1926; reprint, New York: Garland, 1984), 73–104. Isabel Stewart does not mention the course at Waltham (probably because she disapproved of the physician control of the school), although it was clearly modeled after the same European courses that influenced Nutting's model at Johns Hopkins. See Annette Fiske, *First Fifty Years of the Waltham Training School for Nurses* (New York: Garland, 1985), 68–78, and Stewart, *Education of Nurses*, 160–61.

Believing that educational reform was central to professionalizing efforts and clinical improvements, a small group of elite reformers attempted to broaden nursing's scientific content and social outlook. In arguing for an increase in the scientific knowledge necessary for nursing, such leaders first had to fight against deep-seated cultural assumptions about male and female "natural" characteristics as embodied in the doctor and nurse. Such sentiments were articulated in the routine platitudes about female sympathy, caring, and subjectivity (and male objectivity) that graced what one nursing leader described as the "doctor homilies" at graduation exercises.[11] Not unexpectedly, such beliefs were professed more frequently whenever nursing groups pushed for higher educational standards or hospitals experienced nursing shortages.

Even small attempts to improve the students' education met resistance. By the early 1900s the training school at the Massachusetts General Hospital (MGH) had introduced some laboratory and basic science courses. In 1906, when a training school committee sought comments on the program, Dr. James G. Mumford stated the widely held physician opinion that "the nurse in the MGH is being overtrained, in the sense that she is a product of the laboratory, the lecture room and the clinic; with an exaggerated idea of the importance of *science* as compared with the *art* of nursing."[12] As one nursing educator noted, "the clamor for a cheap worker of the old servant-nurse type" was a recurring theme.[13]

Yet many nurses shared the belief that nursing was the embodiment of womanly virtue and the antithesis of objective science. American nursing educator Annette Fiske, for example, although she authored two science books for nurses and had an M.A. in classics from Radcliffe College before she entered training, spent her professional career

---

11. Lavinia L. Dock, *A History of Nursing*, vol. 3 (New York: G. P. Putnam's Sons, 1912), 136. See, for example, Henry Fairfield Osborn, *Science and Sentiment* (New York: The Presbyterian Hospital, 1907), 5–6.

12. Dr. James Mumford to Mrs. Whiteside, December 10, 1906, Box 5, Folder 1 Ga 1, MGH Nursing Records, Rare Books Room, Countway Medical Library, Harvard Medical School, Boston, Mass. See similar complaints from Dr. Joel Goldthwait, William Conant, and Hugh Cabot in the same folder. See also Sylvia Perkins, *A Centennial Review, The Massachusetts General Hospital School of Nursing, 1873–1973* (Boston: School of Nursing Nurses Alumnae Association, 1975), 37–38.

13. Isabel M. Stewart, "Progress in Nursing Education during 1919," *Modern Hospital* 14 (March 1920): 183.

in the 1920s arguing against increasing the educational standards. Rather, she called for a reinfusion into nursing of spirituality and service. For a nurse like Annette Fiske, science was but a minor sidelight to the art of caring on nursing's center stage.[14] Nursing was for her and many others still a womanly art requiring inherent character in its practitioners and training in practical skills and moral values in its schools.

The professionalizing elite in nursing had to contend with these understandings of nursing, yet still press their claims for increased status and autonomy. Defining a role for science in nursing became an essential part of this endeavor. But in so doing the leadership had to tread lightly around the Fiskes in their own ranks who rankled at the demands of more courses, the physicians who feared that nurses really wanted to be doctors, and the hospital administrators who didn't want to pay for more nursing education.

These constraints shaped the writings and teachings that emerged from the nursing educators and students at Teachers College (TC), Columbia University, in New York. In 1899 the Society of Superintendents for Nurses arranged for a course in Hospital Economics for nurses at TC. Under the initial leadership of M. Adelaide Nutting, a Johns Hopkins graduate and former superintendent of their nursing school, the course grew into a nursing department, then a division that offered courses, then a certificate program, a bachelor's degree program, and later a graduate program. While a baccalaureate degree in nursing was still primarily a dream, and many nursing schools did not even require a high school diploma for either student entry or a faculty position, TC became what one historian labeled "the cornerstone for nursing education."[15]

From its inception the TC program was under enormous pressure to provide nursing with skilled and well-trained educators and administrators. "It is primarily for the benefit of the training schools that

---

14. Annette Fiske, "How Can We Counteract the Prevailing Tendency to Commercialism in Nursing?" *Proceedings of the 17th Annual Meeting of the Massachusetts State Nurses Association*, p. 8, Box 7, Massachusetts Nurses' Association (MNA) Papers, Nursing Archives, Mugar Library, Boston University, Boston, Mass.

15. Theresa E. Christy, *Cornerstone for Nursing Education* (New York: Teachers College Press, 1969).

the department exists,'' Nutting wrote in her annual report in 1910–11.[16] She clearly felt that this program would shape nursing's destiny and provide the basis for its acceptance as a profession. In turn, the program's curriculum, as well as the reports and surveys prepared by individual faculty members, continually reflected the demands placed on it by the national nursing community.[17] At the same time the program could not escape the necessity of making the teaching seem ''practical'' to its students. A Columbia physicist, for example, when brought in to teach, first went to St. Luke's Hospital to ask the nurses to show him what they did that required a knowledge of physics. He used their answers to structure his course around their specific problems in a clinical setting.[18]

Keenly aware of TC's critical position in nursing, Nutting strove to provide the most relevant and informed teachers possible. Distinguished practitioners like Haven Emerson in public health, S. Josephine Baker in municipal health nursing, C.-E. A. Winslow in sanitary science, and Edward Thorndike in psychology, gave TC its reputation for having the most advanced and solid education available for nurses. Away from the relentless pressures of nursing practice that controlled hospital-based training, the TC educators stressed underlying scientific principles in each of their courses. Nutting and the other faculty members thus hoped the teaching would be intellectual as well as practical, linking the art of nursing to a scientific base.

In establishing the TC program these educators espoused a belief in the liberating power of science's seeming objectivity and commitment to truth. In emotional tones, Nutting declared that a ''foundation in

16. TC Department of Nursing and Health, ''1910–11 Report of the Department,'' M. Adelaide Nutting Collection, Box 2, Teachers College (TC) Archives, TC, Columbia University, New York, New York. See also the ''1920–21 Report of the Department of Nursing and Health'' located in the same box and depository; Isabel M. Stewart, ''Twenty-Five Years of Nursing Education in Teachers College, 1899–1925,'' *Teachers College Bulletin*, 17th ser., no. 3 (February 1926): 7–21, Isabel M. Stewart Papers, Box 4, TC Archives; and Christy, *Cornerstone for Nursing Education*.

17. Isabel M. Stewart, ''The Reminiscences of Isabel M. Stewart,'' Transcription of taped interviews from the Oral History Research Office, Columbia University, 1916, 325–27, Box 4, Stewart Papers. For a discussion of the continued pressure on the faculty to work for the collective good of nursing, see R. Louise McManus, ''Nursing Research—Its Evolution,'' *American Journal of Nursing* 61 (April 1961): 78.

18. Christy, *Cornerstone for Nursing Education*, 36, and Stewart, ''Reminiscences,'' 325–29.

science or principles" would make possible a "worthier and freer" system of nursing, almost a nursing reformation.[19] Harkening back to the ideas of the "New Learning" of Frances Bacon and other seventeenth-century Puritan reformers, and reformulated in the language of the Progressive Era, was the belief that science could be harnessed to social and political reform. "Pedagogic idealism" and "antiauthoritarianism," central to the scientific vision of the Baconians, was part of this nursing vision.[20]

This understanding of the role of science was clearest in the writing and teaching of Isabel Maitland Stewart, the Canadian-born nurse who was Nutting's protégé and successor at TC. Stewart had been an elementary school teacher in Winnipeg, then retrained as a nurse and practiced primarily in private duty for four and a half years before coming to TC as a student in 1908. She spent the rest of her life as a nursing educator at TC. Critical of the abuse and rigidity in hospital-based training, Stewart's ideas about transforming nursing were shaped by her close relationship to Nutting and her contact with John Dewey and his beliefs in the democratization that comes with liberal education.[21]

Stewart's concern about a science *for* nursing was both pragmatic and political. Influenced by her friendship with the efficiency engineers Frank and Lillian Gilbreth and the general concern in the hospital community for standardization and efficiency, Stewart wrote enthusiastically about the promise of scientific management. She hoped that efficiency studies of nursing procedures and tasks, not unlike those being attempted in industry, would validate different nursing procedures and provide the facts on exploitation and inefficiency that could be used to break the hospital's hold on nursing education. With such studies, she believed nursing's base in sentiment could move on to one in science.

Aware of the disdain towards "industrial" models in the health-care world, Stewart argued for the appropriate modification of such

19. Quoted by Stewart, "Twenty-Five Years of Nursing Education," 14.

20. Wolfgang van den Daele, "The Social Construction of Science: Institutionalisation and Definition of Positive Science in the Latter Half of the Seventeenth Century," in *The Social Production of Scientific Knowledge*, ed. Mendelsohn et al., 32.

21. See Stewart, *Education of Nurses*; Christy, *Cornerstone for Nursing Education*; and Rosalind Rosenberg, *Beyond Separate Spheres* (New Haven: Yale University Press, 1982) on Dewey's general influence on women in education.

models for measuring both nursing procedures and patient outcome. Her pleas for efficiency and standardization were made judiciously to avoid the charge that she was selling out nursing's soul. American jingoism after World War I also provided Stewart's critics with the argument that she was introducing "German efficiency . . . something heartless and brutal."[22] In a carefully worded 1919 article on standardization, Stewart called for the establishment of "experimental laboratories" to begin the organized study of nursing work.[23] Thus, she hoped to create the infrastructure needed to institutionalize nursing's more scientific stance and ultimately liberate it from hospital control.

As an educator rather than a clinician, Stewart saw science primarily as a methodology for examining a series of problems and an ideology for demanding change. Her emphasis on careful inquiry rather than clinical investigation, and her definition of scientific nursing research was extremely broad. When the call for efficiency studies carried less cultural weight she shifted the ground of her argument, but not its basic outline. In a 1929 article titled "The Science and Art of Nursing," she admitted "that the scientific content of nursing is little more than a thin veneer covering a larger body of traditional material and practice gained largely through experience." Calling for an end to "empiric" nursing, she argued once again for a "scientific inquiry" into nursing procedures. By this she now meant the need for "not only bacteriological and physiological and chemical tests . . . but economic and psychological and sociological measurements also."[24]

In 1930 she tried again to institutionalize these ideas by suggesting a nursing research unit for TC. But the beginning of the depression was hardly an auspicious time to launch a search for funding or to convince the increasingly large numbers of unemployed nurses that such an effort was worthwhile. Even among the TC graduates there

22. Isabel M. Stewart, "Possibilities of Standardization in Nursing Technique," *Modern Hospital* 12 (June 1919): 451–54; Fiske, "How Can We Counteract," 8; Faye G. Abdellah and Virginia Henderson, "Nursing Research," in *Principles and Practice of Nursing*, 6th ed., ed. Virginia Henderson and Gladys Nite (New York: Macmillan, 1978), 1064–66; and Susan Reverby, "Stealing the Golden Eggs: Ernest Amory Codman and the Science and Management of Medicine," *Bulletin of the History of Medicine* 55 (Summer 1981): 156–71.

23. Stewart, "Possibilities of Standardization," 454.

24. Isabel M. Stewart, "The Science and Art of Nursing," *Nursing Education Bulletin* 2, n.s. (Winter 1929): 1–4.

seemed to be little understanding or support for such an undertaking. Once back in the hospital they thought the emphasis on underlying principles, much less a research program, was merely an educator's luxury. An alumnae questionnaire revealed that the graduates wanted more "scientific spirit" (as they labeled it) in nursing, but thought that the TC program should have stressed more practical work.[25] Sally Johnson, a superintendent of nurses at MGH and a TC alumna, criticised the distance of the TC faculty from the realities of the training schools: "Where there are three nurses, two orderlies, and a ward helper on and all but one are en route to the operating room, the front door, the out-patient department, and the electro-cardiogram, there is no time for teaching. These are the features of the ward situation over which the faculty at TC have little conception."[26]

The concern of Sally Johnson and the other TC alumnae was, in part, a response to the growing intensity of nursing in the interwar years. Not only was there more to do, but there were more patients. Gone was the almost leisurely nineteenth-century form of caring for semichronically ill patients who lived in the hospital for months at a time. Expanding hospital usage coupled with earlier ambulation meant that more acutely ill patients occupied each hospital bed in a given year. The increasing number of clinical labs and X-ray departments placed new demands on the nurse's time.[27] By the early 1930s, for example, a nurse caring for a diabetic patient had a complicated set of routines that included preparing trays for blood samples, coordinating food intake with insulin injections, and teaching patients how to give their own hypodermics and regulate their diets. The explosion in new equipment and regulations also forced the nurse to monitor an ever more intricate system of requisitions and forms.[28]

25. Response to questionnaires sent to former students in 1923, Box 1, Nutting Collection. It is also clear from their annual reports that the department felt on the defensive about not providing totally "practical" courses; see "Report of the Department of Nursing Education for 1923–24," Box 1, Nutting Collection.

26. "Gleanings," n.d., circa 1935, Box 2, Folder 1 D 12, MGH Nursing Collection, Rare Books Room, Countway Medical Library, Harvard Medical School, Boston, Mass.

27. See each March issue of the *Journal of the American Medical Association* for hospital statistics, and Harry Marks, "Review of Barbara Melosh's 'The Physician's Hand,' " *Technology and Culture* 26 (April 1985): 326–28.

28. Minnie Goodnow, *The Technic of Nursing*, 2d ed. (Philadelphia: W. B. Saunders, 1931), 354; Marion Elizabeth Derry, "We Can Still Serve, Says Retired Nurse in Uniform

Most of this was still being done by students who were supposed to be in training, although they typically worked twelve-hour days, six and a half days a week, and were expected to float from ward to ward when needed.[29] As the TC alumnae noted, as long as students worked, there was only time for a smattering of "scientific spirit" in the typical nursing school. Few in the hospital world were ready to acknowledge that a separation of the nursing service from nursing education would be needed to prepare a nurse who evinced more than a mere spirit of science.

Stewart worked to raise nursing's educational standards and to push for the creation of collegiate programs to solve the dilemma of the hospital's use of student labor. She devoted almost all her energy during the 1930s to an extensive revision of the recommended nursing school curriculum for the National League for Nursing Education, as well as on internal reorganization at TC. Graduate students with an interest in or talent for research were often drafted to work on curriculum projects rather than directed toward advanced clinical work or the laboratory. By 1941, while Stewart continued to call for more nursing research, she clearly meant social science curricular studies.[30] For her, science was increasingly a question of research methods and a political language with which to demand a new form of education. As a faculty member of an education school and one concerned about nursing's continuing problems with its hospital-based training system, she could hardly have been expected to see things in any other way.

Not everyone at TC thought nursing's research focus should take such an educational direction or had this kind of politicized hope for science. By the late 1920s others began to see that science for nursing would have to be based in clinical studies of nursing practice. In 1929, Martha Ruth Smith, a nurse trained at the Peter Bent Brigham Hospital in Boston and at TC, became supervisor of instruction at TC. Facing

Again," *Hospitals* 18 (February 1944): 32; and Shirley Titus, "The Present Position of Nursing in Hospitals in the United States," *Nosokomeion* 2 (April 1931): 288–97.

29. President of the Alumnae Association of the Capital City School of Nursing, Letter to the Editor, *Washington Post*, February 17, 1933, quoted in Harry Dowling, *City Hospitals: The Undercare of the Underprivileged* (Cambridge: Harvard University Press, 1982), 142.

30. Isabel M. Stewart, "The Responsibility of Nursing Educators for Investigating Their Own Problems," *Nursing Education Bulletin*, n.s. 11 (September 1941): 1–7.

classes of graduate nurses, Smith and her colleagues discovered that their students almost came to blows over their "fierce and unquestioning loyalties" to the particular methods and nursing practices of their training schools.[31] In hopes that such allegiances would be based on a therapeutic rather than a loyalty standard, Smith and her colleagues began to teach a course in 1930 for graduate students titled "Comparative Nursing Practice." As Smith wrote, the course was intended to "make science serve the art of nursing."[32]

Building on Stewart's earlier dictums about efficiency and standardization, the course taught students to investigate specific nursing problems in the clinical setting. Control groups were set up to investigate differing procedures and their effectiveness. "Scientific facts" underlying the procedures were enumerated and discussed.[33] As a result, some students and faculty were encouraged to evaluate different nursing procedures through the use of standard laboratory methods. TC's *Nursing Education Bulletin* published the results of their work on such topics as "medical and surgical asepsis," "thermometer techniques," and control of bacteriological contamination.[34]

After Smith left TC in 1931 for a faculty position at Simmons College in Boston and later the first deanship in nursing at Boston University, her course was taught by Virginia Henderson. As both a TC student and faculty member from 1931 to 1948, Henderson became increasingly concerned with the failure of nursing to establish a research program in a clinical setting. It was Henderson who, over the years, trained hundreds of nurses in comparative scientific procedures and became the champion of science in nursing practice.

Henderson was a southerner from a respectable and established Vir-

31. Virginia Henderson, "We've 'Come a Long Way,' but What of the Direction?" *Nursing Research* 26 (May-June 1977): 163. See also Martha Ruth Smith, "The Variability in Existing Nursing Practice and Methods of Determining Validity," *Nursing Education Bulletin* 1, n.s. (1930): 10.

32. Martha Ruth Smith, "The Improvement of Nursing Methods," *38th Annual Report of the National League of Nursing Education* (New York: National League of Nursing Education, 1932), 182.

33. Abdellah and Henderson, "Nursing Research," 1064, and Interview by Susan Reverby with Virginia Henderson, New Haven, Conn., March 24, 1984.

34. Smith, "The Variability in Existing Nursing Practice," 10–17; Martha Erdmann and Margaret Welsh, "Studies in Thermometer Technique," *Nursing Education Bulletin* 2, n.s. (Winter 1929): 8–33; and Virginia Henderson, "Medical and Surgical Asepsis," *Nursing Education Bulletin* 3, n.s. (June 1935).

ginia family. She trained under the progressive nursing educator Annie Goodrich at the Army School of Nursing in Washington, D.C. in the early 1920s. From a close personal as well as academic bond with Goodrich, Henderson gained an idealistic and social perspective on nursing that, she recalled, "bore little relevance to the day to day nursing of doing a series of unrelated tasks."[35] After ten years as a public health nurse, a hospital training-school educational director, and a clinical instructor in a hospital outpatient department, she came to TC to obtain her bachelor's degree. Increasingly censorious of hospital-centered care and nursing that focused on tasks rather than the patient's particular problems and needs, she brought to TC a critical view of nursing as it was then taught and practiced.[36]

Isabel Stewart, recognizing Henderson's research interests and intellectual talents early in her TC career, put her to work on the national curriculum study. Fascinated more by the sciences than by educational theory, however, Henderson enrolled in the bacteriology and physiology courses offered in the nursing division. Her scientific bent was further nurtured by Stewart, who encouraged her to take anatomy, physiology, neuroanatomy, and other such courses at Columbia University's medical school.

Henderson's understanding of a science-nursing relationship soon went beyond Stewart's concern with method and Smith's hopes that science might contribute to the nursing arts. With her training, Henderson began to see the possibility of, in her metaphor, a "complete marriage between nursing and science." She has spent the rest of her career trying to implement the terms of this nuptial contract. In her course "Comparative Nursing Practice," Henderson built upon Smith's model. Her students went to the library to investigate the underlying theories of particular nursing problems. When no scientific theory appeared to help explain a situation, Henderson had her students "list the unanswered questions needing further research." This was an unusually innovative approach to nursing education, where the focus

35. Henderson interview; see also Virginia Henderson, "Commencement Address—Grace New Haven Hospital School of Nursing," June 6, 1961, p. 5, Virginia Henderson Papers, Box 1, Folder 6, Nursing Archives, Boston University.

36. Virginia Henderson, *The Nature of Nursing* (New York: Macmillan, 1966), 6–23. The following information and quotations are from the Henderson interview cited in n.33 above, unless otherwise noted.

was still on the functional division of tasks and the rote learning of procedures. Henderson thus hoped to teach her students to begin to think like questioning researchers.

Henderson saw herself as an outsider at TC, continually arguing for "more advanced clinical teaching than they were doing." Except in the obstetrical nursing-midwifery section, Henderson believed there was very little understanding of the special way nursing could use the underlying basic sciences to change clinical practice. "They really couldn't envision the content," she claimed. "Because the way advanced clinical courses had been taught, with the exception of midwifery, was just a watered-down course or two in a hospital, really an imitation of what physicians do."[37]

Stewart had argued continually that nursing was not medicine and had something very different to offer. As she noted, nurses were not interested "in duplicating, but in complementing and rounding out the efforts of [physicians] and in filling in some of the gaps in the care of patients."[38] But she failed to grasp that to do so would require the development of a clinical science research and educational program, not merely university-based research institutes committed to studying the nursing role and curriculum.

It was Henderson who had a differing vision of what science could mean, and do, for nursing. The physiological approach of her TC professor, Caroline Stackpole, influenced Henderson's evolving ideas on nursing. Focused upon Claude Bernard's notions that health depended upon "the constancy of intercellular fluids" and physiological balance, Henderson sought to apply these concepts to the link between a patient's behavior and physical state. In some ways Henderson's evolving ideas restated nineteenth-century notions of the body as a closed energy system and combined them with the contemporary understanding of physiology's lessons for patient treatment. At a time when many doctors remained skeptical of experimental physiology's ability to solve any clinical problem, Henderson sought a way to use

37. For corroboration of Henderson's contentions see outlines and course descriptions in Box 2, Stewart Papers. For a view of Stewart's interests that stress her clinical concerns, see Christy, *Cornerstone for Nursing Education*, 75–112. Christy's history of the TC division is quite hagiographic and reflects an attempt to show how much the division supported what became important nursing concerns in the 1960s.

38. "Report of Isabel M. Stewart's Trip," draft copy, p. 4, Nutting Collection, Box 9.

physiological theory to define a scientific base for nursing.[39] In language that sounded much like that of Harvard physiologist Walter Cannon, Henderson wrote "that emotional balance is inseparable from physiological balance" and "an emotion is actually our interpretation of cellular response to fluctuations in the chemical composition of the intercellular fluids."[40] Henderson was attempting to resolve in nursing's clinical practice what one historian has labeled a "common" problem of twentieth-century medicine, "the tension between the cognitive nature of laboratory science and the practical imperatives of clinical practice."[41]

Henderson was not merely concerned with individual body reactions. Influenced by Edward Thorndike's teaching on psychology, she focused on social and cultural environments as much as on individuals. Experiences with the patient focus of rehabilitation medicine further refined her thinking. She was thus beginning to search for a way to use this approach to restoring health as the basis for a nursing education and research program.

By the mid-1940s Henderson began to formulate a perspective for advanced clinical nursing that had "content that was different from medicine's." In a course for advanced students in medical-surgical nursing, Henderson and a small number of like-minded instructors developed an approach that was "unique because it was patient-centered and organized around major nursing problems rather than medical diagnoses and diseases of the body systems."[42] It was the

39. See John Harley Warner, "Physiology," in *The Education of American Physicians: Historical Essays*, ed. Ronald L. Numbers (Berkeley: University of California Press, 1980), 48–71; Gerald L. Geison, "Divided We Stand: Physiologists and Clinicians in the American Context," in *The Therapeutic Revolution: Essays in the Social History of American Medicine*, ed. Morris Vogel and Charles Rosenberg (Philadelphia: University of Pennsylvania Press, 1979), 67–90; Gerald L. Geison, ed., *Physiology in the American Context, 1850–1940* (Bethesda, Md.: American Physiological Society, 1987); and Saul Benison, A. Clifford Barger, and Elin L. Wolfe, *Walter B. Cannon: The Life and Times of a Young Scientist* (Cambridge: Harvard University Press, 1987).

40. Henderson, *The Nature of Nursing*, 11. Henderson also contends that some of her thinking was shaped by the physiology courses she took at the Columbia Medical School and the microbiology courses taught at TC by Jean Broadhurst.

41. Joel D. Howell, "Cardiac Physiology and Clinical Medicine? Two Case Studies," in *Physiology in the American Context*, ed. Geison, 290.

42. Henderson, *The Nature of Nursing*, 14; Abdellah and Henderson, "Nursing Research," 1065. Around the same time the Yale University School of Nursing was also beginning to use the case method of teaching, rather than the functional method.

beginning of teaching nurses to care for a whole patient, not just to perform a series of tasks.

However, much of this work remained undeveloped. Henderson, like the other nursing division faculty, was overburdened by work and was expected to teach a variety of subjects. Another nursing educator, recalling her grueling years on the TC faculty, commented: "We taught everything. We were said not to occupy chairs but benches."[43] Furthermore, few of the TC faculty, as in nursing in general, had doctorates, and even fewer had doctorates in fields other than education. They therefore had neither the time nor the training to do systematic clinical research.

In the hospital-based nursing schools the situation was even worse. Although the hours devoted to basic science teaching increased in the early twentieth century, much of it consisted of lectures on countless facts, leading to what one critic called "mental indigestion." In 1932 less than a third of the schools had instructors with a college degree, and the typical school gave over 10 percent of its teaching time to theory and 90 percent to practice (See tables 6.1 and 6.2). Over a fifth of the schools had no full-time instructors.[44]

Nor was it clear where advanced, clinically trained nurses would have practiced, or done research, once they completed their education. With the battle to gain acceptance for a baccalaureate education for nurses still to be won, the idea that a nurse might be either a specially skilled clinician or a researcher garnered little support. Advancement in nursing meant administrative or teaching positions, not a career in clinical or laboratory research. Neither the hospitals nor the universities would create a place for such a nurse. Even when the Rockefeller Foundation supported the showcase collegiate nursing program at Yale, their contribution was penurious compared to the funds lavished on the medical school.[45] Clinical science research and advanced training were reserved for physicians or basic scientists.

43. Oral History interview with Ruth Sleeper by Mary Ann Garrigan and Lois Monteiro, January 1965, transcript in Box 2, Folder 5, Martha Ruth Smith Papers, Nursing Archives, Boston University.

44. Margaret Bridgman, *Collegiate Education for Nursing* (New York: Russell Sage Foundation, 1953), 55; Committee on the Grading of Nursing Schools, *The Second Grading* (New York: The Committee, 1932), 55, 155.

45. Sister Dorothy Sheahan, "The Social Origins of American Nursing and Its Move-

Table 6.1.
Medical and nursing school curricula, 1928–29

	Hours for selected subjects[a]		
Subjects	Nursing[b] highest	Medicine[c] highest	Medicine lowest
Anatomy	90	1267	480
Biochemistry	30	363	99
Physiology	—	612	224
Pathology	15	473	220
Bacteriology	28	432	124
Pharmacology/Materia Medica	50	279	104
Obstetrics/gynecology	37	368	168

Sources: Committee on the Grading of Nursing Schools, *The Second Grading* (New York: The Committee, 1932), 157, and *Final Report of the Commission on Medical Education* (New York: Association of American Medical Colleges, 1932), Appendix tables 111–12.
[a]Total required median hours: 631 for nursing, 3,914 for medicine.
[b]Figures for 1,397 nursing schools responding to survey.
[c]Figures from 13 medical schools selected by random.

The nursing and medical cultures had by the 1940s made very different places for research in clinical science. In the early 1920s numerous clinicians and medical school faculty still refused to bow before what one physician labeled "the false gods of the German physiological school" that assume "a man [sic] gropes darkly at the bedside but sees clearly in the laboratory."[46] But by the late 1920s medicine had differentiated the clinical teacher and researcher from the practitioner as foundation largesse and university support paid most of the costs, and the creation of the teaching hospital provided the site and necessary patients. Clinical scientist-physicians with an interest in "disease and therapeutics" found a place on the medical school faculties.[47] Ironi-

ment into the University" (Ph.D. diss., New York University, 1980), ch. 3. I am grateful to the author for lending me a copy of her thesis.

46. Dr. Charles Emerson, "Comments—Annual Congress on Medical Education and Licensure," *Journal of the American Medical Association* 74 (March 13, 1920): 757. See also Saul Jarcho, "Medical Education in the United States, 1910–1956," *Journal of the Mt. Sinai Hospital* 26 (July–August 1959): 339–85.

47. Kenneth M. Ludmerer, *Learning to Heal: The Development of American Medical Education* (New York: Basic Books, 1985), 52, 212, 219–33. See also A. McGehee Harvey, *Science at the Bedside: Clinical Research in American Medicine, 1905–1945* (Baltimore: Johns Hopkins University Press, 1981).

Table 6.2.
Percentage of nursing schools planning to give at least as many hours as recommended by the National League of Nursing Education in selected subjects

Subject	1929	1932
Anatomy	51	68
Bacteriology	22	38
Chemistry	29	46
Materia Medica	51	69
Principles and Practice of Nursing	49	59
Pathology	52	58
Gynecology	92	91
Obstetrics	49	65

Source: Committee on the Grading of Nursing Schools, *The Second Grading* (New York: The Committee, 1932), 158.

cally, nursing always had the link to hospitals that medicine had to create, but it lacked the political power and societal approval to transform it into a clinical research base.

In this context, Henderson found it increasingly difficult to gain support for the kind of teaching and research she was attempting to create. Emphasis on correct methods or curriculum vastly overshadowed any clinical research. In 1944 Annie Goodrich wrote to her disciple, encouraging her to keep her clinical focus and applauding her work. When it appeared that Henderson had been passed over for a promotion at TC, Goodrich reminded her that "Stewart . . . I fear with many others do[es] not interpret the art and science of nursing as the *Practice* of nursing."[48] In a more recent interview Henderson noted: "I was always more interested in the substance than the method— while so many others were so afraid to be criticized for not doing it correctly that they focused on the method, not the substance."[49]

Goodrich could sustain Henderson as an individual and friend, but she could not change the educational climate at TC or the attitude toward nursing research in the hospital. When another nursing educator, R. Louise McManus, replaced Stewart as head of the TC division

48. Annie Goodrich to Virginia Henderson, March 3, 1944, Box 3, Henderson Papers. The underlining and capitalization are by Goodrich.
49. Virginia Henderson to Ellen Baer, telephone conversation, October 10, 1985, and quoted in Baer, " 'A Cooperative Venture' in Pursuit of Professional Status: A Research Journal for Nursing," *Nursing Research* 35 (January–February 1987): 21.

in 1947, it became clear that Henderson's approach was not being supported. When McManus asked Henderson to stop teaching both the classroom and in-hospital clinical aspects of her course and to concentrate only on the classroom, Henderson resigned.[50]

During her TC years, Henderson began to formulate a theory of nursing that would become more fully stated in her 1966 publication, *The Nature of Nursing*. Building upon her personal experience in nursing and her understanding of physiology, she tried to place nursing in a continuum with medicine, while providing it with its own explanatory model for practice. With her clinician's understanding, Henderson argued that the nurse had to place herself figuratively "inside" patients in order to become their "counterpart, alter ego, or helper."[51]

Henderson's vision linked research in the basic sciences and the testing of procedures for effectiveness with the patient's needs in order to strengthen the nurse's clinical stance. Even in 1966 her reviewers and admirers noted how necessary and farseeing her concept of nursing was.[52] Bedside nursing and clinical practice remained at the center of her research concerns, but Henderson also remained a maverick and outsider, focusing upon historical-bibliographic work and continually arguing for research on nursing practice.

Science, with its multiple meanings, thus proved a difficult vehicle to harness for nursing's escape from hospital control. When economic and political factors finally made possible the shift from student to staff nursing by World War II, the difficulties of hospital power over nursing and the working lives of nurses remained.[53] In the face of rising nursing shortages and mass discontent over the staff nursing position in the 1950s, nursing research, when it did occur, focused more on the nursing role and the nurse herself than on nursing practice. The lack of support or understanding of the

50. Susan Reverby interview with Henderson, March 24, 1984. For a different interpretation of TC's emphasis on clinical content, see Theresa Christy's interview with R. Louise McManus, *Cornerstone for Nursing Education*, 105–6. Not surprisingly, McManus wrote an article titled, "Isabel M. Stewart—Foremost Researcher," *Nursing Research* 11 (January 1962): 4–6; see discussion in Baer, " 'A Cooperative Venture,' " 18–25.

51. See both her "Commencement Address," 14, and *The Nature of Nursing*.

52. See numerous reviews and letters in Box 1, Folder 1, Henderson Papers.

53. See Reverby, *Ordered to Care*, 180–198, and Melosh, *"The Physician's Hand,"* 159–206, for further discussion.

need for any other kind of research, the growing concern with high
turnover rates in the hospitals and nurses' dissatisfaction with their
work, the cold hand of the education schools, and the assumptions
that science in nursing meant methodology or the addition of more
courses in the underlying biological sciences, continued to guide
nursing higher education. Growing awareness that nursing needed
more of a theoretical orientation to justify its demands for more authority led to philosophical studies of nursing as a process and to
the development of "grand theory," but not to either more clinical
or laboratory research.[54]

The institutional basis for change was created very slowly. In the
post–World War II years the number of nurses with both baccalaureate
and graduate degrees began to grow. Federal funding for advanced
nursing education, coupled with changes in medical therapeutics and
technology, helped to generate both the supply and demand for nurses
with different kinds of training and orientations to their field.[55] Drawn
into the university and away from the hospital's control, nursing education had to meet higher standards for acceptance and to gain support
for various types of research.

At TC, Stewart's dream of a nursing research institute was finally
realized when the Kellogg and Rockefeller Foundations funded the
Institute of Research and Service in Nursing Education in 1953. Seen
primarily as an educational research/field service program, however,
it focused more on nursing roles and administration than clinical practice.[56] In 1952 a journal titled *Nursing Research* began publication to
encourage and report research by nurses. Until quite recently, however,
it too was shaped by nursing's commitment to "structure not content,"

54. The most influential postwar figure was Martha Rogers at New York University;
see her *An Introduction to the Theoretical Basis of Nursing* (Philadelphia: J. P. Lippincott,
1970). For a discussion of the impact of Rogers and her followers on nursing education
and theory in the 1950s and 1960s, see Oral History interview with Dean Claire Fagin by
Susan Reverby, June and August 1982, School of Nursing, University of Pennsylvania,
and Rozella M. Schlotfeldt, "Defining Nursing: A Historic Controversy," *Nursing Research* 35 (January–February 1987): 64–67.

55. For an overview of the effect of these changes on nursing research and theory
development see Susan R. Gortner and Helen Nahm, "An Overview of Nursing Research
in the United States," *Nursing Research* 26 (January–February 1977): 10–33.

56. Helen L. Bunge, "A Review of the First Six Years, 1953–59, with Suggestions
for the Future," Institute of Research and Service in Nursing Education Papers, Box 1,
TC Archives; see also Louice C. Smith, *Helen L. Bunge: Nurse, Teacher, Scholar* (Madison:
University of Wisconsin Nursing School, 1979).

as Henderson labeled it. In a widely read editorial in 1956, Henderson still had to inquire: "Research in nursing practice—When?"[57]

As increasing clinical specialization and the nurse-practitioner movements of the 1960s developed with the help of federal funds, expanding feminist consciousness, and a nursing revolt against the limitations of the administrative track, the importance of Henderson's views were acknowledged and she was resurrected as the grand lady of nursing research. Twenty-one years later, in yet another guest editorial, she could admit that "the emphasis *is* changing." But, she sagely argued: "Nurses are still loathe to take responsibility for designing the methods they use; for undertaking studies that, if the findings were applied, might revolutionize practice. They are, perhaps, less comfortable in collaborating with physiologists and physicians than with social scientists, less likely to expect or ask for a colleague relationship if they work with physicians on questions of health care."[58]

Nursing today is increasingly preoccupied with encouraging more research, but is still divided over what this means. Nurses no longer debate *if* there should be a nursing-science relationship, but rather what that relationship should be. Is nursing a science with a coherent theoretical base and methodology, or an applied science that draws upon the biological and social sciences?[59] However, both sides of this intellectual debate cling to the belief that science—as objective method and/or knowable laws—can save nursing from a professional abyss.

Nursing's creation as gender-appropriate work for women and controlled by the hospitals shaped its founding ideologies, educational structures, professionalizing effort, and place in the health-care hierarchy. In turn, these factors determined the terms the science debate would use. To a Florence Nightingale or an Annette Fiske, science in nursing could not be separated from the conception of woman's role, service, and morality. For an early twentieth-century *science-interested* educator like Isabel Stewart, science was a neutral and objective methodology to harness to nursing's need for a more liberal curriculum, to

57. See Baer, " 'A Cooperative Venture,' " 21, and Virginia Henderson, *Nursing Research* 4 (February 1956): 99.
58. Virginia Henderson, "We've 'Come a Long Way,' " 163–64.
59. Susan R. Gortner, "The History and Philosophy of Nursing Science and Research," *Advances in Nursing Science* 5 (January 1983): 1–8, and Jacqueline Fawcett, *Analysis and Evaluation of Conceptual Models of Nursing* (Philadelphia: 1984).

rationalize its work load, and to improve its professional standing. For a *science-oriented* clinician like Virginia Henderson, however, science drew upon various disciplines that could be used to create an effective clinical nursing practice and theory.[60] Stewart's views were perhaps a more accurate reading of the contemporary possibilities for nursing, but Henderson's were more prescient. Each vision of the science-nursing relationship has continued to contend for the right to define, in Henderson's words, "the nature of nursing."

The hospital's continued pressure on nursing to focus upon patient needs kept a nurse like Virginia Henderson interested in patient-centered clinical study rather than more obscure research. It forced nurses to consider if they have created, or will create, different and effective ways to understand the human reaction to illness. But as our contemporary media headlines about the prevailing nursing shortage suggest, working nurses now have other options and can abandon the hospital when its demands become outrageous or its pay scales too demeaning. Whether science in Stewart's broad vision, or in Henderson's clinical stance, can help to solve this current crisis in the health-care system remains to be seen. But it is clear that the "legitimate daughter" is seeking new terms for her relationships.

60. These categories are used by Kathryn Pyne Addelson, "The Man of Professional Wisdom," in *Discovering Reality: Feminist Perspectives on Epistemology, Metaphysics, and Philosophy of Science*, ed. Sandra Harding and Merrill B. Hintikka (Dordrecht, Holland and Boston: Reidel, 1983), 165.

7

Doing Well or Doing Good: The Ambivalent Focus of Hospital Administration

DAVID ROSNER

The field of hospital administration has developed with three inter-twined and sometimes contradictory goals in view. First, health ad-ministrators have been responsible for the business and financial aspects of hospitals and clinics. Problems of personnel administration, financial management, cost accounting, data analysis, reimbursement metho-dologies, laundry, food, and other housekeeping functions all fall into the normal realm of the institutional administrator. Hospital admin-istrators, therefore, are identified with a set of generic management skills that are aimed at increasing the efficiency and financial security of their institutions. Second, hospital administrators have had the re-sponsibility for providing the most basic social service—the care of dependent people at the most vulnerable points of their lives—at birth, illness, or death. The administrator has had the responsibility of plan-ning for and organizing patient discharges, home care, and other health-related services. Third, administrators have been responsible for main-taining the internal moral and social order of the institution. They have acted as guardians for patients, arbitrators, and intermediaries between the various professional groups. These three sets of objectives have been achieved historically through informal and formal training in the institutions and graduate programs in hospital and public health administration.

Recently, these goals of service, social guidance, and efficient management have appeared to be in conflict. Before the 1940s administrators often saw their role first, as a provider of moral and medical service, and second, as financial agents. But an ideology of the centrality of businesslike efficiency has emerged as a dominant theme in the administrative literature. In the past two decades the field of health administration has sought to align itself more closely with the generic fields of business management, apparently undermining the social and medical service aspects of their historical mission. This essay explores the origins of the apparent conflict in the United States during the first three decades of this century. I posit that today's seemingly intractable differences between a social and medical service orientation and a business enterprise have historical roots. But, contrary to some, I posit that the history of this conflict indicates that the apparent dominance of business ideology is a transient phenomena. The traditional social service ideology that informed the administrators' education and reasons for entering the field, along with public expectations of their role has tended to undermine business-based rationales in popular and professional discourse. Even in today's market-oriented world, dominated by hospital chains and for-profit systems, it is shortsighted to assume that the traditional social service rationales for hospital care are being supplanted.

The history of training in hospital administration is closely related to the history of charity hospital growth in the United States. Between 1875 and 1925 the enormous growth in the number and complexity of hospitals created a demand for administrators. In that time period the number of hospitals grew from just over 170 to about 7,000 and the number of hospital beds increased from 35,000 to 860,000. In addition, the newer institutions were substantially more complex than those from earlier in the nineteenth century, which were either very large, long-term care institutions or smaller charity facilities. The overwhelming preponderance of new institutions were 100–300-bed facilities where the average length of stay was significantly shorter.[1]

1. See David Rosner, *A Once Charitable Enterprise: Hospitals and Health Care in Brooklyn and New York, 1885–1915* (Princeton: Princeton University Press, 1986). See also Michael M. Davis, *Hospital Administration, A Career: The Need of Trained Executives*

The unique social conditions of the nineteenth century created a special environment for the developing field of hospital administration. For many decades throughout the late nineteenth and early twentieth centuries, when most hospitals were considered part of the extensive network of charity institutions, a majority of hospital administrators were women. Especially in the numerous smaller charity institutions scattered throughout the nation, many nurses, nuns, and laywomen who functioned as caretakers within the facilities rose through the ranks to assume major roles as ward or institutional managers. The significant role of women as administrators continued even as recently as 1929, when they made up nearly 40 percent of all head administrators in the country. In a 1929 survey of superintendents in the 7,610 institutions in the United States and Canada, Michael M. Davis reported that 20 percent were nurses, 8 percent were sisters, and 11 percent were laywomen. Of the 61 percent remaining, 37 percent were male physicians, 10 percent were laymen, and the remaining 14 percent were unspecified.[2]

The role that women have played in shaping modern health administration has hardly been recognized. In the years when the health system grew dramatically, hospital and clinic administration was seen as the natural perserve of largely single, middle-class women whose social role was to maintain the harmony, the stability, and the cohesiveness of their communities. Just as the married woman ran the household, single women, often sisters in Catholic institutions or nurses and laywomen in smaller ethnic facilities, were appropriate candidates to run the community's voluntary institutions. In these generally smaller institutions they were responsible both for the caring and business functions of the facility. As late as 1928, one woman administrator noted that "a hospital superintendent should have a working knowledge of business methods. I am confident that many hospitals need and want as superintendent women who have health, business ability and some

---

for a Billion Dollar Business, and How They May Be Trained (New York, 1929), for a brief description of the importance of this rapid growth on the functions of the administrator.

2. Davis, *Hospital Administration*, 8–9; this data was collected by the American Medical Association. It is significant to note that prior to the 1930s hospital administration texts often assumed that women would play a leading role in the institution. See, for example, John Hornsby and Richard Schmidt, *The Modern Hospital, Its Inspiration, Its Architecture, Its Equipment, Its Operation* (Philadelphia: W. B. Saunders, 1913), 253.

understanding of medical and nursing problems."[3] For most of the
first third of the century caring and financial abilities were considered
to be equally necessary for the hospital administrator. Women, therefore, with their claim on the household and emotional lives of the
community, made excellent candidates for administrative positions.

The importance of women in the administration of many early
twentieth-century institutions grew out of the unique blend of moral,
religious, medical, and social services that hospitals were expected to
provide. A brief look at the names of nineteenth-century institutions
shows the close affiliation of these facilities with particular ethnic or
religious communities—Lutheran, Jewish, Cabrini, St. Vincent's, Montefiore. Much of the impetus for organizing these facilities emanated
from the social condition of the immigrant communities that began
to send patients there. Dependence on the larger community was often
a by-product of the extraordinary disjuncture between basic human
needs for shelter and clothing and their availability in communities
where housing was generally inadequate at best. Abandoned children
might live for long periods of time in a foundling hospital rather than
an orphanage; out-of-wedlock births indicated dependence on social
institutions such as maternity or women's hospitals; general charity
facilities often saw demands for their services rise and fall with changes
in local economic conditions among the unskilled and semiskilled
workforce. While sickness was one form of dependence that increased
the demand for hospitals, the social surroundings of a community made
the institution the appropriate center for care for the poor or the immigrant. In this setting women's traditional role as caretaker could
merge with career aspirations, creating career paths unavailable in the
male-dominated outside world that locked women out of many professions, government service, and business.

Women's role as protectors of the moral life of the nation added a
degree of legitimacy to their positions as hospital administrators. In
late-nineteenth- and early-twentieth-century urban society, where dependence, poverty, and illness were often interpreted as interlocking
indications of the general morality—or immorality—of patients, medical cure was seen as intimately linked to the success of moral reform
within the institution. Hence, the administrator, as the person respon-

3. May Ayres Burgess, quoted in Davis, *Hospital Administration*, 29.

sible for the institution, largely controlled the program that would teach patients acceptable standards of moral behavior. Internally, facilities reflected the underlying moral goals of the originators and the head administrator. The superintendent was responsible for the daily management of the institution and functioned as the patriarch or matriarch of the extended family that the hospital was supposed to resemble. The facility's administration was modeled on the ideals of the middle-class family of late-nineteenth- and early-twentieth-century America: the Superintendent and/or matron served as mother or father; nurses, sisters, long-term patients, and young housestaff physicians played the role of older children with varying degrees of responsibility for the housekeeping chores required in the institution; and newly admitted patients, not yet socialized into the life of the institution, were effectively the "infants" in need of constant guidance and supervision by parents and siblings alike.[4] Only the trustees, the institution's spiritual leaders, escaped the confining environment of the "house," as it was called.[5] Since opportunities for males in other areas of American political, economic, and social life left the hospital relatively open, there was room for women to assert their leadership qualities without direct challenges.

In light of the unique administrative structure of the hospital, there was an indistinct separation of traditional nursing and administrative functions in many smaller charity facilities for much of the first decades of the century. In the Brooklyn Nursery and Infants' Hospital, for example, the head administrator was responsible for the "entire supervision of the House, and control of the servants and nurses," as stated in the facility's constitution. But, in addition to these traditional administrative roles, she was required to make certain that the children's "deportment is proper at the table" and that "on Sunday the inmates of the house [were] called together, and [were] present at

4. See Charles E. Rosenberg, *The Care of Strangers: The Rise of America's Hospital System* (New York: Basic Books, 1987).
5. See Charles E. Rosenberg, "Inward Vision and Outward Glance: The Shaping of the American Hospital," *Bulletin of the History of Medicine* 53 (1979): 346–91; Charles Rosenberg, "And Heal the Sick: The Hospital and the Patient in Nineteenth-Century America," *Journal of Social History* 10 (1977): 428–47; Morris Vogel, *The Invention of the Modern Hospital* (Chicago: University of Chicago Press, 1980); and Rosner, *A Once Charitable Enterprise*, for extended discussions of the structure of the nineteenth- and early-twentieth-century facilities.

[Sabbath] services."[6] Separating out the qualities necessary for clinical and administrative duties in many smaller hospitals was difficult or impossible until the 1940s. "The former superintendent was also a director of nurses," complained one female superintendent, "I am not, and the task of separating the two positions in the public (and private) mind is requiring great persistence as well as care."[7] Generally, this early generation of female administrators was drawn from the ranks of hospital nurses or sometimes former patients who had proven their mettle. Their salaries were low. In 1929 over 50 percent received less than $2,000 a year plus room and board.[8]

The last tumultuous decade of the nineteenth century and the first decades of this century inflicted tremendous damage on the older maternalist relationships within the charity hospitals, undermining the traditional role of the female head administrator. As financial problems increasingly plagued hospitals and as medical staffs began to play a more central role in these charity facilities, trustees sought new types of personnel to administer their institutions. Increasingly, they turned to men with a background in both medicine and business. While the goals of the institution still revolved around providing human services, the new stated mission of the institution tended to de-emphasize older charity ideals in favor of the new rising credibility of medicine and business. With the de-emphasis of social service and the growing emphasis on science and business, women, generally perceived as lacking business sense and scientific training, were eased out of their prominent positions in the hospital hierarchy, making way for men with medical or management backgrounds.

The traditional association of the hospital with charity care gave the institution a clear class identification that trustees were eager to abandon, and the movement of men into administration signaled an important change in the social structure and mission of the institution. This shift helped trustees in their efforts to shed their institutions of the image of a charity facility. Furthermore, as medicine became a more accepted justification of a hospital's function and physicians became more integral to the financial and service structure of these

6. Brooklyn Nursery and Infants' Hospital, "Constitution and By-Laws," Annual Report, 1892–1893, 11.

7. Quoted in Davis, *Hospital Administration*, 29.

8. Davis, *Hospital Administration*, 16.

institutions, trustees sought administrators who were more intimately associated with medicine rather than charity, who could identify potential problems associated with the medicalization of the institution and its business interests. Hence, when possible, trustees turned to physicians to administer their institutions. By 1929 fully 37 percent of all administrators were male physicians. In teaching hospitals, the percentage was even higher, hovering around 53 percent.[9] "Standards of hospital administration have been practically revolutionized within the past five or ten years, and the standards of hospital managers have changed within the same time," announced one important hospital administration text in 1913. In addition to fulfilling the traditional housekeeping chores, the new administrator must "keep abreast of medical and surgical progress, to know what new apparatus of a medical or surgical kind should be bought and used. He must know the laws of asepsis, and at least enough about the character of the communicable diseases to guard not only against their appearance . . . but to prevent their spread."[10] Medical expertise became a new criteria for the efficient manager, challenging social service as the primary administrative function. "If the modern superintendent is not a surgeon or internist . . . he must at least be sufficiently well informed on all of these subjects to engage in intelligent conference with members of his medical staff," remarked the authors of *The Modern Hospital* in 1913.[11]

The redefinition of the hospital administrator reflected a fundamental change in the underlying political economy of the institution. Between the late 1890s and the advent of the depression, the institution changed its mission, reorganized its services, and altered its financial base. First, the older role of the hospital as a charitable institution was undermined by a new rationale based on medical intent. Hospitals emerged as the workshops of physicians, and social service departments were added to the new medical institution. Second, as hospitals increasingly sought to attract patients from the middle or upper classes of society, they sought to build services with more amenities and greater comforts than had previously been necessary. Private and semiprivate wards began to replace the charity ward; private wings and

9. Ibid., 12.
10. Hornsby and Schmidt, *The Modern Hospital*, 253.
11. Ibid., 253–54.

private nursing was introduced into facilities that previously made few if any class distinctions regarding patients. Similarly, visiting medical personnel came to be ubiquitous in institutions where only a few decades earlier few physicians could be found on the wards on any regular basis. By the 1920s the institution was reorganizing in response to the new needs of potential customers, and the basis for the maternalist, female administrator faded. While the public image of the institution was that of a social service, women began to complain that trustees showed preference for males interested in becoming head administrators. "There has . . . been great injustice shown toward the woman executive," complained one hospital administrator from Pennsylvania. "A woman builds up on a substantial foundation but [w]hen the institution has expanded in its capacity for increased service, in its popularity with the public, in its wholesome influence upon the community, the question seems to be raised in the minds of [these trustees], should we not pass on to a man's control, and this often when a woman has mortgaged her health in her impassioned service to the institution."[12]

This administrator was not only bemoaning the passing of a career track from females to males, she was also noting a transformation of her institution from one that was community and family based to one that was to be managed by people with little connection to its charitable origins. She worried about the uneasy alliance between health care and business. In the view of many, the new vision of the institution and its administrators lacked the strong and coherent ideology of the older charity institution. The 1920s marked the beginning of a period of turmoil within hospital administration.

Perhaps the most significant indication of this increasing disorder was the call for formal training in hospital administration from administrators themselves. S. S. Goldwater, the head administrator of Mt. Sinai Hospital in New York City from 1902 to 1929 and a major actor in the shaping of the New York public hospital system and Blue Cross, reflected the frustration that many physicians and laymen experienced in the rapidly changing hospital environment of the early twentieth century. "The country has drifted into its present chaotic condition because there was nobody whose business it was to furnish guidance in matters of medical administration," he complained in

12. Quoted in Davis, *Hospital Administration*, 30.

1919. "Incomparably the best way to treat the matter is to have the study of medical administration organized and directed under university auspices."[13] Repeated often throughout the 1920s, the demand of hospital administrators for formal training reflected their increasing sense of drift during a period of tremendous disruption in the relationship of the administrator to his or her institution.[14] As hospital administration exited from the relative stability of a culture of maternalism and charity, there was a strong sense that the traditional values and roles of administration were of little relevance in the new environment of modern medicine. But there were few alternatives to this older notion of the administrator as the moral, social, and organizational voice of the institution. A new basis for administration was required and many turned to the university as a source of inspiration and focus.

In 1922 the Josiah Macy Jr. Foundation responded by forming a committee to evaluate the need for more formal training among health administrators. In their concluding report the committee developed a mission statement for future education courses, one that merged traditional service ideals with a broad mandate of educational reform along the lines of modern business administration. "An interpretation of the principles involved in hospital functions, organization and tendencies and a presentation of their relationships to the broad problems and activities of community life . . . should be the basis of training for hospital executives," the report remarked. "A philosophy of community responsibility in matters of health is rapidly growing," it continued.[15] For those involved in developing formal educational goals for hospital administrators during the 1920s, the first order of business was to merge the community and medical service function of the hospital with a new set of business skills.

Perhaps the most promising development of the 1930s was the organization of an M.B.A. program in health administration at the University of Chicago. The only formal business program for hospital administrators, it began with the goal of providing the foundations

13. S. S. Goldwater, "Civilian Medical Administration and the Need for Trained Leaders," in S. S. Goldwater, *On Hospitals* (1919; reprint New York: Macmillan, 1947), 26.

14. See the "Report of the Committee on the Training of Hospital Executives," in *Principles of Hospital Administration and Training of Hospital Executives* (New York: Josiah Macy Jr. Foundation, 1922).

15. Ibid., 8; see also S. S. Goldwater, "Ideal Aims of Hospital Organization," in *On Hospitals*, 4–5 (1922; reprint 1947).

upon which the dual responsibilities of caring and managing could be met. It sought to provide a place where administrators "absorbed in institutional detail" could stand back and reflect on the broader social currents that affected their job as managers of social services.[16]

These early efforts at formal education acknowledged the traditional missions of the institution, seeking to ground the role of the manager in the earlier service mandate of the charity hospital. The new manager was to maintain the service orientation of the facility while augmenting his management skills with ideas and concepts borrowed from the business community. Organized during the depression and coincidental with the publication of the Committee on the Costs of Medical Care, the Chicago experiment was part of a broader attempt to restructure education. But in that restructuring, the administration could not quite shake its nineteenth-century moorings. Rather than radically depart from the charity ideals of the nineteenth and early twentieth centuries, the Chicago program substituted voluntarist language of the twentieth century for traditional class-bound charitable identifications.

In many educational programs the tensions between a charity and a business focus remained relatively muted as formal education in administration moved primarily into schools of public health rather than into business schools. The object of all courses was to design delivery systems less concerned with business notions of efficiency or service costs. Furthermore, even when administrators came from one of the few M.B.A. programs in health administration, they quickly adopted the paternalistic (or more appropriately, maternalistic) ideals of caring for a community's sick, dependent, and helpless. In community institutions managers could only institute business measures to improve efficiency and effectiveness and to balance the budget if the measures were in compliance with the goals of the caring professions. The trained administrator could not afford to maintain true allegiance to his academic training in management techniques. The very skills that this

16. M. M. Davis, "Development of the First Graduate Program in Hospital Administration," reprinted in *Journal of Health Administration Education* 2 (Spring 1984): 122. There were other shorter courses provided for a variety of administrators throughout the 1920s. New York University, the Illinois Training School for Women, McGill University, Marquette University, Yale University, University of Cincinnati, and Harvard University School of Public Health all provided either special short courses or attenuated curricula from 1910 through the 1920s. None, with the possible exception of Marquette, provided more than a short sequence of courses and most were not offered regularly.

new administrator brought from his student days would undergo a fundamental change when faced by the culture of caring and the realities of hospital practice. When hospital administrators—whether female or male—"borrowed a volume from industry" they did more than crudely adopt business principles as if there were no distinctions between money-making corporations and charitable enterprises. Rather, they essentially transformed business concepts to suit their needs as administrators of a public trust.

S. S. Goldwater stated the evolving rationale for the field of hospital administration, one that guaranteed that the field would remain separated from other business fields: "The hospital is a social institution whose true origins are deeply embedded in the human character. . . . It is the response of prudence and sympathy to man's hatred of suffering and his fear of death."[17] Here he adopted service as the primary motive for hospital organization. Elsewhere he differentiated between the hospital definitions of efficiency and accountability, which were generally intertwined with ideals rooted in what was essentially the most human of human enterprises: providing care for the community's dependent and vulnerable. In that context it is not surprising that the ideas borrowed from industry underwent a mutation that often made them unidentifiable by the business communities in which they first appeared. By the Depression years hospital administration defined its mission as the application of industrial organization tools to the unique and complex setting of a human service where the bottom line could not be measured by mere profits and losses but by human happiness and comfort:

> If you were asked what you considered the most important single quality in a hospital administrator what would you say? . . . I would answer, "sympathy and compassion." Not the emotional type of compassion which gives way to tears and ends in helpless despair, but the kind which arouses action, which intuitively grasps the meaning of a critical situation, which senses the need of appeasement, and eventually does something. The future will see a widening of the beneficent influence of this type of compassion to the extent that men of good will can be enrolled in the ranks of administrators.[18]

17. S. S. Goldwater, *On Hospitals*, 20.
18. Ibid.

Goldwater sought to make a distinction between a business manager and a health administrator. He differed from his female counterpart of thirty years earlier only in rhetorical style, not content. He wanted sympathy and compassion—traditional administration ideals—but augmented by a hard business sense.

The distinctions between health and other types of business administration were not merely due to older administrators' bringing forward old notions of *caritas*. Both business and health administrators through the first half of this century used the rhetoric and language of science, management, and the assembly line. But the hospital administrator's success was not measured in terms of dollars but in terms of human comfort and well being.

S. S. Goldwater wrote a letter to C.-E.A. Winslow in 1928 that sought to explain his reasons for entering health administration and revealed some of the basic ideals that informed the early generation of hospital administrators:

> I originally dedicated myself not to medical or public health work, but to economics. With an ethical background and with the love of and belief in justice that characterizes the youthful enthusiast, I speedily arrived at the conclusion that a mere analysis of economic conditions without a social objective was hardly worthwhile. . . . This line of thought led me straight away back to . . . health and suggested that any system of applied economics designed to satisfy human needs would eventually have to be directed by . . . health officers. I at once decided to abandon economics [to begin] a [public] health career.[19]

In this letter Goldwater disclosed the mixed baggage of hospital administration during its early years. It was at the same time a profession that not only defined its mission as doing well financially but also doing good for its clients.

For most of this century the hospital has been the central focus of health administration programs. There has rarely been a question regarding the ultimate objective of the administrator to organize for health as well as for the institution's economic security. Despite the rhetoric

19. S. S. Goldwater to C.-E.A. Winslow, quoted in S. S. Goldwater, *On Hospitals*, xix.

of the business community it is unlikely that the cultural and social rationale of the institution could be abandoned without seriously eroding the support of the community and the nation. If today is a critical moment for health-care administration it is not because the institution has changed but because administrators are abandoning the institution. Today, some trained administrators are organizing health benefits packages in corporations or consulting firms; others are organizing Preferred Provider Organizations or Health Maintainance Organizations for corporations. In these new settings it is unclear whether the hospitals' focus on care will be a central factor in determining administrators' identity. If the administrators lose that identity their field will suffer, along with the institutions and its patients.

These new work settings may exert new pressures on their administrators, pressures that ultimately affect the very definitions of administration. Administrators will now be working in a culture that often measures success by the extent to which one limits health coverage, shifts costs to the patient, excludes categories of patients because of inadequate coverage or because of race, or forces people out of expensive beds. As corporations become more involved in creating their health benefit packages, health administration may, for the first time, cease to be intimately linked to the problems of health-care provision.[20] Ironically, the health administrators' concern with costs and profit might very well limit their ability to shape the content of programs and definitions of service with the "sympathy and compassion" that Goldwater called for. Health administrators are thereby in danger of losing their special identity as managers of medical and social, rather than business enterprises.

20. See Paul Starr, *The Social Transformation of American Medicine* (New York: Basic Books, 1982).

8

Coming of Age: Local 1199 in the 1960s

BRIAN GREENBERG

During the breakthrough in labor organization in the 1930s, union membership in the United States increased fivefold: almost two-thirds of production workers were covered under collective-bargaining agreements by the end of World War II.[1] In basic industry, union coverage was complete or nearly so.[2] Still, not all workers were caught up in the union tide of the thirties. Workers in hospitals, as well as those in most service industries, were little affected. Indeed, voluntary, not-for-profit institutions were specifically exempted from the provisions of the 1947 Taft-Hartley Act.

1. This chapter is drawn from a full-scale study, Leon Fink and Brian Greenberg, *Upheaval in the Quiet Zone: A History of Hospital Workers' Union, Local 1199* (Urbana, Ill.: University of Illinois Press, 1989). We tell the story of a union of hospital workers and in so doing pursue a range of issues confronting workers, unions, the health-care industry, and the larger society in which the themes of workplace conflict are played out. In our research we look closely at the organizing process itself—how and why workers traditionally outside the reach of labor unionism suddenly, and often successfully, engaged in collective action. Second, we explore the labor union as institution, assessing the limits of its role as a catalyst for social change. Finally, we analyze the forces in the industry, the economy, and the political community at large, which, in important ways, defined the opportunities for workers and their representatives.

2. David Brody, *Workers in Industrial America: Essays in Twentieth-Century Struggle* (New York: Oxford University Press, 1980), 158–73.

170

Beginning in the 1950s, hospitals became the low-wage employer of last resort for newly arrived immigrants and for southern black and Hispanic migrants to cities in the North. By 1970 black and Hispanic workers made up between 70 and 80 percent of the service and maintenance departments of many voluntary hospitals in New York City.[3] Service workers, usually female, toiled as cooks, aides, and laundry and maintenance workers in an expanding hospital industry. The low status of service and maintenance workers in hospitals and their lack of legal bargaining rights, as well as the special status society accorded their employer (notably, the moral sanction against striking helpless patients) combined to forestall union interest in organizing hospital workers. However, in the late 1950s, Local 1199, a six-thousand-member union of pharmacists and drugstore employees rooted in the left-wing industrial unionism of the thirties, began a concerted effort to organize workers in New York City's hospitals.[4]

In 1957, looking for new areas in which to expand 1199, Leon Davis, president of the union almost from its beginnings, recruited Elliott Godoff, who since the 1930s had led numerous, mostly unsuccessful, efforts to unionize New York City hospital workers.[5] Unable to make any headway among workers at several proprietary (small, for-profit) institutions, Godoff turned to organize the city's voluntary hospitals, specifically targeting Montefiore Hospital in the Bronx, where he had a few long-standing contacts. Over the course of a prolonged campaign at Montefiore from December 1957 to August 1958, organizers for 1199 signed up a majority of the eligible workers.[6] The next phase of the union's campaign to gain recognition embraced

3. Judith Layzer, *Ethnic Survey of Hospital Employees: New Occupational Possibilities* (New York: Office of the Mayor, 1970), 9.

4. By the mid-1980s 1199 represented some 150,000 workers in nineteen states plus the District of Columbia and the Commonwealth of Puerto Rico, making it the largest union of voluntary hospital workers in the country. According to 1981 figures, the Service Employees International Union, which organizes in large numbers of nursing homes and state hospitals as well as in voluntary hospitals, has enrolled some 250,000 health-care members. Also active in the health-care field are the American Federation of Teachers and the American Nursing Association.

5. In the 1930s Godoff successfully organized Maimonides Hospital in Brooklyn. Unfortunately, this history of 1199 was begun after Godoff's death in 1975.

6. See Leon Fink and Brian Greenberg, "Organizing Montefiore: Labor Militancy Meets a Progressive Health Care Empire," in *Health Care in America: Essays in Social History*, ed. Susan Reverby and David Rosner (Philadelphia: Temple University Press, 1970), 226–44.

an elaborate set of maneuvers that involved city government, the Central Labor Council, the endorsement of important public figures such as Eleanor Roosevelt and Senator Herbert H. Lehman, and the threat of a strike. Only hours before a December 8, 1958 strike deadline Montefiore officials agreed, pending a certification election, to recognize Local 1199 as the sole collective-bargaining agent for its service and maintenance employees.

After its victory at Montefiore, 1199 began organizing workers in other hospitals across the city. Confronted by more determined opposition from management than they had at Montefiore, thirty-five hundred hospital workers at seven of New York's major voluntary hospitals walked out on May 8, 1959. The unprecedented forty-six-day strike that followed ended in a stalemate. Instead of formal union recognition, both sides agreed to a Statement of Policy establishing a quasi-public agency, the Permanent Administrative Committee (PAC), charged with supervising labor relations in the hospitals. Having been denied formal recognition, 1199 spent three frustrating years consolidating its de facto organizational strength in the city's hospitals. In 1962, 1199 struck again, and by an adroit combination of militant rank-and-file action and effective political pressure, the union successfully challenged the PAC. Hospital workers in New York City finally won their collective-bargaining rights in 1963 when they were enrolled under the state's labor relations acts.[7]

In May 1963 Leon Davis, still recuperating at home from a heart attack he had suffered in February, met with a reporter from the *New York Herald Tribune* to discuss the union's future. Despite his physical infirmities, Davis was in a positive mood. In New York City collective bargaining in voluntary hospitals was now the law; also, the union had just passed an early test when workers at Mt. Sinai Hospital voted twenty to one for representation by Local 1199. Surveying the hospital field, Davis expressed his belief that the Mt. Sinai vote would be the first of many union victories in the next several years.[8]

Much as Davis predicted, by the end of the sixties 1199 had quadrupled its membership. Equally important, a significant number of the

7. See Brian Greenberg, "The Making of a Union in the Hospitals," in *The History of Sociology of Technology*, ed. David Hoke (Milwaukee: Milwaukee Public Museum, 1982), 259–68.
8. *New York Herald Tribune*, May 26, 1963.

new members were professional and technical workers—laboratory technicians, social workers, therapists, clinical workers, and so on— who 1199 had organized into a separate guild division. By 1965 the union had won the right to represent hospital workers throughout New York State. Moreover, in 1966 and then two years later, 1199 made considerable progress in raising the income of hospital workers. Within five years after passage of the 1963 law, the minimum weekly salary for hospital workers almost doubled.[9] Local 1199's progress on two fronts—extending union organization to professional and technical workers in the hospitals and raising the standard of living of hospital employees—truly represented the union's "coming of age."

"PEACEABLE KINGDOM"?

Local 1199's early efforts to build a union in New York City's voluntary hospitals focused on the achievement of two complementary objectives: the expansion of the union's organizational base and the establishment of the union's legitimacy as the collective-bargaining agent for hospital service and maintenance workers. Even though Leon Davis was certain that the union's failure to engage professional hospital workers in the 1959 strike had been one of its "biggest weaknesses," 1199 did little to bring these workers into the union prior to 1963.[10] Apparently convinced that the union could rid itself of the PAC only through militant confrontation, 1199's leader de-emphasized organizing among professional and technical workers. Thus, in April 1963 Godoff explained to the general council of the drug division that 1199 was slow in organizing professionals "not because we didn't want to, but because they feared the militant struggles we were conducting and were not prepared to enter into them."[11] Yet the reluctance

9. Sara Gamm, *Toward Collective Bargaining in Non-Profit Hospitals: Impact of New York Law* (Ithaca, N.Y.: New York State School of Industrial and Labor Relations, 1968), 67–68.

10. Minutes, Executive Council, June 19, 1959; June 27, 1959; and February 15, 1960, National Union of Hospital and Health Care Employees Archives, Labor-Management Documentation Center, New York State School of Industrial and Labor Relations, Cornell University, Ithaca, N.Y. Unless otherwise noted, further direct quotations in the text derive from oral interviews conducted by Leon Fink and/or Brian Greenberg between 1975 and 1985. The tapes and transcripts, where available, have been deposited with the union archives.

11. Minutes, Drug Division General Council, April 3, 1963, 1199 Archives.

of professionals to strike does not, however, fully explain their resistance to joining a union. In the *1199 News* of August 1962, Harold
Garelick, a research technician at Montefiore who had been a union
steward since 1958, wrote that his coworkers wanted "an organization
of professional employees and for professional employees."[12] In response, the union announced in the same issue that it was forming a
professional organization that would function as a "separate group to
deal exclusively with the needs of professional and technical
workers."[13]

The problem of enrolling professional and technical hospital workers
as union members was one issue addressed by 1199's executive council
through the fall of 1963. Among the changes adopted by the council
was the formation of the Guild of Professional, Technical, Office, and
Clerical Hospital Employees. Like the union's drug and hospital divisions, the guild would keep its own records, collect its own dues,
and elect its own delegate assembly. By January 1964 the guild had
some five hundred members, mainly professional and technical workers
from Montefiore and Maimonides hospitals.[14]

Special literature was produced for guild organizing campaigns. In
"a message to technicians and professionals in the voluntary hospital,"
the union outlined what the "GUILD CAN ACCOMPLISH." Although
acknowledging that "economic issues are uppermost in everyone's
minds," the leaflet stated that the guild would also work "to give
organizational expression on all professional issues." These issues
included a fair job classification system based on educational experience, salaries commensurate with responsibilities, educational opportunities for advancement available through hospital-financed tuition-
aid programs, and licensing legislation.[15]

Guild publications tried to convince skilled workers that professionalism and unionism were fully compatible. Most of the literature
included a picture of Albert Einstein along with his statement "I con-

12. *1199 News*, August 1962.
13. Ibid. At this point it was called the Guild of Medical, Diagnostic Research, and
X-ray Technicians.
14. Gamm, *Toward Collective Bargaining*, 65–66; *1199 News*, January 1964; and
Minutes, Executive Council, October 11, 1964, and November 9, 1963, 1199 Archives.
15. *A Message to Technicians and Professionals in the Voluntary Hospital*, 1199
Archives.

sider it important, indeed urgently necessary, for intellectual workers to build an organization to protect their own interests." Having thus given the guild impeccable credentials, a pamphlet, "Professionals and Economic Security," carried a typical endorsement: "As a pharmacist I know that 1199 has established standards for retail store Rx men which are 25 to 50% higher than what we receive in the voluntary hospitals." In addition to citing other benefits, organizing victories, and successful grievances, the leaflet made special reference to union-sponsored social and cultural events under the heading "1199: A Swinging Union."[16]

Guild organizing proceeded slowly and mostly at institutions where 1199 already represented the service and maintenance workers. The guild's first director, Jesse Olson, recalled that the task was always somewhat easier when the organizer could point out to the professional staff how much more porters working in the same hospital were earning since they had become union members. Nevertheless, fewer than 20 percent of the 5,000 hospital employees who joined 1199 in 1965 were guild workers.[17] A typical union election in this period might find service and maintenance workers voting in numbers five times greater than guild members.[18] Unlike the hospital division, in which all of an institution's service and maintenance employees voted as a unit, professional and technical workers in the guild usually voted by department— with one significant exception.[19]

A major advance in the growth of the guild occurred in 1967 when more than one thousand workers at the Albert Einstein College of Medicine (AECOM) and its affiliated units at Bronx Municipal Hospital Center became 1199 members.[20] Two features distinguished this campaign: AECOM was the first medical school, rather than hospital, that 1199 attempted to organize, and the college's guild chapter included nonprofessional as well as professional members. Still, most AECOM guild members were professional workers who, as one early activist

16. Union leaflet, "Professionals and Economic Security," 1199 Archives.
17. *1199 News*, October 1965.
18. Gamm, *Toward Collective Bargaining*, 45.
19. *1199 News*, June 1967.
20. The Albert Einstein College of Medicine is a medical school operated by Yeshiva University with affiliated units at Jacobi, Van Etten, and Lincoln hospitals and at Bronx neighborhood health centers.

noted, "wanted to be treated like professionals." Therefore, despite its unique aspects, unionization of AECOM reflected the critical issues that the guild would always face.

In late 1966 workers at AECOM, led by Bernie Minter, an electrical technician, and Manya Shaffron, a research assistant in the pediatric department, launched the Albert Einstein Employees Organization (AEEO) as an unaffiliated association of college employees.[21] An elected representative council met with college administrators to present the workers' modest demands: a 10 percent across-the-board wage increase, health coverage, and access to the institution's swimming pool. Indeed, the college had just closed the employees' health service facility at Jacobi Hospital and, as one member of the representative council recalled, AEEO members found the denial of health coverage while working at a medical school to be particularly galling.[22]

Not surprisingly, the AEEO ran into a stone wall in their negotiations with the college administration. Minter met Davis, an old friend, by chance at a peace rally during the spring of 1967 and asked him if 1199 would help the AEEO. Davis had some doubts because the medical college was not a hospital, but Minter found that convincing Davis was easier than convincing AEEO members to affiliate with 1199. As a research facility, Albert Einstein had a "flexible kind of atmosphere," and many workers expressed fear that "the union would come in and take over." As professionals they were also reluctant to join a union whose members were predominantly service and maintenance workers.

Minter used the college administration's hard-line stand as an argument for affiliation with 1199. Diane Bianculli, then a recent high school graduate working as a technician trainee in the histology lab and known among fellow AEEO members as "the Kid," recalled Minter ridiculing the college's claim that a 10-percent wage increase would bankrupt the institution. All the employees really wanted was to be regarded "on the same level as [the] toilet paper," Minter argued,

21. Unsigned leaflet to the Albert Einstein Employees Organization, May 1967, 1199 Archives.

22. Information about the AEEO comes from an interview with Diane Bianculli, May 28, 1982.

pointing out that even as the price went up Albert Einstein did not hesitate to pay for what it considered necessary. How could workers hide behind their "professionalism" and refuse to affiliate with 1199 when the college's administrators made it clear that the employees were not "as important to the functioning of the college as are supplies, furniture, etc."[23] Such arguments finally led to an overwhelming five to one vote in May 1967 to join the union, but because many workers still identified with their professional association, the new organization was called "AEEO/1199."[24]

After its workers affiliated with 1199 events at Albert Einstein followed a fairly predictable course. Soon after the election AEEO/1199 sent a mass delegation to meet with the college's administration while outside of the medical school some one thousand employees marched to demand union recognition. With a strike deadline of July 24 approaching, Charles C. Bassine, chairman of the college's board of overseers, prompted by city officials, intervened and agreed to a union election for all employees except supervisors and confidential secretaries.[25]

In preparation for what would, in October 1967, prove to be a successful union certification election, the executive committee for AEEO/1199 issued "Sense and Common Sense." In this pamphlet the executive committee stated that "it may be wise to pause at this junction, to sit and discuss some of the issues raised by some of our fellow employees" at Albert Einstein, particularly the issues of "Professionalism and Union Membership" and "Unions and Medical Schools." Workers who thought that they could "do all right" for themselves "by wheeling and dealing" were exhorted to "think about it the next time you pay for an X-ray or to be examined by a staff physician." The original leadership of the AEEO had recognized that forming "some kind of technical guild" would not work: "As long as any one group in this College remains alone and tries to better conditions for itself only, that effort is doomed to failure." Working conditions "affected everyone in the institution, from glasswasher to

23. Unsigned leaflet to the Albert Einstein Employees Organization, May 1967, 1199 Archives.
24. *1199 News*, November 1967.
25. *New York Times*, July 22, 1967, and July 24, 1967.

research assistant and from porters to senior secretaries. Our problems
are common to everyone—the solutions are also."[26] Consequently the
Einstein chapter is unique within 1199 in not having a separate guild
and hospital division membership.

As a child of the militant trade unionism of the thirties, Local
1199 had a deep-seated commitment to organizing all workers in
the health-care industry, regardless of their skill or individual differences, into one union. But the early years of the hospital campaign
convinced the union's leaders that they had no choice but to adopt
separate divisions. According to Davis, 1199 tried "to accomplish
the same thing" in the hospitals as it had in the drugstores, that is,
industrial organization, "but we recognized . . . that we can't just put
workers together regardless of their background and station of life, in
their job and how they make a living." Jesse Olson, looking back on
the experience a dozen or so years after the formation of the guild in
1964, insisted that "we would never have been able to organize 21,000
white-collar workers" if 1199 had not established a separate division.

At the same time that they pleaded necessity, 1199's leaders also
made a more positive argument in defense of the union's separate
divisions. Differences in skill, race, ethnic background, and other
distinctions have historically fragmented American workers and the
trade-union movement. Yet by creating two divisions within the union,
Davis insisted that 1199 avoided the conditions that prevail, for example, in the hotel or construction industries, where ten or twenty
unions are the rule. He wrote in 1963 that workers should vote for the
union because "1199 has divisions for all hospital workers—the
skilled, the unskilled, the professional, technical and office personnel."[27] For Davis, separate divisions are better than separate unions;
or, as Olson observed, separate divisions represented not a failure "but
a success" of industrial unionism.

Even as 1199 established the guild, the union was adopting other
structural changes in 1963 aimed at unifying the organization's leadership. It was up to the union, Davis told the executive council, to
build "a leadership of all three divisions, not just of any one division."
The three divisions would be given a large measure of autonomy, but

26. "Sense and Common Sense," a leaflet distributed by the Executive Committee
AEEO/1199, October 12, 1968, 1199 Archives.
27. *1199 News*, June 1963.

the union must be integrated "from the top. We want the top leadership to be '1199'—not drug, or hospital or Guild. As one union we must meet together, act together, have one point of interest, the union." Unity was the key. "If we succeed in this," Davis predicted, "we will have achieved the millennium. We will have proved that the lion and the lamb can live together."[28]

Despite the vigor with which 1199's leaders championed the union's divisional structure, there is evidence that they were also made uncomfortable by it. In 1967 the union engaged in another internal evaluation of its operations. At a meeting to review the guild administration, the staff discussed the current status of organizing among licensed practical nurses (LPNs). Just two years earlier, Local 1199 had founded the Guild League for Licensed Practical Nurses, which, by June 1967, had fifteen hundred members as well as two LPNs on the guild staff.[29] During the discussion Davis asked, "Should the LPN League be a separate entity???" Olson replied that there was no need for a "separate structure" for the LPNs, "as a matter of fact they enjoy mixing with other delegates at the [guild] assembly." The consensus of the staff was unequivocal: "DROP THE LEAGUE. Encourage the LPN's to mix with others."[30] Union organizing literature later referred to an LPN league, but made it clear that the league was an integral part of the guild.[31]

In 1976, 1199 did establish a fourth division, the League of Registered Nurses (RNs). Although Bianculli conceded that without a separate division organizing the RNs probably "would never have gotten off the ground," she proposed that now that the nurses are in the union they should be educated to understand that separate divisions are not necessary. 1199's leaders have accepted the premise that the only way all hospital workers will be organized together in one union is through the separate divisions. When Davis made this point in reference to the need to revise the union's constitution in 1963, he stated that "the best we can work toward is mutual re-

28. Minutes, Executive Council, September 7, 1963; October 11, 1963; and November 9, 1963, 1199 Archives.
29. *1199 News*, June 1967.
30. Minutes, Review of the Union Administration, May 15, 1967, 1199 Archives.
31. Leaflet, "Why Mount Sinai LPNs Should Join the 1199 LPN League," July 23, 1970, 1199 Archives.

spect, interest and moral responsibility for each other.''[32] If not quite the millennium, Davis still set a high standard of cooperation for the union to attain.

A LIVING WAGE

In the effort to establish its legitimacy as the collective-bargaining agent for hospital workers, 1199 had inevitably subordinated the winning of wage and other demands to the task of increasing its membership. But by 1966, having achieved a secure position in New York City's hospitals, 1199's leaders decided to abandon their cautious approach to collective bargaining. Norman Metzger, the personnel director at Mt. Sinai Hospital, characterized labor-management relations between 1963 and 1966 as ''a piece of cake.'' In retrospect, Metzger believed that 1199 was only trying ''to lull us into a sense of security that the union was not really a problem.'' For the hospitals, this modern day ''Era of Good Feelings'' proved short-lived: ''1966,'' Metzger declared, ''was the moment of truth.''

With a special ''Let's Fight Poverty'' issue of *1199 News* in February 1966, the union launched its campaign to gain significant wage increases at nineteen of the city's voluntary hospitals.[33] As they did throughout the 1960s, union leaders drew explicit parallels between their wage demands and ''the overall struggle of American Negro workers . . . to fight their way out of poverty and into first-class citizenship.''[34] Seeking wage parity for its members with the city's municipal hospital workers, 1199 tried to arrange joint talks with the voluntary hospitals under contract. No progress was made and in June, workers from almost every institution gathered for about two weeks in front of the director's office demanding negotiations. Finally, on July 7, following a noontime walkout, officials at Maimonides Hospital agreed to bargain. An agreement was reached under which the workers gained a 24-percent wage increase: an immediate 10-percent raise, a

32. Minutes, Executive Council, September 7, 1963, 1199 Archives. Through the 1970s the union appeared to have in many ways fulfilled Davis's aspirations. Only recently have the economic and cultural differences recognized in the formation of discrete divisions begun to haunt 1199.

33. *1199 News*, February 1966. The existing contracts were five-year pacts that contained a reopener clause, for wages only, at the start of the fourth year. If a wage increase could not be agreed to, the issue had to be arbitrated.

34. *1199 News*, September 1966.

7 ½-percent increase the next year, an additional 2 ½-percent increase in June 1968, and a 4-percent payroll contribution for family health benefits.[35]

Local 1199 quickly announced that it would settle for no less than the "Maimonides formula" at the other hospitals. Employees at several New York institutions, but particularly at Montefiore and Mt. Sinai, began a campaign that involved a pattern of on-again, off-again work stoppages. Despite such provocation, hospitals never made a serious effort to force arbitration; both sides hoped that continued unrest would lead to government intervention. On July 12, Mt. Sinai officials wired Governor Nelson Rockefeller, Lt. Governor Malcolm Wilson, and New York City mayor John V. Lindsay asking them to intervene in order to avoid "a catastrophe."[36] Lindsay was the first to act, assigning Deputy Mayor Timothy Costello to conduct secret negotiations with both sides.

The catastrophe that Lindsay hoped to avert went beyond the usual concern caused by any disruption in health services. By July 1966 the possibility that the wage campaign might touch off a race riot had to be considered. New York's mayor was keenly aware that the civil rights movement once dominated by Dr. Martin Luther King's philosophy of nonviolence had given way to cries of "Black Power" and "Burn, Baby, Burn." The *New York Times* reported that during the negotiations Davis told Costello that the growing discontent of the black and Hispanic community in New York could lead to "a blood bath that would make Watts look like a playground."[37] Whether or not Davis actually made this statement, it is unlikely that city officials needed to be reminded of the long, hot summers then convulsing the nation. In the three years that followed the 1965 race riot in the Watts section of Los Angeles, some three hundred violent racial disturbances took place, marked by fifty thousand arrests and more than eight hundred casualties. In 1966 alone more than a score of riots in cities across the nation required the national guard to restore order.[38]

The possibility of violence lent a sense of urgency to the negotiations

35. Ibid.; *New York Times*, July 13, 1966, and July 14, 1966; Gamm, *Toward Collective Bargaining*, 66–68, 74.
36. *New York Times*, July 13, 1966, and July 14, 1966.
37. Ibid., July 21, 1966.
38. Harvard Sitkoff, *The Struggle for Black Equality, 1954–1980* (New York: Hill and Wang, 1981), 200–202.

between the union and the hospitals. After a weekend of marathon bargaining, Mt. Sinai agreed to the "Maimonides formula." The next day New York's other voluntary hospitals followed suit. Only Montefiore expressed open dissatisfaction. Calling the agreement by Mt. Sinai's administrators a "dangerous surrender of principle," Dr. Martin Cherkasky, director of Montefiore Hospital, publicly lamented their "capitulating to Local 1199."[39] The *New York Times* agreed that the hospitals were bowing "to harassment by strike, exercised in defiance of both law and contract, [which] sets a precedent of great danger to the community." But what really raised the editors' ire was the inevitability that the hospitals would "pass their higher outlays on to patients and the community in the form of higher fees for all hospital services. All levels of government will feel the impact in inflation of the charges they must meet under the new Medicare and Medicaid programs. Blue Cross rates will also feel the upward pull."[40] In this statement, the *New York Times* had its editorial finger on one of the most significant changes in the contemporary health-care industry—the fact that for most New Yorkers a hospital stay was increasingly paid for by a third party, either a voluntary health insurance plan (usually Blue Cross) or, since 1965, by Medicare and Medicaid. More to the point, all increases in hospital wage rates and fringe benefits, as well as in expenses for personnel administration, were considered to be part of the legitimate cost of providing patient services that could be passed along to a third-party payer.[41]

After 1966, according to Norman Metzger, bargaining between hospital management and labor became something of a game; both sides learned "that reimbursement was the name of the game and that negotiations had to take a certain form." From the hospitals's perspective, not only would the union not seriously negotiate, but, once the talks reached a crisis, "ipso facto somebody would come in with a pile of money." As far as the hospitals were concerned, they "were a conduit" for the "public money" that paid the bills.

Metzger may be reading further into the past what would be a more accurate description of hospital management and labor negotiations after 1968. Clearly, Cherkasky's response to the 1966 settlement is

39. *New York Times*, July 19, 1966.
40. "The Hospital Surrender," *New York Times*, July 20, 1966.
41. Odin Anderson, *Blue Cross since 1929: Accountability and the Public Trust* (Cambridge, Mass.: Ballinger, 1975), 81–86; *Hospitals*, October 16, 1973.

evidence that the participants had not yet fully learned the rules of the game. Moreover, the 1966 talks had at first involved bargaining only between hospital management and the union.[42] Not until 1968 did the hospitals begin pressing heavily for direct government and Blue Cross involvement in the bargaining process. Perhaps Metzger then was closer to the mark when he concluded that 1966 was a "sign of the future," whereas 1968, when a new agreement was negotiated, "was the future."

On March 7, 1968, *New York Times* reported that in order to conduct joint bargaining fifteen hospitals had formed the League of Voluntary Hospitals.[43] The league's position, articulated in a series of newspaper advertisements, was based on three premises: (1) any work stoppage or strike was illegal; the main issue was "respect for the law"; (2) union wage and benefit demands would exact a tremendous price, pushing up the cost of hospital care by twenty-five dollars per day; and (3) the hospitals and patients both were innocent victims in that government and medical plan funds now had to meet a major share of hospital costs. League statements continually emphasized that "it is not our money. . . . It is yours." Because hospitals were only "custodians of public funds," the league called for the direct participation of the mayor, governor, and Blue Cross in the negotiations.[44]

For its part 1199 was also unyielding, announcing that its major demand, a $100-per-week minimum salary, was "not arbitratable, not negotiable, it's irreducible."[45] Once again the union linked its wage demands to the moral and social imperatives of the civil rights movement. Davis wrote in *1199 News,* "What sense, logic, reason or justice is there in talking about the abolition of poverty and making contributions to the Poor People's Campaign (as some of the hospital trustees have done) while opposing a minimum wage that would be a long step towards the objective?"[46] Union leaders, aware that in the hospital

42. For example, only after the agreement did Maimonides announce that room rates would go up by eight dollars a day. See the *New York Times,* July 24, 1966.

43. *New York Times,* March 7, 1968. John Connorton, director of the Greater New York Hospital Association, maintained that the league took a different approach, a more "rock-em, sock-em" attitude.

44. See the *New York Times,* June 21, 1968; June 27, 1968; and June 28, 1968.

45. *Wall Street Journal,* June 19, 1968. At this point workers in municipal hospitals were earning a minimum weekly salary of just over ninety-six dollars.

46. *1199 News,* May 1968. The Poor People's Campaign refers to the ongoing Southern Christian Leadership Conference demonstration in Washington, D.C.

league they faced a tougher opponent than in 1966, appropriated twenty thousand dollars to cover the costs of a media campaign to explain why the workers "feel they must strike."[47] Under the headline "HOS-PITAL CRISIS," a June 24 union advertisement stated simply that hospital workers would no longer accept "poverty wages. . . . We want all the opportunities for advancement and education available to other Americans." Although recognizing that the demanded minimum wage would add to the hospitals' financial difficulties, the union insisted that the workers would no longer "act as involuntary philanthropists for the voluntary hospitals. . . . The hospitals cannot continue to balance their books on the shoulders of poor people any longer."[48]

Collective bargaining in 1968 was again conducted in a crisis atmosphere, prompted in part by the potential for racial violence. And much as before, last-minute negotiations in which city and state officials played a role brought a settlement that satisfied almost all union demands. According to Metzger, despite the drama, the 1968 negotiations showed, as did those in 1966, that the hospitals and the union were not engaging in adversary bargaining. In fact, he claimed, "the only thing different in 1970, '72, '74, was the hotel [where the negotiations were held]. . . . We both discovered what it was all about, and you just had to play it out." The brinkmanship of hospital and union, in Metzger's view, was more for effect; it was a means of applying pressure on government officials to step in and provide the financial wherewithal for a settlement, rather than a way to force the other party to compromise. The *New York Times* agreed. Its editors took note of the reluctance of the governor, the mayor, and Blue Cross to get involved in the negotiations, and observed that "government officials have always been wary of entering private labor disputes, especially when they are asked, in effect to bring the money."[49] Although concerned that rising hospital costs would cause an upward "inflationary spiral," after the settlement was reached the paper warmly praised Lindsay and other public officials for helping to "avoid a disaster."[50]

Metzger seems justified, then, in concluding that by 1968 collective bargaining between the union and the hospitals had become little more

47. *Wall Street Journal*, June 19, 1968.
48. *New York Times*, June 24, 1968.
49. Ibid., June 21, 1968.
50. Ibid., July 2, 1968.

than finding out how much the government was willing to pay. Yet it would be a mistake to view the 1968 settlement as no more than a cynical deal or an elaborate charade; to do so confuses means with ends. Both the union and the hospital league approached their negotiations knowing that nonparticipants held the keys to a settlement. From the league's perspective, the form of the negotiations was necessary to convince government and health insurance officials that the hospitals had no choice but to raise per diem rates. And if such tactics were required in order for the league to meet union demands, the leaders of 1199 were willing to play along.

For the union and its members the goal was a better life, which was possible only through a substantial rise in wages. During the 1968 negotiations, 1199 advertisements had quoted Martin Luther King, Jr.: "Many of the poor people work in our hospitals. They work fulltime jobs at parttime wages. People are always talking about menial labor. But no labor is menial unless you're not getting adequate wages."[51] Ten years earlier low wages had forced many hospital workers to supplement their salaries with public assistance. With the 1968 "breakthrough," however, they finally earned a weekly salary greater than the minimum standard established for a family of four living in New York City.[52] One Mt. Sinai worker quoted in *1199 News* after the 1968 settlement observed, "We had a time getting this pact but we can enjoy it with dignity. And after the next contract we'll hold our heads higher still."[53] Moe Foner, former executive secretary, summed up the union's philosophy: "But, remember, fundamentally this is a union. And it's a union [that] exists to service members and their families. . . . We believe that their interests coincide with the interests of the general society, of the good things in the general society. But that's . . . our aim, that's what we're out to do." Perhaps more than at any other moment since 1199 began organizing in the hospitals, the 1968 settlement represented the point when the union finally achieved this goal.

The leaders of 1199 ended the 1960s optimistic about the union's

51. *New York Times*, June 24, 1968.
52. Ibid., June 28, 1968. Citing government statistics, the union claimed that it took $272.50 per month or the equivalent (allowing for taxes) of $85 per week take-home pay for a family of four to live in New York City.
53. *1199 News*, September 1966.

future. Firmly entrenched in New York, they announced that they expected to use the 1968 settlement as a springboard from which to organize hospital workers in other major eastern cities.[54] Although worried about the resources needed to undertake a national campaign, no one on 1199's executive committee questioned that the union had the "moral right to organize hospital workers." Theirs was the only union that understood that organizing hospital workers was not simply a trade union task but involved "human rights, civil rights." Committing itself to a campaign based upon "union power and soul power," Local 1199 formed a national organizing committee and asked Coretta Scott King, the widow of the Reverend Dr. King, to be its honorary chair.[55]

Despite union leaders' high expectations, 1199 encountered serious problems implementing the "union power and soul power" strategy. In 1969 a dramatic and bitterly contested three-month strike in Charleston, South Carolina, ended in a compromise that 1199 was unable to claim as a victory. Although more successful in Baltimore, the national organizing campaign badly misfired in Pittsburgh. The Pittsburgh campaign's collapse in early 1970 forced union leaders to reassess their reliance on union power and soul power. In 1199's subsequent campaigns at hospitals in Philadelphia and New York City, the union again directed its organizing efforts at mobilizing the work force.

1199's efforts to establish the union in New York benefited from the expansion of health services fueled by public spending in the 1960s. By the mid-1970s, however, the union was operating in a more restrictive and competitive environment. Even the passage in 1974 of amendments to the Taft-Hartley Act ending voluntary hospital exemption from the National Labor Relations Act of 1947—an apparent victory for 1199—proved to be a mixed blessing. Hospital managers, often abetted by the presence of other unions competing with 1199 for members, turned the provisions of federal labor law to their advantage. For example, in the late 1970s the union made little progress organizing registered nurses due to legal maneuvers by the hospitals as well as to opposition from other unions and from state nursing associations. Although 1199 was still expanding in the 1970s, it did so at a slower rate after the changes in the Taft-Hartley Act.

54. *Wall Street Journal*, July 2, 1968.
55. Minutes, Executive Council, July 17, 1968, 1199 Archives.

Old formulas failed 1199 in the seventies at the negotiating table as well as in organizing campaigns. Contract bargaining between 1199 and the city's voluntary hospitals continued to conform to the pattern established in 1968 until 1976 when the state adamantly refused to provide more money. And not only in New York did government officials begin to make strenuous efforts to regulate and contain the rising cost of health care. The expansive 1960s, which had fostered the union's great economic strides, was succeeded by an era of more constricted cost controls.

By the close of the seventies, confronted by more effective opposition from management, increased competition from other unions, and fiscal limits imposed by changes in the health-care industry, 1199 found its momentum markedly slowed. To meet "the tough challenges of the 1980s," Leon Davis told the fourth annual convention of the National Hospital Union in December 1979, 1199 needed "to reach out to every state and every hospital and nursing home in the nation. We just don't have the resources to do it alone. We need to unite in one powerful national union."[56] As an antidote to 1199's languishing fortunes, Davis initiated merger discussions with the Service Employees International Union. Despite approval of a unity resolution by the convention, the attempted merger exposed unbridgeable divisions within 1199 itself, and in the early eighties 1199 was torn apart by a bitter internecine struggle.

Despite the many serious issues that remained, the 1960s represented 1199's coming of age. Within six years after collective-bargaining rights were legally extended to employees in New York City's voluntary hospitals, the union's hospital membership had grown significantly and come to include licensed practical nurses, laboratory technicians, and other skilled professional workers.[57] As a result of the 1968 contract, hospital workers were for the first time earning a living wage. While 1199's leaders may have been overconfident in 1968, their self-assurance is understandable in light of the rapid and extensive growth of the union through the mid-sixties.

56. *1199 News*, January 1980.
57. Minutes, Hospital Division Stewards Council, January 8, 1963, 1199 Archives. By March 1969 1199 had 19,000 hospital division members and 8,000 guild members. See *1199 News*, March 1969.

CONCLUSION

Times Past, Times Present

ROSEMARY A. STEVENS

For a book on hospitals and communities, two broad historical statements should be made. First, hospitals continue to be subject to the
drives and perceptions of an array of communities, as they have for
at least the past hundred years. These communities represent social
power structures—communities of interest—rather than the community
of patients served by the hospital. Second, the definition of the institution we call the hospital is not and never has been set. American
hospitals in the 1980s can be described as one of the great medical
and economic success stories of the twentieth century, as profligate
institutions involved in massive waste, as symbols of the inadequacies
of competition and the marketplace in providing services for the whole
population, as a healthy aspect of the U.S. labor market, and as a
cause of rising ambivalence about their appropriate role as social institutions. Past and present are inextricably linked.

The degree and nature of changes taking place in the 1980s need to

Research for this paper was done as part of a larger study of the history of U.S. general
hospitals and was supported by the Commonwealth Fund, by research grant 5-ROI-LM
03849 from the National Library of Medicine, and by a Guggenheim fellowship. See
Rosemary Stevens, *In Sickness and in Wealth: American Hospitals in the Twentieth Century*
(New York: Basic Books, 1989).

be fully appreciated by historians as a context to our work in history. But historians can also contribute to present-day debates by defining continuing, unresolved issues, identifying the hospital's various constituencies, suggesting theories to explain present changes, enabling the present to be seen in a longer time frame than is customary in political debates, and exposing underlying patterns, structures, and beliefs. I begin by describing major structural changes affecting hospitals in the 1980s and then move, via four specific illustrations, to the relationship between history and policy, times past and times present.

TRANSFORMATIONS IN THE PRESENT

With annual expenditures approaching $200 billion (more than 4 percent of the gross national product) hospitals have become one of this country's largest enterprises. Recent changes affecting this enterprise are the consolidation of freestanding hospitals into competing national and regional systems; the growth of investor ownership of hospitals and contract management; the restructuring of hospital boards into corporate constellations; and the removal of services from the hospital domain—including those that have been central to hospital development in the past, such as pathology, radiology, and surgery, which are being increasingly performed in freestanding surgical centers. Home-care services are now available for procedures as diverse as parenteral nutrition, orthopedic traction, and kidney dialysis, processes that would have been hospital-based, without question, in previous decades. Hospitals are experiencing, to some degree, a technological dismantling. Meanwhile, the full consequences of major changes in Medicare reimbursement procedures (in 1983) geared to recognize "diagnosis related groups" (DRGs) cannot yet be predicted. Hospital admission rates are dropping after an upward trend that has lasted for decades.

For historians in the future the 1980s may prove to be as challenging a period of institutional transformation as the years between 1870 and 1910.[1] Three changes are particularly significant. First, the institution

1. The best accounts and interpretations of this transformation are Charles E. Rosenberg, *The Care of Strangers: The Rise of America's Hospital System* (New York: Basic Books, 1987), and "Inward Vision and Outward Glance: The Shaping of the American Hospital,

that has been recognized as a hospital for the last seventy or eighty years may be fast disappearing. At one end of a range of possibilities, the typical hospital of the future may be at the hub of a multipurpose health-care system, offering health insurance programs, primary-care centers in outlying neighborhoods, home care, associated nursing-home care, and rehabilitation services. Such a hospital may also be responsible for various real estate ventures, including medical office buildings, parking lots, and surgical centers. At the other end of the spectrum, the hospital may become little more than an intensive care unit, merely one of a variety of health-care institutions, as hospital technologies are diffused into freestanding organizations and into the patient's home. Different hospitals may well move in different directions. Thus the hospital system of the future may become even more diverse than it is at present; less standardized than at any time since the 1920s.

Second, the concept of a hospital as a "community hospital," a unit that is administratively responsible to local power structures and functionally responsive to local interests, is under serious question. Hospitals have become big businesses and systems have become the watchword of the day. Besides the development of the major profit-making chains, such as Hospital Corporation of America, the not-for-profit hospitals have been banding together through mergers and, more widely, in mutually supportive alliances. The largest of the alliances, Voluntary Hospitals of America, served 250 health-care institutions with combined revenues of $7 billion by the early 1980s. Such systems provide hospitals with joint purchasing arrangements, the ability to raise capital, consultants and expertise, joint ventures among hospitals and between hospitals and groups of physicians, and a vehicle for lobbying on the national level. At the same time, corporate headquarters for a particular hospital may be half a continent away.

Third, the hospital industry in the 1980s is infused with the combined ethos of competition, managerialism, and profit making. Whether profit

---

1880–1914," *Bulletin of the History of Medicine* 53 (1979): 346–91; David Rosner, *A Once Charitable Enterprise: Hospitals and Health Care in Brooklyn and New York, 1885–1915* (New York: Cambridge University Press, 1982); Morris J. Vogel, *The Invention of the Modern Hospital: Boston, 1870–1930* (Chicago: University of Chicago Press, 1980); and Joan E. Lynaugh, "The Community Hospitals of Kansas City, Missouri, 1870 to 1915" (Ph.D. diss., University of Kansas, 1981).

making in medicine is good or bad, how profits should be defined and which communities or individuals benefit from any profits (investors, consumers, physicians, or institutions) have become urgent matters for debate. Not least is the vexed question of whether so-called not-for-profit hospitals should continue to be tax-exempt.[2]

Most of the changes subsumed under the three broad categories of institutional transformation, the growth of systems, and the acceptance of profit making are phenomena of the last fifteen years. Rapid changes to any large-scale social institution inevitably provoke unease. The uncertainty generated by the speed of change is demonstrated by the rapid growth of consulting groups and conferences at which hospital administrators, trustees, physicians, and experts from the legal and accounting professions, from academia, and from policy fields share the knowledge they are creating on the arcane intricacies of preferred provider organizations (PPOs) or DRGs, on capital, on regulation, on tax law, and on "the future." But the change has also taken place in a climate of rapid financial expansion. In this the transformation of the hospital industry is different from that of other major systems, including the automobile and steel industries. The amount of money spent on American hospitals almost quadrupled between 1970 and 1980, rising faster than other elements of national health expenditures. Despite attempts to keep costs down, hospital expenditures doubled between 1979 and 1987. In the 1980s hospital care has represented more than 40 percent of all U.S. health expenditures.[3] Here is a major social organization dedicated to spending more while apparently, in some ways, doing less.

The ironies, inconsistencies, and concerns about hospital change in the 1980s pose questions about the identity and definition of the hospital's communities. From the historian's perspective present changes

2. The flavor of these debates is captured in *For-profit Enterprise in Health Care*, ed. Bradford H. Gray (Washington, D.C.: 1986); Regina E. Herzlinger and William S. Krasker, "Who Profits from Nonprofits?" *Harvard Business Review* (January-February 1987): 93–106; and Eli Ginzberg, "For-Profit Medicine: A Reassessment," *New England Journal of Medicine* 319 (1988): 757–62.
3. R. M. Gibson, D. R. Waldo, and K. R. Levit, "National Health Expenditures, 1982," *Health Care Financing Review* 5, no. 1: 1–31; American Hospital Association, *Hospital Statistics, 1988 Edition* (Chicago: American Hospital Association, 1988), table 1.

also lack adequate explanatory theories. In what terms and on behalf of which communities are present changes to be measured? If hospitals are seen as an industry, the moves toward institutional diversity, industrial consolidation, and a focus on management, marketing, and profit making can be justified in terms of increasing managerial efficiency. Indeed, it is easy to argue, as Milton Friedman did more than twenty years ago, that without the constraints of professional control, the health-care industry might have behaved like other industries and that long ago we would have had department stores of medicine and health-care systems.[4] Under this argument the medical profession makes a convenient, not entirely guiltless, villain. Wisps of technological determinism linger on in explanation of present trends as the belated recognition of a necessary process of industrial consolidation, in which the model of the health-care business moves, inexorably, from a decentralized cottage industry to centralized large-scale corporations.

In the early 1980s we heard this line of argument in statements from some of the more articulate hospital futurologists, that by the year 2000 hospitals might be controlled by fifteen or twenty huge national conglomerates, some technically for-profit, some not-for-profit, but all continuing to maximize their income.[5] Conventional wisdom is now that this will not occur. I believe that we are heading toward more variety rather than more conformity. However, such predictions beg the question of whether hospitals are in fact a legitimate "industry" and, if so, what this means; let alone whether *any* service industry can reasonably be compared to any manufacturing industry. With hospital costs continuing to rise rapidly, there are obvious questions about the meaning of efficiency. Efficiency for what and for whom? With 10 to 15 percent of Americans uninsured or underinsured for hospital care, such questions have moral, distributive, and political implications. Whose views about hospitals will prevail?

It is too simple to suggest, as Paul Starr did in the early 1980s, that recent events can be explained by an era of professional control giving

4. Milton Friedman, *Capitalism and Freedom* (Chicago: University of Chicago Press, 1962).
5. Readers are invited to sample the editorial material in journals such as *Modern Healthcare, Business and Health, Health Affairs*, and *Health Care Management Review*.

way to one of corporate domination of the health-care system.[6] Powerful new actors are appearing on the scene in the form of more assertive federal agencies, consumer groups, and major purchasers of care, changing the power structure through which decisions are made. Hospitals collectively have become a vast system of diverse interests.

It now appears misleading, too, to assume that the central problem facing the U.S. medical profession is the sacrifice of its "cultural authority" to corporations. True, the traditional professional values of independent, private, fee-for-service practice, with its cherished clinical freedom, have lost much of their currency in the 1980s. However, the fact that these are passing does not mean that professional authority is automatically on the decline. Rather, the nature of medical authority is undergoing a major transformation. In theory, at least, (and, I believe in practice) the medical profession of the future may exert even more collective power in and through health-care systems than in the past— but they will exert this power through policy making and corporate regulation, rather than through the occupational monopoly that was so successful a vehicle for professional prestige between 1870 and 1970.[7] Thus the notion of professional dominance, reinterpreted, will probably be with us for many more years.

Another conceptual oversimplification is to assume that hospital decision making is subject primarily to the vagaries of a controlling oligopoly as suggested, for example, in Relman's term, the "medical-industrial complex."[8] This term is useful in dramatizing the concentration of management power in large organizations, especially hospital systems, the increase of profit-making activity (and its associated rhetoric) in health care, and the networks of mutual interest, logrolling, and backscratching that exist among a wide variety of players—from hospital lobbying groups to the stock and bond markets, insurance companies, and banks. However, such organizations are unlikely to band together on a sustained basis to form a real oligopoly, a unified, controlling force for the hospital industry; their day-to-day interests

6. Paul Starr, *The Social Transformation of American Medicine: The Rise of a Sovereign Profession and the Making of a Vast Industry* (New York: Basic Books, 1982).

7. Rosemary Stevens, "The Future of the Medical Profession," in *From Physician Shortage to Patient Shortage: The Uncertain Future of Medical Practice*, ed. Eli Ginzberg (Boulder, Colo.: Westview Press, 1986), 75–93.

8. Arnold S. Relman, "The New Medical-Industrial Complex," *New England Journal of Medicine* 303 (1980): 963–70.

are too disparate. Hospital decisions will continue to be made by bargaining and negotiation among many different groups, both within the hospital and among the hospital's external communities. (And this is true for investor-owned hospitals as well as voluntary hospitals, as the former is well aware.) Strategic alliances develop around specific issues, but they will not necessarily be sustained once those issues are addressed.

In the 1980s the major communities of interest are the provider organizations, with their associated army of health-care experts in the major legal, accounting, and hospital consulting firms; health-care occupations; the investment community; organized groups of payers; and a grab bag of coalitions among consumers, business, medical, and political groups. None of these groups is monolithic. Provider associations representing academic medical centers, local government hospitals, investor-owned chains, and voluntary hospitals may have conflicting views on specific legislation, such as paying for teaching services in hospitals or reimbursement for capital investment. Healthcare occupations have a well-known history of internecine warfare. Nurses may have different views of hospital development than doctors and both from other groups of workers. Strikes can influence policy for any of the hospital's departments. Groups of insurers are in active competition. Political ideology runs the gamut from a belief in competition among hospitals to belief in government-sponsored national systems. The communities are, in short, fractured and constantly regrouping, forming shifting alliances around temporary agreements.

In the mid-1980s not-for-profit hospitals had an interest in aligning themselves with investor-owned chains into a "private sector" representing two-thirds of all hospitals in the United States, forming a combined front vis à vis government with respect to Medicare and Medicaid reimbursement systems.[9] As we enter the 1990s, however, we see their interests diverge and new alignments form. In some respects voluntary hospitals may now have more in common with local government than with investor-owned hospitals, as part of a "public sector" less concerned with profit making than with providing a guaranteed menu of services.

Within hospitals, moreover, decisions have to be negotiated among

9. For further discussion see Stevens, *In Sickness and in Wealth*, 321–65.

monopoly interests.[10] Among these communities of interest are groups
as diverse as executives sensitive to the expectations of a major accounting firm that is handling the hospital's latest bond issue, and
unionized, striking maintenance workers. These communities are both
served by the hospital in one guise or another. While it is useful to
explore the track records of professional and interprofessional behavior
over time, only the foolish would predict with any certainty which
group will line up with others around specific issues. It is out of this
constant process of realignment and negotiation—in times present as
in times past—that decisions about the hospital industry will be made.

In short, the goals of hospitals are fluid, their purposes various, and
their future dependent on the exercise of power, negotiations, and the
flow of money among a complex network of communities. We have
in the 1980s rapid organizational change; a need for plausible explanatory theories of what is happening to the hospital system, as well as
to individual hospitals; a shifting array of interested communities; and
an institution without a readily definable future. In this shifting context
historians should be challenged to relate past and present, trained as
we are to deal, inductively, with scattered evidence, complexity, continuity, and change.

PAST AND PRESENT

Four historical themes illustrate the ways in which the past may
illuminate the present in clarifying the relation of hospitals to their
communities. They are: (1) the ambiguity of the hospital's role and
the advantages of this ambiguity to the survival of hospitals as institutions with different utilities for different groups; (2) the importance
of economic trajectories (money streams) as a driving force for change;
(3) the symbolic importance of the hospital in America; and (4) the
uses of rhetoric by the hospital's communities. All of these are linked

10. Hospitals and health-care systems are similar to other organizations in this respect;
indeed, there is a fruitful field for comparative organizational analysis of hospitals on such
themes as the role of monopolies and the nature of expertise in organizations, and in
negotiated decision making. See, e.g., Michel Crozier and Erhard Friedburg, *Actors and
Systems: The Politics of Collective Action* (Chicago: University of Chicago Press, 1980).
On hospitals the classic source continues to be Eliot Freidson's edited collection, *The
Hospital in Modern Society* (London: Free Press, 1963).

by the relationship between communities, power, and ideology. All are important in looking at American hospitals, past and present.

The first theme is the ambiguity of the hospital mission. The modern American hospital has always been more than a hotel for the sick. It has long been a multipurpose institution with vague goals, adaptable technologies, and fuzzy functional margins. Hospitals have had neither one product nor even a definable set or balance of products. Like all organizations, they have constantly interacted with their environments—medical, social, economic, and political. As a result, the concept of the hospital has been both adaptive and abstract, and there has never been a clear definition of what the American hospital is. Indeed, there have been debates since before World War I about how responsive the hospital is (and should be) to physicians (as the doctor's workshop); how broad a role the hospital should play as a community health-care institution; and to what extent the American hospital should be properly seen as a financially self-sufficient institution with no particular social commitment to serve those who cannot pay.

In terms of the hospital's growth and survival, this ambiguity has been one of the historical strengths of hospitals as institutions. Elsewhere I have called this characteristic "constructive ambiguity."[11] Ambiguity of role has been a useful vehicle for hospital adaptability and change and for responsiveness to the dominant communities of interest, as they, in turn, have shifted and changed. The twentieth-century hospital has survived and prospered under one label—that of "hospital"—through great transformations of function and role, including the process of medicalization and upward mobility in clientele between 1870 and 1910; further shifts in medical function and the patient population as tonsillectomies and appendectomies became widespread in the 1920s and 1930s and as upper-class women entered hospitals for their deliveries; enormous changes in medical treatment as sulfonamides became accepted in the 1930s and antibiotics after World War II; the rise of machine technology from the 1950s; and an increasing focus on aging and chronic disease, stimulated by Medicare, from the mid-1960s. Within the hospital walls occupational roles have grown and changed through the advent of an army of specialized

11. Rosemary Stevens, "The Changing Hospital," in *Applications of Social Science to Clinical Medicine and Health Policy*, ed. Linda Aiken and David Mechanic (New Brunswick, N.J.: Rutgers University Press, 1986), 80–99.

technicians and a huge support staff that maintains the physical and administrative structure of the institution, from laundry workers to computer experts. Nurses' roles have changed significantly. The hospital too has changed by having its own authority affirmed as an organization responsible for the quality of medical care, a responsibility affirmed by the courts of law, versus the traditional authority of physicians. In these and other respects hospitals have been defined by change, under the umbrella of apparent semantic consistency. The ambiguity inherent in their role has allowed for constant transformation.

The message here, of course, is that present changes, while dramatic, are not revolutionary. From the historical perspective it would be much more surprising if hospital services and structures stood still. Moreover, within the present changes there are strong threads of continuity. In the phenomenal success of hospitals as adaptive twentieth-century American organizations, physicians, administrators, and boards of trustees continue to be major communities of interest. Their various agendas affect the type of services offered, the hospital's location, its architectural prominence and design, and the roles and prestige structures of its various occupations.

The second topic is money. The hospital's operating income, as well as its sources of capital over the years—representing the interests of external communities—have always played an important part in defining and molding the hospital's activities. To some extent money is a shorthand symbol for social preference as exercised by larger communities of interest. But money has also been an important defining force in American hospital history because of the large-scale development of hospitals as private institutions.

Rosner's work on hospitals in New York has traced the general shift in hospital care from charity to purchase well before World War I.[12] My work on hospitals in Pennsylvania and Kingsdale's in Baltimore show a dependence of many of the new hospitals on the sale of services before the turn of the twentieth century.[13] Hanckel's analysis of the

12. Rosner, *A Once Charitable Enterprise*, n. 2.
13. Rosemary Stevens, "Sweet Charity: State Aid to Hospitals in Pennsylvania, 1870–1910," *Bulletin of the History of Medicine* 58 (1984): 287–34, 474–95, and J. M. Kingsdale, "The Growth of Hospitals: An Economic History of Baltimore" (Ph.D. diss., University of Michigan, 1981).

1910 hospital census reveals again the heavy dependence by hospitals on patient fees, particularly outside the Northeastern states.[14] The idea of hospital care as something to sell was buttressed by the growth of what came to be known as third-party payment; that is, insurance reimbursement for the middle class in the 1930s, 1940s, and 1950s and increased government responsibility through Medicare and Medicaid from the late 1960s. Virtually all U.S. hospital income now comes from third-party payments.

The development and the effects of third-party reimbursement form one of the major themes of hospital history in the twentieth century. Among these effects are recognition of the idea that hospital care in America is something to buy and sell, rather than to be provided collectively by the state; the development of contractual relationships between hospitals and government agencies; the maintenance of institutional autonomy in the face of rapid medical and social change; the encouragement of the hospital as a center for high technology rather than for community health, and for inpatient over outpatient care; and, until the last few years, supply-induced demand for the expansion of hospital care, since cost-plus reimbursement was available.

Third-party payment does not spring up all of itself. We have only to look at present-day ventures into discounting hospital services for selective groups of insurers, or into the politics of Medicare and Medicaid reimbursement, to see the active intervention of interest groups— including, of course, the hospitals themselves, represented primarily by their administrators. In retrospect, one of the major events in reimbursement was the separate development of Blue Cross and Blue Shield in the 1930s and 1940s, the direct result of the desire by hospitals (and the American Hospital Association, in the person of C. Rufus Rorem) not to antagonize physicians by setting up insurance schemes that would also include physician fees. Politics, marketing, and money continue to be interlinked.

When hospitals were heavily dependent on individual paying patients their marketing efforts were obviously directed to this clientele. A good example is the establishment of National Hospital Day in the early 1920s to "sell" the hospital to potential consumers through open

14. Frances Stuart Hanckel, "American Hospitals in 1910" (Sc.D. diss., Johns Hopkins University, 1985).

days, fairs, and radio spots. This focus on selling hospital care to individual consumers reappeared in the 1980s, with marketing plans developed to entice individuals to subscribe to particular insurance schemes.

Until the 1960s local communities were important in raising money for capital expansion for voluntary hospitals, through fund drives, donations, and bequests. Federal Hill-Burton construction funds became available in 1946 but still depended on community matching funds. Capital is now raised largely through loans and on the bond market, and the brokers of such funds form a new—and powerful—community of interest. In this sense one can say that hospitals have always responded to the dictates of the marketplace. Historians have much to contribute to present-day debates by clarifying the interlocking system of money, power, and communities of interest in the development of American hospitals as instruments of capital acquisition and distribution; that is, as truly a part of a "capitalist" system.

Just as money symbolizes more, in terms of power, than its fiscal elements, so do American hospitals embody cultural values that go beyond their overt role as patient-care institutions. The third theme is the symbolic or cultural significance of hospitals in modern America—and how this may be changing in the late twentieth century. Because American hospitals developed at the time they did, most significantly between 1870 and 1910, they assumed an unusually important function as the embodiment of social aspirations—of progress, science, efficiency, and humanitarianism. The hospital stood high above the hurly-burly, restlessness, pressure, and pragmatism of the American culture of money making at the turn of the century. Thus Henry James, visiting America in 1905–6, saw the great hospitals (Presbyterian in New York and Johns Hopkins in Baltimore) as symbols of stillness, whiteness, poetry, manners, and tone—necessary values, he considered, in the vulgar materialism of modern America.[15]

It is not coincidental that American hospitals have been among the most luxurious and costly structures ever built. In 1878 a writer for *Harpers Magazine* described the elevator of the New York Hospital, which was larger than that of a fashionable hotel, as so smooth in

15. Henry James, *The American Scene* (Bloomington: Indiana University Press, 1968), 319–20.

motion that it was like a mechanical means of getting to heaven.[16] American hospitals have constantly been reequipped and rebuilt in the twentieth century. Look around you today—they remain more luxurious, more machine conscious, and more aggressively "modern" than hospitals in other countries. The American hospital since the 1870s has been a focus for community pride, conspicuous waste, and cultural display.

In these respects hospitals have been important and continuing symbols of American civilization. It was not through the momentum of autonomous science or even because of economic pressures that the American hospital of the depression and New Deal years developed rapidly as a center for specialized medical techniques. Hospitals were also symbols of hope. Similarly, it was not merely as public works projects that huge amounts of federal money were poured into hospital construction during the New Deal. The twentieth-century American hospital found an invaluable niche as an emblem of American aspirations.

At least part of the unease about hospital change now being experienced may be attributed to the assault on the hospital as an important cultural symbol and the lack of an equally powerful mythology to displace it. Hospitals can be seen as falling to the base forces of materialism; that is, as being seduced by the raw power of the competitive marketplace from the idealized values of science and humanitarianism. Here, too, understanding the past illuminates the present. Indeed, the interrelationships among institutions, systems, interests, and ideologies are the stuff both of policy and of history.

The fourth and final point concerns the relationship between hospitals and external power structures, and the relationship of both of these to the uses of political rhetoric. Charles Rosenberg has shown conclusively how U.S. hospitals have long reflected prevailing social norms in areas such as social class, race, and the occupational relationships between men and women; and how they have also responded to larger social movements. Three relatively recent examples are the civil rights movement, the women's movement, and the ideology of competition. Hospitals have served, at one and the same time, as emblems of what society would like to be and as reflections of what it is. Hence the

16. "Hospital Life in New York," *Harper's New Monthly Magazine* (1878): 171–89.

paradox in the 1980s that the American hospital system can signify at
one and the same time the marvels of a society in which organ trans-
plantation has become commonplace and the evils of a society that
affronts human dignity in its refusal to provide insurance for all
patients.

American hospitals have so long been mirrors of American class
that the existence of the class system in medicine has been virtually
taken for granted. As the 1960s have receded into history the brief
efforts under Medicaid to bring the poor into the mainstream of medicine (that is, to create one, undifferentiated standard and place of
service) seem merely a temporary disturbance in a segmented and
stratified system. In the 1980s, as in the early 1900s, richer and poorer
Americans are segregated both within and between different institutions. Studies of the troubled relationships between hospitals and immigrants in Miami and Los Angeles in the 1980s evoke much earlier
scenarios, in New York or Philadelphia, for example, in the 1890s.

However, hospitals are not merely symbols of cultural aspirations
or mirrors of their environments. Successful organizations work to
influence and to change these environments. As hospitals and their
associations have become powerful institutions, they have used ideology for political ends. They have developed, in effect, as their own
community of interest. American voluntary hospitals have shown themselves to be extraordinarily adept politically, presenting themselves as
public or private institutions, as socially or business oriented, or as in
a state of collapse or success, depending on the advantages inherent
in the prevailing milieu. A vivid example is the rhetoric of voluntary
hospitals in the 1930s. Throughout that decade their supporters proclaimed their imminent demise. Nevertheless, through careful ideological positioning, these hospitals emerged from the 1930s as
politically stronger institutions than they had been in the 1920s. During
the 1930s the voluntary hospitals differentiated themselves in kind from
both profit-making and governmental institutions. They also committed
themselves, together with their associated Blue Cross schemes, to the
voluntary ethos as something quintessentially American—a home-
grown alternative to socialized medicine. Voluntarism became a major
unifying theme for hospitals in the 1930s and 1940s, just as managerialism, competition, and corporate enterprise are the organizing
themes of the 1980s.

In the cases of both the 1930s and 1980s changes in rhetoric do not necessarily assume fundamental changes in organization or in goals. Rhetoric greases the wheels of change, allowing for temporary alliances among disparate interests, but under the umbrella of diverging ideologies business may continue much as usual. Just as it is important to distinguish ideology, rhetoric, and reality in interpreting the past, some of today's changes may be only in the labels. For example, names of some of the new corporations may seem to suggest to policy makers a major change of mission, names like Sisters of Sorrowful Mother Management, Milwaukee, or Alexian Brothers Health Management Inc. But Roman Catholic hospitals, like other hospitals in this country struggling to make ends meet with little or no endowment funds, have always been overtly businesslike. Throughout this century these hospitals have relied on providing services to those who could pay and expanding their market for new patients in order to meet their expenses. Once again, continuity is interwoven with change, below the noisy level of rhetoric.

Within the four themes of the ambiguity of the hospital, the importance of money as a driving force for change, the hospital as an important American cultural symbol, and the uses of rhetoric by hospital communities, times past can indeed inform times present. American hospitals continue to be economically driven. They are socially stratified to an extent far greater, for example, than hospitals in Britain. The relationships between physicians and hospitals have been formed out of the predominant patterns of private practice in American medicine, characterized by a relatively autonomous staff of attending physicians. Physicians are now becoming more organized participants on the hospital scene. Indeed, they have a vested interest in becoming so. Nevertheless, to a large extent they are still not employees of the institutions.

American hospitals hold themselves out as centers of high technology and expertise. Despite the creation of large-scale hospital systems, individual hospitals (including those belonging to different systems) compete with each other at the local level, leading to duplication of services in the name of competition. They are heavily geared toward the exigencies of the reimbursement system. Their efforts inevitably turn outward toward negotiations with private third parties and with government agencies and legislators. American hospitals are peculiarly "American." Their roots lie deep in their own history.

Through the present period of uncertainty and rapid change thread the old tensions of American civilization—between materialism and idealism, individualism and collectivism, uniformity and diversity, social stratification and egalitarianism, and (more recently) belief in technology versus disappointment and anxiety over its effects. The hospital's communities have extended into the economic and political sphere, yet communities have always been defined around areas of common interest. Hospitals of the 1980s have to be seen in terms of money and power, as much as in terms of altruism, science, and medicine.

Despite the many uncertainties and hospital closings of the late 1980s, American hospitals, collectively, are thriving institutions. Their ambiguity of function and of ideology; their responsiveness to a wide range of communities of interest, marked in particular by the flow of funding; their uses of prevailing ideology; and the enthusiasm of their adherents for the latest rhetoric characterize the hospitals of the 1980s just as much as they did in earlier decades. Meanwhile, the links between history and policy are both challenging and elusive. Present events inevitably inform our perspectives as historians, sometimes in ways difficult to assess. In turn, the past is peculiarly important for those grappling with the present: policy analysts, hospital administrators and boards, physicians, government officials, fringe-benefit managers, and individual investors.

Since hospitals are now embroiled in institutional, political, and economic change, one would expect to see an increasing amount of research from the perspective of institutional, political, and economic history. More important, however, are attempts to come up with theories to explain recent changes and to identify underlying themes and attributes in the ongoing history of hospitals in America, attributes that may continue into the future. It is perhaps too much to hope that explanations of the past will be used to understand present-day changes—but we can try. American hospitals can be better understood by explaining the American past than by comparing American and foreign hospitals in the 1980s or 1990s.

Bibliography

Notable Books on the American General Hospital

Dowling, Harry F. *City Hospitals: The Undercare of the Underprivileged*. Cambridge: Harvard University Press, 1982.

Fink, Leon, and Brian Greenberg. *Upheaval in the Quiet Zone: A History of Hospital Workers' Union, Local 1199*. Urbana: University of Illinois Press, 1989.

Melosh, Barbara. *"The Physician's Hand": Work Culture and Conflict in American Nursing*. Philadelphia: Temple University Press, 1982.

Reverby, Susan M. *Ordered to Care: The Dilemma of American Nursing, 1850–1945*. Cambridge: Cambridge University Press, 1987.

Rosenberg, Charles E. *The Care of Strangers: The Rise of America's Hospital System*. New York: Basic Books, 1987.

Rosner, David. *A Once Charitable Enterprise: Hospitals and Health Care in Brooklyn and New York, 1885–1915*. Cambridge: Cambridge University Press, 1982.

Snoke, Albert. *Hospitals, Health, and People*. New Haven: Yale University Press, 1987.

Stevens, Rosemary. *American Medicine and the Public Interest*. New Haven: Yale University Press, 1971.

————. *In Sickness and in Wealth: American Hospitals in the Twentieth Century*. New York: Basic Books, 1989.

Thompson, John D. and Grace Goldin. *The Hospital: A Social and Architectural History*. New Haven: Yale University Press, 1975.

Vogel, J. Morris. *The Invention of the Modern Hospital: Boston, 1870–1930*. Chicago: University of Chicago Press, 1980.

Contributors

RIMA D. APPLE, Ph.D., Assistant Editor, *Isis*, Department of the History of Medicine, University of Wisconsin–Madison.

EDWARD C. ATWATER, M.D., Associate Professor of Medicine and the History of Medicine, Department of Medicine, University of Rochester Medical Center.

VANESSA NORTHINGTON GAMBLE, M.D., Ph.D., Assistant Professor, Department of The History of Medicine and Department of Preventive Medicine, University of Wisconsin–Madison.

JANET GOLDEN, Ph.D., Visiting Assistant Professor, Department of History, Temple University.

BRIAN GREENBERG, Ph.D., Associate Professor, Department of History, University of Delaware.

JOEL D. HOWELL, M.D., Ph.D., Assistant Professor, Department of Internal Medicine, Department of History, and Department of Health Services Management and Policy, University of Michigan.

DIANA ELIZABETH LONG, Ph.D., Director, Women's Studies Program and Associate Professor, Department of History, University of Southern Maine.

JOAN E. LYNAUGH, R.N., Ph.D., F.A.A.N, Director and Associate Professor, Center for the Study of the History of Nursing, University of Pennsylvania School of Nursing.

SUSAN M. REVERBY, Ph.D., Director and Associate Professor, Women's Studies Program, Wellesley College.

CHARLES E. ROSENBERG, Ph.D., Janice and Julian Bers Professor of History and Sociology of Science, Department of the History and Sociology of Science, University of Pennsylvania.

DAVID ROSNER, Ph.D., Professor of History, Baruch College and City University of New York Graduate Center.

ROSEMARY A. STEVENS, Ph.D., Professor and Chairman, Department of the History and Sociology of Science, University of Pennsylvania.

Index

214

Library of Congress Cataloging-in-Publication Data
The American general hospital : communities and
  social contexts / editors, Diana Elizabeth Long and Janet
Golden.
    p. cm. — (Publication of the Francis Clark Wood Institute
for the History of Medicine, College of Physicians of Philadelphia)
    Bibliography: p.
    Includes index.
    ISBN 0-8014-2349-X (alk. paper)
    1. Hospital and community—United States—History. I. Long,
Diana E. II. Golden, Janet Lynne, 1951– . III. Series.
    [DNLM: 1. Hospitals, Community—history—United States.
2. Hospitals, General—history—United States. WX 27 AA1 H8]
RA965.5.H68   1989
362.1′1′097309—dc20
DNLM/DLC
for Library of Congress   89-7264